THE BANQUET

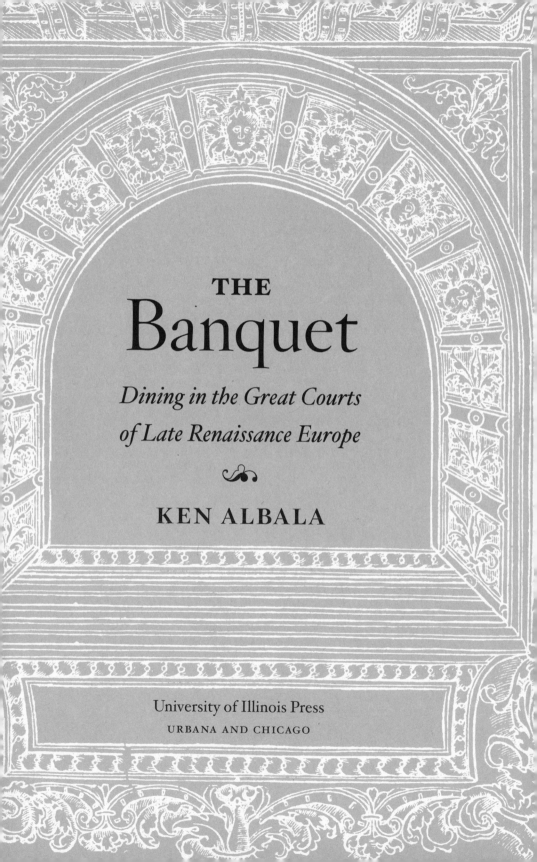

THE
Banquet

Dining in the Great Courts
of Late Renaissance Europe

ॐ

KEN ALBALA

University of Illinois Press
URBANA AND CHICAGO

Library of Congress Cataloging-in-Publication Data
Albala, Ken, 1964–
The banquet : dining in the great courts of
late Renaissance Europe / Ken Albala.
    p.   cm. — (The Food series)
Includes bibliographical references and index.
ISBN-13: 978-0-252-03133-5 (cloth : alk. paper)
ISBN-10: 0-252-03133-4 (cloth : alk. paper)
    1. Dinners and dining—Europe—History.
2. Food habits—Europe—History. I. Title. II. Series.
        TX737.A42   2007
    394.1'2094—dc22   2006017927

CONTENTS

PREFACE

Some men are born with titles, some achieve titles, and some have titles thrust upon them. The last of these explains *The Banquet*. It works, though. The word itself derives from a board or bank mounted by a street performer or mountebank, or set on trestles for dining. Thus banquets could be staged anywhere, because in Renaissance-era Europe, homes lacked a fixed room with stationary tables for dining. The term took an odd twist in England, where it denoted the final portable dessert course of sweetmeats and fruit. Elsewhere it meant an entire meal, the grandest that could be imagined at European courts. So important were these meals that they were recorded for posterity in cookbooks, menus, and as rules for kitchen organization and table manners. Just as weddings and gala events are photographed or videotaped today, banquet literature affords us a snapshot of the past, admittedly edited and embellished, but nonetheless revealing the aesthetic preoccupations of our forbears. For a fleeting moment we are able to peer through the brocade curtains of the past, to catch the wafting scent of cinnamon and ginger, to gaze upon the glimmering table settings and towering sugar sculptures, and perhaps even to imagine the vibrant flavors and sultry textures of this brilliant bygone cuisine. My goal here is thus partly voyeuristic. But because attitudes toward food also reflect deeper thought structures and are essentially expressions of identity (of self, community, state), then this tale is merely a history of western Europe told through the lens of food and fine dining. It is a history of ruling elites in a period that was changing demographically, politically, and of course, culturally.

Moreover, the cuisine analyzed here is largely unknown to American readers. Aristocratic diners in sixteenth- and seventeenth-century Europe indulged in what are arguably among the most elaborate creations ever to have emerged from a kitchen. There were monumental pies flecked with gold leaf, roasted fowl redolent of spices and rose water, savory stews brimming with unctuous morsels, truffles, nuts, and candied citron. It was a cuisine that in some ways will seem familiar:

chicken, veal, and fish were favorites, as were vegetables like asparagus and artichoke. In other ways, it will appear utterly foreign. The flavor combinations will shock and surprise, as will the predilection for organ meats and whole calves' heads. Above all, the sheer volume of food and the structure of the meal will perplex our modern sensibilities.

This cuisine was anything but monotonous. Aristocratic diners consumed a staggering variety of ingredients, mostly local and seasonal and much of it wild, but some was imported from the far ends of the earth. Cooks and banquet managers paid surprising attention to the freshness of their ingredients and sometimes sought to preserve simple pristine flavors and aromas. They were also keen judges of food's provenance, knowing exactly where to find the best seafood, and the choicest cheeses, fruits, and wines. Many of these foods were assigned names by place of origin, much as we do today. Food workers invented new cooking techniques, implements, serving methods, and styles of presentation that truly elevated the meal to a form of high art.

Cooking in the late Renaissance was also quite different from medieval cuisine that preceded it, as well as from French haute cuisine that followed. Perched between these two grand traditions, the sixteenth and seventeenth centuries have often been overlooked in culinary histories of Europe. But in these years there appeared some of the largest and most comprehensive cookbooks ever written. Dining manuals, carving guides, and what we would call general food reference works—many comparable to those being published today—were best sellers. There was a thriving culture of food all across Europe reflective of the general artistic efflorescence of the era, and coinciding precisely with the styles art historians refer to as mannerism and the baroque.

The neglect among food historians has left the late Renaissance to be treated either as a coda to the elaborate cuisine of the late Middle Ages or an actual hindrance to the culinary revolution of the mid-seventeenth century. Only following La Varenne, when a stock and butter-based cuisine replaced the strange sweet-and-sour and spicy (backward) medieval flavor preferences, could cooking attain perfection, these authors insist. (Flandrin, Revel, etc.)[1] In their view, only when food would taste of itself should the term *gastronomy* be applied. The tendency has been to treat culinary history as a series of advances leading toward the present: here is the first roux, the first béchamel sauce, the first modern service in courses. This is a positivist approach that has been abandoned in practically all historical subdisciplines, and now that culinary history has come of age, it is time to apprehend the past on its own terms. That is, we must evaluate this cuisine as an expression of the culture that produced it without reference to our taste preferences. Such objectivity will be absolutely essential as we mentally tuck into some dishes that will, to our sensibilities, seem perverse if not downright repulsive.

Rather than focus on such oddities for their shock value, the goal here is to determine why people ate as they did and what it reveals about them, their aesthetic preferences, values, fears, and prejudices. A good deal of energy will be devoted to describing ingredients and aristocratic dining habits in detail. This is not so that one might re-create banquets of the past, though there is nothing wrong in doing so, but rather to understand the importance of dining as one among the many resplendent art forms of the period.

By treating cuisine as an art form, I hope to open further avenues of inquiry for all periods of culinary history. For one, the language of gastronomy is fairly threadbare and lacks a good critical vocabulary for discussing food. Modern professional chefs have their own terminology for describing recipes and procedures, but historians have little to work with when comparing stylistic periods, certainly nothing compared to art historians or music historians. Speaking of cooking as an art, this is not merely to suggest that cooking is difficult and requires great planning and imagination and therefore should be considered art rather than mere skill, but rather that the same aesthetic values inform all artistic media. It should be possible, therefore, to borrow terms or even invent them if necessary, in order to explain this cuisine as a distinct style. One simple example will clarify the need for a precise lexicon. Musicologists speaking of the madrigal refer to the way several separate voices each carry their own distinct melody, intertwining and responding to the others. *Polyphony* describes this without any further explanation. The culinary historian, when facing the same stylistic approach to ingredients that compose a dish, has no such suitable term. Think of several flavors, each distinct and pronounced, sharply contrasting rather than melding to form a homogenous and intensified taste experience. The sharpness of vinegar stands out against the sweetness of sugar, the warm aroma of nutmeg and cloves, and the richness of stewed wildfowl with fruit. *Polysipid* as an adjective or *polysavory* as a noun directly describes this style. And not coincidentally, this way of combining discrete elements in a composition is replaced in music and in cooking at about the same time, in the course of the seventeenth century. Such neologisms will be found throughout the text, and the reader is kindly referred to the glossary if the context alone should prove insufficient.

Speaking of aristocratic dining from the 1520s to the 1660s as a unified style poses certain problems. Stylistically this period covers both mannerism and the baroque, before the classical tendencies of the era of Louis XIV take precedence. These terms will be used throughout the narrative, as will the phrase *late Renaissance,* not only because the culinary arts bring to perfection many of the innovations of the fifteenth-century Renaissance, but because no other suitable term for this time span exists. Thus as historians of drama loosely refer to the Tudor and Stuart periods as Renaissance drama, so too will it be used for cooking, though not without serious qualification. This period also corresponds nicely to the history of culinary publication. It follows the appearance of the first printed cookbook—Martino of Como's *Liber de arte coquinaria,* which was embedded in Platina's *De honesta voluptate* of around 1470. This is, in terms of style, the last of the great medieval cookbooks, but still points the way to the next period. Its popularity alone through the sixteenth century warrants some consideration here. The same can be said of Rupert of Nola's Catalan cookbook, which is still in most respects a medieval work. This study ends around the time of La Varenne in France in the 1660s, not because his cooking was truly as revolutionary as some claim, but because the latter seventeenth and eighteenth centuries do witness many decisive changes in the evolution of cooking. Because this new approach to cooking was not directly felt outside France and to a certain extent England for several decades, some titles published in the late seventeenth century have been included—most notably the work of Bartolomeo Stefani in Mantua in the 1660s, some banquet management guides, as well as many English cookbooks of the same era, appearing just before or during the Restoration.

Within this time, from the mid sixteenth to mid seventeenth century, were published some of the most ambitious and comprehensive cookbooks and dining manuals ever written. There were the works of Christoforo di Messisbugo in Ferrara, Domenico Romoli in Florence, and then the magisterial *Opera* of Bartolomeo Scappi. Shortly on its heels follow the many books on banquet management, the *scalco* literature by Giovanni Battista Rossetti, Cesare Evitascandalo, Vittorio Lancelotti, and Antonio Frugoli, among others. There is also an extensive carving literature written for *trincianti,* of which Vincenzo Cervio and Mattia Geigher are representative. Outside Italy, coverage here will strive to be as international as possible. There are the works of Lancelot de Casteau in what is today Belgium, Domingo Hernandez de Maceras and Francisco Martínez Montiño in Spain, and several extraordinary English cookbook authors such as Robert May and William Rabisha. As with the art of the period, focusing on any single national cuisine obscures the very international nature of culinary trends, and this book is intentionally comparative across national lines. Having said that, readers should be aware from the outset that this study focuses heavily on Italy, where most culinary literature was written, and covers Spain, France, and England and tangentially the Netherlands and Switzerland. German-speaking regions are only included when the texts are in Latin or when authors discuss Germany. This is merely the result of my own inability to tackle sixteenth-century German. There were several cookbooks written, and Marx Rumpolt's is the most important of these.

To clarify another point, I use the term *dining* in its modern sense, but dining in the sixteenth and seventeenth centuries referred to a midday meal. It shifted in subsequent centuries later and later in the day, so that the first meal *disjejeunare* (to un-fast or break fast) eventually became the evening meal. In the Renaissance the evening meal, supper or *cena,* was normally the smaller of the two. Confusingly, a banquet, the grandest of all meals, was usually held in the evening. The majority of meals analyzed here will be banquets, in the broader sense of the term, but many will be smaller suppers and even ordinary meals when authors describe them.

Lastly, there is also what must be considered an ancillary culinary literature and certain arts that indirectly describe aristocratic eating habits. There are burlesque poems, depictions of banquets in paintings and especially food in still life, as well as a vast literature condemning noble customs either from a medical standpoint or a moral and religious angle. There are also books on individual ingredients or types of dishes—on wine or salads, for example. Surprisingly, even titles that purport to explain dining habits of the ancient Greeks and Romans end up saying a lot about contemporary practices. Thus this book is designed to take account of any resource offering clues about what wealthy people were eating, or wished they could eat, even though it focuses on cookbooks and menus.

But what exactly is a banquet? Ottaviano Rabasco in his *Il convito* of 1615 offers the most complete taxonomy of banquet types. Normally the banquet was merely an extended elaborate form of dinner, held around noon, though he stipulates that it could be served earlier, two hours before noon, at ten o'clock or eleven o'clock if no breakfast or *colezione* was eaten first thing in the morning. Banquets could also be held in the evening, but normally the evening meal, supper or *cena,* was held a few hours before sleep, and so was smaller and lighter.[2] Menus of the period do consistently list both banquets and suppers. There were no hard and fast rules about mealtimes though, and sometimes even a lunch or *merenda* could occur in the late afternoon. This was actually one of the most typical complaints of physicians, that courtiers ate practically round the clock, and by the clock, Rabasco reminds us, there were three that could be followed: "that of the stomach, that of the [clock] tower, and that of the kitchen." In other words, though hunger pressed and the clock struck time, one might have to just wait until food was prepared.[3]

Rabasco also distinguishes between private banquets, intimate and among friends, and grander public banquets. It is the latter that concerns us most here. This was the time to show off the most exquisite foods, of highest quality, in great quantity, and particularly showcasing produce and wines from one's native region, whether it be "salami from Bologna, olives, confections or moscatello from Genoa, marzolini in Florence, in Siena cheese from the Crete, marzipan in Piacenza, etc."[4] Marzolini are cheeses, as are those from the Crete Senese, presumably something like pecorino from Pienza.

As for the occasion, weddings were common enough along with baptisms, but first place is accorded victory celebrations, reception of foreign princes or ambassadors, and even lesser occasions such as receiving a doctorate or being ordained.[5] The banquet guides make clear, though, that the most typical form was the public reception of princes and magistrates. Banquets are thus explicitly political in nature, and include both overt messages honoring guests and more subtle interchanges of meaning, as will be discussed later.

Before describing the details of topics such as kitchen organization, ingredients, cooking methods, and the experience of fine dining in this period, it would make sense to begin with a gradual approach to the topic from a broad perspective, so that readers may grasp how this material will be discussed. On the one hand, the primary intent is merely to describe what foods were eaten and how they were cooked; on the other hand, what these choices reveal about the past is also the topic here. Thus we must begin with the broader question "why did late Renaissance diners make the food choices they did?"

ACKNOWLEDGMENTS

Honestly, offering thanks is the best part about writing a book. First there is my pal Andy Smith, series editor, Willis Regier, director, and all the people at the University of Illinois Press, for signing me on with not much more than an idea. I am proud to be included in this food series. Next, an enormous thank you to the International Association of Culinary Professionals Foundation, Martini and Rossi, and Torani Syrups for awarding me a juicy grant to research this project in Europe, as well as to the University of the Pacific for an Eberhardt Research Grant. Thanks to the eternal city of Rome, which proved more of an inspiration for this book than I could ever have imagined.

Thanks to the staff of all the marvelous research facilities that invited me to pore over their cookbooks: the Biblioteca Apostolica Vaticana, the Library of Congress, and the Folger Shakespeare Library, where I was overjoyed to find so many old friends and mentors still lurking, the State Library in Sacramento, and a special thanks to Sean Thackrey, winemaker, for inviting me to use his astonishing collection of rare wine books. Thanks to the wonderful staff at the Schlesinger Library at Radcliffe, where I found my final two sources just under the wire.

I must also thank the people at Arnaldo Forni Editori for their remarkable series of facsimiles and prompt service getting them to my desk. This book would truly have been unthinkable without them. The same goes for Tom Jaine at Prospect Books and to the fantastic Fons Grewe Web site, where I found many of the texts used in this study. Thanks to Thomas Gloning, whose bibliography and Web site proved indispensable. As always, a huge thank you goes to the Interlibrary Loan people at the University of the Pacific and to Robin Imhof for tracking down obscure books for me.

Then, thanks to all the people who have helped me along the way, colleagues in the history department and in modern languages and classics for help with obscure terms. Thanks to our work study student Joseph Nguyen for photocopying, downloading, and printing more pages than would seem humanly possible, and thanks to Marilyn and Terri for their years of support.

Thanks also to all my friends (I dare not say foodies) on the ASFS Listserve, whose furtive ideas and rantings inspired my own in ways that I cannot even begin to recount. Thanks to the many sundry assorted scholars whose comments in symposia and conferences, from Oxford, Australia, and Italy, to Boston and New York, as well as my authors in the Food Culture series. I have pilfered ideas from all of you. Then, thanks to those remarkable food historians I have stumbled upon by chance: Terence Scully, whose translation of Scappi should appear soon, Timothy Tomasik, who lent me copies of the sixteenth-century French cookbooks, Rachel Laudan, Barbara Ketcham Wheaton, Johnna Holloway, and Fiona Lucraft for getting me a copy of *Le grande cuisiner.* Thanks to Suzanne Rindell and Alice McLean for reading and responding to ideas.

Lastly, to my family, Joanna, Ethan, and Benjamin, Sadie, Persephone, and especially Bumblebee and Maxie, with whom I shared many nibbles and my lap—we will never forget you. Thanks for once again tolerating my edomania and giving me the time to write. And thanks to my dear dear friends with whom I absolutely love to eat and drink, especially Lisa, who patiently listened to practically every idea in its infancy.

*Acknowl-
edgments*

CHRONOLOGY

	ITALY	SPAIN	FRANCE	ENGLAND
1520				
1530				
1540	Messisbugo		*Livre fort excellent* *Grand cuisiner*	
1550				*Proper Newe Booke*
1560	Romoli	Willich		
1570	Scappi	(Swiss)		
1580	Rossetti			*Good Huswifes Handmaide*
1590	Cervio			Dawson
1600		Granado Maceras	Lancelot (Belgium)	
1610	Evitascandalo Rabasco	Montino		Markham Murrell
1620				
1630	Lancelotti Frugoli Crisci			
1640	Giegher Vasselli		Vonlett	
1650	Del Turco Colorsi		La Varenne	Cooper *Archimagirus*
1660	Liberati Stefani			*Compleat Cook* May, Rabisha
1670	Mattei		*Ecole Parfait* De Lune, L. S. R. Massialot	

The Banquet

CHAPTER I

Setting the Stage — Setting the Table

To start, consider all the variables involved in choosing food. Most people who have ever lived ate whatever they could get their hands on, but for those who can choose, and especially the elite, there are quirky personal preferences, considerations of cost and availability, as well as the complex cultural baggage that dictates what is edible and what is repulsive. For those with discretionary income, deciding what to eat was a very complicated affair, involving deep-seated notions of how food would affect the body and spirit. For those entertaining others it could be fraught with peril, choosing just the right foods to please every palate, to display wealth or savoir faire.

Naturally, the factors that enter into food choice are highly variable and change from place to place, over time, and from person to person. For some people, concerns about a food's origin and about agricultural practices are most important. In the sixteenth century a rare and delicate peach from one's own estate, carefully tended and matured to perfection, was often presented as tangible evidence of a landowner's pride of place and mastery over nature. Today, the organic enthusiast may seek out a similar peach but for very different reasons. Concern for the environment, one's health, and the plight of the small farmer may override all other considerations, even exorbitant cost. In both cases the consumer's values are revealed: landholding and power in the former, physical and environmental health in the latter.

The time and difficulty of food preparation may also inform the individual's choice. Some opt for the convenience of grabbing a quick snack on the go, while others value the time and energy devoted to cooking a meal from scratch as an expression of their devotion to those with whom they share the meal. Presentation may also be a consideration. Food can be elegantly plated, garnished with exotic ephemera, or served from a common bowl passed around the table. The former denotes worldliness and taste, the latter familiarity and commensality. Other factors include how the food is consumed, what sensory perceptions the dish conveys, and, of course, what effects are anticipated from eating such a food. Is it perceived to be fattening or healthy, a sinful indulgence or nutritious? Lastly, all people have vivid associations with particular foods and meals, sometimes peculiar to the individual and sometimes shared within a family, group, or nationality. A dish may only appear at certain festive occasions, may be nostalgically linked with childhood, or associated with a particular social group.

Although people may claim they eat certain foods simply because they enjoy them, food preferences reveal much more than the chemical reception of positive sensory stimuli. Taste and dining preferences point to broader values, desires, and sometimes explicit food ideologies. Like any ideology, this term denotes a conscious way of behaving, in this case eating, intended both to set the individual or group apart from others but also as a dietary program that promises a kind of transformation of the self. The dieter is promised a slim figure, popularity, and perhaps romantic love. The devout Jew who keeps kosher upholds the unique covenant made with God, and by eating manifests his submission and becomes righteous. The vegetarian rejects systematic cruelty toward animals and thus becomes ethically just through the abstention from flesh. The extravagant prince earns the respect and honor of his courtly guests both by spending a fortune and by dazzling them with the wit and sophistication of his banquet. In each case the ideology reflects an entire world outlook encompassing aesthetic, political, and social values. A food ideology should be distinguished from a cuisine, or generally recognized sets of ingredients, procedures, and flavor combinations handed down through generations. Eating according to the tenets of a food ideology enacts the idealized self, changing the individual from an average consumer into someone distinct and extraordinary. In the case of the Renaissance banquet, one becomes a courtier only by eating like one, as well as dressing, speaking, and behaving as a courtier should.

Food choices reveal personality traits as well as cultural aspirations. They are, most important, indicators of identity both conscious and subconscious. The intrepid cook who hunts down the most "authentic" ingredients and pulls off an exotic meal for friends flaunts not only culinary skill but the individual's relationship to and appropriation of the "other" culture, even if ostensibly denoting a willingness to try strange new things. Conversely, someone who refuses to taste the odd and unfamiliar probably has other reservations about strange people. The meal is thus never a routine ingestion of fuel but a complex message being communicated to others, scripted and otherwise. Even when one dines alone, eating can be a reaffirmation of the self. Think of the dialogue that occurs in the mind of the ravenous health enthusiast confronted with an indulgent morsel. It may be "I deserve this treat" or "to hell with my physician's warnings," or "I am strong, I can resist you, fiendish piece of cake." Whatever the apparent meaning of the meal, there is always some underlying script, especially when eating with others.

Naturally, people eat many different kinds of meals and choose them with the intention of communicating the right message to the right audience. One would not reheat half-eaten leftovers when trying to impress a potential lover, just as one would not spend a fortune on extravagant ingredients for a hurried everyday meal eaten in solitude. Every meal has, in a sense, its own coded message. This is not to say, however, that it is always readily perceived or interpreted correctly by others. What may be intended as cozy informality to someone preparing a meal might be interpreted as crass effrontery or laziness by an invited guest. Equally, a meal of roast beef offered to a vegetarian might be construed as a calculated insult. As with all language, there can be miscommunication. Despite this, an outsider observing or commenting on an eating event can usually decode the intended message without too much difficulty.

In the case of meals recorded in the past, the task of the interpreter is somewhat more complex. The vocabulary of food has changed, the syntax and much of the grammar too. That is, the ingredients are different, we cook them differently, and serve them in a different order. Understanding the logic in past food practices is much like translating an archaic language: a great deal depends on the context. Sometimes we still miss the jokes. This difficulty is compounded by the fact that accounts are usually delivered secondhand. They may be through the eyes of a witness or on the pages of an authority who may be projecting her own values onto the meal. Naturally, when a banquet planner or chef describes his own creations, we must always anticipate a certain degree of hyperbole.

With these cautions in mind, it is still possible to decode eating habits throughout history and, by examining food preferences, ultimately uncover the values and preoccupations of people with whom we cannot communicate. For example, consider the message intended by an aristocratic hunter who invites his social inferior to partake in his catch. The exchange, while ostensibly displaying friendship, may also be reinforcing deference, dependence, and mutual obligation. The key lies entirely in the context. Serving a guest a food widely regarded as an aphrodisiac sends a different kind of message if in an intimate setting. Ordering an outlandish and highly spiced dish to be shared among friends can, again depending on the context, be intended as a challenge to see who has the most daring palate. Those who can withstand the hottest or most revolting food have affirmed their superiority over those who have bowed out. This is, even if in sublimated form, a reenactment of basic hard-wired rutting instincts. In fact, in each of these examples, the meal re-stages, if you will, a central human drive to dominate, to woo, to challenge. Each is also a kind of play.

Any meal, past or present, thus contains a script. It might be said that every participant in the eating event is equally an actor. Sometimes the roles are rigidly cast, particularly in the case of formal aristocratic dining, but the parts can also be improvised and negotiated in the course of a meal. In this respect, a meal is a form of theater. In the case of the banquets described here, this is literally the case, replete with an audience, stage sets, props, and interludes. A state banquet serves as propaganda, displaying the wealth and power of the host, purveying a message of stability, order, and hierarchy. But it also functions on much more subtle levels. Is the produce imported from the far ends of the earth? This may be intended to display trade networks or the breadth of colonial empires. Is the meal restrained and frugal? Perhaps a prelate intends to impress guests with his own piety and self-control. Does the chef try his hardest to present innovative grand creations, or does he present traditional fare firmly associated with national identity? All these factors make the meal a highly structured and carefully staged performance.

Not only the context of the performance but also the associations of particular foods and preparations are crucial to explaining what the meal may have meant to those present. Certain foods had explicit meanings no longer current, just as word meanings subtly shift over time. Melons and eels, for example, would have struck any elite diner in the sixteenth century as particularly toothsome but also dangerous foods, which in excess would lead to illness. A sweet and finely ground chicken and almond dish (the original *blancmange*), on the other hand, was considered good for convalescents, easy to digest, and thus would have been included in a menu where guests might choose to eat "light" fare. The appearance of eyeballs on a plate or staring at you from within a pie would, of course, be received with horror today, but does not seem to have bothered the Renaissance diner. The meaning of food evolves over time, despite the persistence of associations such as caviar, truffles, and rare wines with elegance and special occasions.

The actors themselves had a great impact on the underlying message. Careful consideration of who was performing will also yield clues about the subtext of a meal. For example, in the case of the small Italian city-states from which most dining books in this period originate, it is important to remember that few of these rulers really held much power. They might even be considered weak when compared to nation-states like Spain and France, which had been struggling for dominance of the peninsula for the first half of the sixteenth century. It was in this setting that Machiavelli wrote *The Prince,* as a call to a powerful leader to unite the peninsula and liberate it from the barbarians. A few of these petty despotisms had expanded geographically and had greater titles affixed to their names (the Gonzaga went from Marquises to Dukes in 1530, and Cosimo de' Medici became Grand Duke of Tuscany in 1569), but they were still relatively small compared to kingdoms and The Empire. The papacy was in no better position as a temporal state. What this suggests is that their displays of power were not born of self-confidence but out of a real need to cement relationships and broadcast a message of strength and stability. But it all masked an underlying fragility, especially for the smaller cities threatened by their larger neighbors. Ferrara is a perfect example, and it was indeed swallowed by the Papal States in 1598. It should not be surprising that it is in such cities that some of the most dazzling banquets were held, nor that accounts of them were published for everyone to read. The great banquets of the d'Este, in context, can be read not so much as dazzling displays of wealth and power but as an attempt merely to communicate to other states the impression of strength.

As Machiavelli himself made clear to his would-be liberator of Italy from the barbarians, everything is a matter of appearance. The semblance of piety, the apprehension of power and ruthlessness, the reputation of virtue, are all more important than the actual possession of these traits. The banquet management books sound much the same note, particularly in their authors' insistence that the honor of the banquet manager, or *scalco,* depends on the performance of the meal, as does the reputation of the prince himself. This is especially the case when foreigners are present; everything is carefully calculated to enhance the standing of the prince, both in the banquet itself and in the printed accounts that will be carried abroad.

The importance of putting on a good show and publishing the results may even explain why the truly powerful courts in the sixteenth century produced few cookbooks or accounts of their banquets. Their power spoke for itself. Only when the foundations of state threatened to crack did the cookbooks and courtly dining guides proliferate. Perhaps it was not by chance that such works were first published in seventeenth-century Spain, as its glory began to wane. This may be coincidental, but in any case careful attention to who is throwing the banquet and why, who is invited and for what reason, can be as revealing as what appears on the plate.

The very fact that banquet accounts are published is evidence enough that these are spectacles not only for those present but for the courtly gossips and avid readers—banquet managers or *scalchi* at other courts eager to learn exactly "how to" throw the perfect banquet. Princes themselves would have been anxious to "keep up with the d'Este." Though they may have been rulers of small, relatively insignificant states, they still hoped to project an image of taste and sophistication.

Banquets could also become a matter of overt competition. Without real battles to wage, the Medici, Gonzaga, and papal court fought with their forks. There were not only catering guides but also cookbooks, books on manners and comportment, gardening and hunting guides— books containing all the information necessary for a rising courtier. That the reader might not yet be sure how to do it explains the proliferation of works in these genres. These books were a form of propaganda for the courts that produced them. They were also bestsellers for wannabes hoping to gain access to these courts and fearful lest they cut an inelegant caper, commit a faux pas over the pheasant, or, worse, let it fall off the carving fork into her ladyship's lap.

Guidebooks were also important because service at table was one of the primary routes of patronage for aspiring lesser nobles, junior cadets in obscure and impoverished families, and those on the margins of respectability. Service was the surest way to have your name, face, and well-turned leg noticed by those in power. Thus a prince was sending a message not only to his elite guests and foreign dignitaries but to his courtly staff, and even to the general public when they were invited to gawk. Everything was an elaborate performance in cooking, serving, and eating. It was also a mummery or "dumb show" for the real power relations that took place outside the banquet hall. In ritualistic form the unequal status of diners was enacted in the seating arrangements, and especially in who was invited to serve whom. Patronage networks were in silent form made perfectly clear, perhaps even more so than with a modern corporate management flowchart that only graphically represents subordination. Here it is acted out for everyone to see. It would also become perfectly plain when insubordination threatened to disrupt social harmony. As in any form of theater, when the suspension of disbelief is destroyed, the ceremonial insult transforms into the real, and when a conscious affront occurs in a meal, the illusion is broken, and the image of stability and harmony is shattered.

Equally important as communicating to underlings is the presence of visiting foreign dignitaries. In the delicate maneuvers of diplomacy, both in Italy and the nation-states, entertaining political equals, or their representatives, in style was another component of the drama performed at the banquet table. Animosities and rivalries were temporarily buried, the banquet table becoming a kind of proscenium separating the real from the play acting of polite conversation and nibbling. Offering and accepting food, literally from one's own plate, was seen as a gesture of good will. Giovanni della Casa explains these acts, as well as the inherent danger of condescension toward those who consider themselves equals. Not eating with gusto, or worse, refusing food, could be interpreted as an act of broader defiance, much as it would be at any table. In della Casa's *Galateo,* a guidebook for courtly behavior, the author explains

> I do not believe that it is proper to offer something from one's own plate unless the person who is offering it is of a much more exalted rank; then the person who receives it will consider this an honor. Between men of equal rank, it will seem that the person who is offering is somehow making himself the superior of the one to whom he is offering it, and sometimes what is given may not be to the other person's taste. Besides, this shows that the banquet does not have sufficient dishes and that they are not evenly distributed, for one person has too much and another not enough, and this could embarrass the master of the house. Nevertheless, in this matter we must do what is done, and not what should be done, for it is better to be impolite with others than to be correct all by oneself. But whatever is proper, you must not refuse what is offered to you for it will seem that you either despise or rebuke the man who is offering it to you.[1]

Clearly della Casa understands the dangers of these customs but is willing to advise submission when necessary. His comments also explain why banquet guidebooks are scrupulous about providing the exact same sets of dishes to each group of diners. Not to do so would be considered a calculated insult on the part of the host. So too, it seems, is failure on the part of guests to share their food as these strange rituals began to be played out, always keeping in mind that one only offers food to social inferiors and always accepts food from superiors.

What then did the typical banquet of the sixteenth and seventeenth century say? What script was encoded in the food itself? Much of the message is plain enough. The sheer volume and variety of food speak loudest: "Make no mistake about it, I am extremely wealthy." Keeping in mind that this is an era of relatively few luxury items, beyond decorating your palazzi and buying nice clothes and jewels, expensive foods were the best way to flaunt your wealth. Spices and sugar in particular, in copious doses—one would never want to seem tightfisted with them—not only proclaim the lengths a person will go to flavor food but are also the most conspicuous form of consumption. Spices are literally consumed and their rarefied aroma is even more evanescent than the meal itself.

Beyond extravagant seasoning, the variety of meats, fowl, and fish, much of which was hunted or caught, communicates a message that is more complex than a mere display of wealth. Here it is privilege. Although pedigreed nobles were not as abundant in Italy as elsewhere, and were sometimes even less endowed than their mercantile neighbors, serving wild game was still the preserve of the nobility. Ordinary peasants could in fact hunt, and much of their diet was no doubt supplemented by the odd hare or pigeon that wandered by. But hunting as a daily leisure activity was the exclusive privilege of the landed nobility and their guests, particularly when dealing with large game like boar and venison, requiring many men, equipment, and horses. Throughout the Middle Ages there was an explicit association of large game with nobility, and in many places there were legal restrictions on who was allowed to hunt and where. Many nobles set up their own fenced-in hunting parks when the wild forests and game populations shrank. And of course hunting also served as a training ground for war, as well as a diversion for the bloodthirsty in times of peace.

The Renaissance courtier was still a warrior, but he was also becoming something of the scholar, art collector, and man of taste. It seems that this in part explains how and why dietary preferences were changing. Eating large quantities of food was no longer socially acceptable, nor was wolfing it down. The civil gentleman "does not devour like the wolf, nor does he chomp vigorously like a goat, nor gnaw on bones like a dog."[2] But it went much further than mere manners. Appreciating the proper balance of spices, or the perfect degree of cooking by the most complex methods invented, ran in tandem with good taste in paintings and poetry. This may explain the gradual shift toward lighter whiter meats such as veal and capon, and delicate viands over large game animals associated with violence and hunting.

By the Renaissance, large game still appeared, but more often we find smaller morsels and tiny elegant wildfowl gracing the banquet table. These would have been captured by a trained falcon, and this too had long been a noble recreation. Smaller birds were also caught with sticky quicklime smeared on tree branches. The sheer number of birds served, sometimes hundreds in one meal, suggests that they were probably purchased from tradesmen as well. In the case of domestic fowl it is not so clear. Nobles often kept dovecotes, towers, and coops, especially in rural areas, specifically for raising pigeons. Even in cities they could be supplied by the family estate beyond the walls. Wealthy city folk typically owned rural holdings that they would lease to sharecroppers who would regularly send a proportion of their produce to their landlord. In any case, wherever their provenance, by the sixteenth century, fowl is the food most readily associated with nobility. Lighter-fleshed fowl included pheasant, partridge, pigeon, and capon. Add the turkey recently introduced from the Americas, guinea fowl from Africa, and also the old standbys—peacock, geese, and other waterfowl. In the erotic dream banquet described in Francesco Colonna's *Hypnerotomachia Poliphili,* written in the fifteenth century, this shift is already apparent. Along with cordials redolent of musk, roses, and unicorn horn, each course contains a different fowl: capon, partridge, pheasant, and peacock.[3] This preference for lighter delicate meats would predominate for the next two centuries.

Although tastes had not become entirely domesticated (nor had courtiers themselves), the proliferation of more dainty foods does send a new kind of message to diners: although vast quantities of food are still fashionable, we also know fine food when we see it. We have taste and discernment and sensitive palates.

As an analogue to fowl, and suitable for Lent and other fast days, fish were another favorite gracing courtly tables. In particular were large species such as sturgeon and salmon, but also eels, oysters, and shellfish. In a sense they provide a conceptual replacement, and are also hunted, or at least captured. They fulfill the association of noble eating with wild foods, even if hunting them is less glamorous and done by professional fishermen. Again, with fish too, it is not merely the large, expensive, and in a manner of speaking "hunted" fish that appear, but small supremely succulent morsels that can be eaten in dainty mouthfuls. Ease of eating, cleanliness, and polite manners may also explain the shift to smaller pieces of food presented, as well as the obsession with elegant carving.

This is not to suggest that medieval diners were outright slobs, gouging huge hunks of flesh from whole carcasses or tossing half-eaten limbs behind their backs—the image we conjure up of Henry VIII as portrayed by Charles Laughton. One can easily go too far in imagining the rude, uncouth, and uneducated medieval warrior suddenly transformed by Renaissance culture into the graceful witty courtier. It was certainly not so simple as that. Nor can a dramatic and immediate distinction be drawn between medieval and early modern cuisine. But there is a gradual shift in the style of what appears on the plate, the garnishes—and indeed that there is a plate. The oyster, for example, though hardly rare or expensive, fits the bill nicely for foods most highly esteemed by Renaissance courtiers. It comes in just the right mouthful, with a beautiful package, and with just the hint of venereal association to titillate the palate. Oysters can also appear anywhere in a meal, as a starter, within a main course, or with the fruit course. The message here is indeed that the meal should be fraught with flirtation from beginning to end, something made difficult if not unsavory with greasy fingers.

Lastly, fresh domestic meat also typically appears on noble tables—as opposed to preserved. Veal in particular is preferred, but also beef—indeed every imaginable part, along with kid and lamb. This is not to say that cured meats and hams are disdained—in fact quite the opposite. They are standard in first courses, typically cooked and served cold. But they do not receive the central placement in the meal nor the variety of preparations that the more highly esteemed and "lighter" foods do, notably fowl, veal, and sturgeon. Furthermore, the more exquisite the presentation of these items, again the more highly esteemed. This probably explains the obsession with pies. Why serve something simple and unadorned when it can be dismembered, seasoned, sauced, and garnished all in a grand container made just for the occasion from something as fleeting as dough? On a similar level, sugar transformed into incredible stage-set sculptures depicted mythological scenes or some attribute of the guest of honor, ringed by columns, garlands, flowers, and animals. These were the real centerpieces of the Renaissance banquet, even though they usually appeared at the beginning of a meal, at least in Italy.

Despite the preference for a few species, there were surprisingly few foods that courtiers would not eat. A notable exception to this is that beans rarely appeared, and then usually fresh. Garlic and onions too were a rarity, no doubt because of their supposedly offensive odor. Cesare Evitascandalo advises that it would not be good "to place in the midst of a banquet table onions, garlic, scallions, anchovies and similar things, though it may seem to some a pretty invention, it will not however be honorable, for besides the stink they bear, they will suggest that the diners are rustics."[4] These items were nonetheless served cooked or included as ingredients in composed dishes. In the French cookbooks onions became a standard aromatic.

In the minds of courtiers only a few foods were firmly associated with lower classes. Renaissance banquet menus, in the sixteenth century especially, included practically anything that could be obtained, provided it was cooked with discretion and served with panache. Foods that dietary authors of this period typically associate with lower classes (tripe, sausages, herring, and simple porridges or polenta) still find their way into elite banquets. This fact itself is revealing. Not only was there little aversion to cheap foods, body parts, and lowly vegetables, but diversity and abundance for its own sake seems to have been the primary goal. A menu often reads like a taxonomic catalogue of every variety of fish, fowl, or flesh. Courtiers may have been found ogling at the grand presentation dishes, but they could also choose from an enormous variety of dishes prepared from a wide array of creatures and plants both rare and expensive and perfectly ordinary.

This suggests that at most banquets, the superiority of courtly diners was so apparent and undeniable that there was no fear of debasement by eating lowly or common foods. This is not to say that others did not have explicit ideas about what foods are appropriate for people at opposite ends of the social spectrum. But courtiers themselves seem to have paid no heed to such associations. Apart from a few items they valued the most, any other food could be found beside it. For example, artichokes and asparagus are the most typical vegetables, but we also find cabbages, turnips, and a slew of other ingredients that would normally grace the peasant's soup pot.

A detailed account of the ingredients used in Renaissance banquets and how they were cooked appears in following chapters, but the question remains, why were certain fowl and fish so highly esteemed, and what message did serving them communicate to guests? It might be useful to decode an entire menu found in one of the banquet management guides to answer this question. Giovanni Battista Rossetti offers some of the most extensive menus of the sixteenth century in his *Dello Scalco*. Without doubt the most fascinating of these involve serving an entire meal composed of one ingredient. It is as if abundance and variety itself could no longer impress, then culinary virtuosity, wit, and allusion take their place. The same shift occurs in cookbooks at the same time.

For the time being, here is the scenario. A dinner, which in this case means a meal before noon, was held during Lent in the month of March, sometime before 1584, when the book was printed. Because held during Lent, there were no meat or fowl dishes. We are only told that both cavaliers and ladies were present, but not how many. Judging from the fact that all the dishes were presented in multiples of four, we can guess that it was a fairly small number, given that large banquets and weddings included up to sixteen sets of every cooked item. The meal is not intimate, though; smaller dinners or suppers could have as few as two plates of every cooked food. For five consecutive days similar dinners were served, each highlighting one single species of fish. Only on the fifth day does Rossetti confess that he gave up his interesting exercise in culinary invention. It is also worth noting that as *scalco,* Rossetti takes credit for devising the menus; the cook was merely handed the order to prepare everything.

The successive dinners all follow the same basic structure, two courses followed by a fruit course. Because these are not banquets, no cold first course appears, nor a course of confections at the very end. This was a comparatively small meal, and simple in structure. In each of the three courses there were fifteen separate preparations. Balance and harmony between the courses appears to have been of utmost importance, as well as their balanced arrangement on the table. Everything in the first two hot courses was composed of sturgeon, the most highly esteemed fish by all contemporary accounts owing to its delicate white flesh, but also no doubt because of its size and cost. There were, therefore, thirty sturgeon dishes in multiples of four—or 120 servings in all. Because it was expected that every person should be able to choose any of the dishes, each of the sets of dishes was placed in the vicinity of a small grouping of people, and again, this was a small dinner. In another banquet, also served in multiples of four, we are told that there were twenty-four guests.[5]

Something else becomes apparent while progressing through the roster of dishes served. Practically nothing has been wasted. Several whole sturgeons would have been required for this meal, and nearly every anatomical part makes an appearance. Unlike typical meals, where the taxonomic variety itself seems to have been the goal, here it appears to be the anatomical specificity of each dish. Little in the postmodern culinary repertoire can beat the ingenuity here.

The meal began with the head cooked in a white sauce sprinkled with pomegranate seeds. This was followed by sturgeon meatballs in a sauce served on slices of bread. Then slices of sturgeon in a pistachio sauce arrived. These were all ceremonially carried to the table to accentuate the dramatic effect. Next came sturgeon pies, then sturgeon under cherries and jujubes—a small date-like fruit. Then another kind of sturgeon pie, a soup of sturgeon "milk" (milt or fish semen) with herbs, white cabbage with sturgeon belly, crushed chickpeas with salted sturgeon, sturgeon tripe on German bread, sturgeon removed from its pastry shell with spicy sauce, sturgeon eggs and beaten sturgeon in a thick soup with sops, pieces of sturgeon in the German fashion with French mustard, fresh caviar, and lastly sturgeon meatballs cooked in a baking tin.

The second course replicated the traditional second course of roasted food, and appropriately included sturgeon on a spit with garlic and rosemary, grilled sturgeon, thin strips or *tagliadelle* of sturgeon fried with orange garnish, beaten sturgeon dressed in a crab shell, and large slices of sturgeon stewed with green sauce. Then proceeded a tart of sturgeon milt with spinach, stuffed rolls of sturgeon on a spit, poached sturgeon belly cut into batons and put into crescent-shaped pastries (*fiadoncini*) with candied citron and then fried, pieces of sturgeon stuck with sea squash to replicate larding, sturgeon *accarpionato* (fried and seasoned with vinegar) then grilled on paper, sturgeon beaten with caviar and herbs in snail shells, rolls of sturgeon with fried leeks, fried slices of sturgeon with fried parsley, sturgeon milt baked and served on biscuits, and finally tiny meatballs stewed then fried with rosemary and sage fritters.

The fruit course was just that, though that term was defined much more broadly to include nuts, truffles, fennel, and cardoons as well as various fruits. It looked much like any fruit course, and one can imagine the diners somewhat relieved not to find mock fruits made of sturgeon. Such things were common though, made of sugar or marzipan.

Without doubt the ingenuity of the *scalco* and skill of the cook in pulling off all these techniques was the main message being communicated here. The dishes also often mimicked other preparations normally made of meat or other ingredients. Notice the sturgeon pasta. But more important, the repertoire of cooking procedures, being rehearsed with one ingredient, flaunts the inventiveness and *virtù* of the kitchen staff. Just as a mannerist painter would go out of his way to reproduce every possible variation of the human form twisted into every possible and impossible position, or the architect who would invent subtle reconfigurations and playful references to standard classical ornament, so too the cook here is telling a kind of inside joke. Wordplay and macaronic poetry of the period function the same way. Only those who know the standard dishes can appreciate the humor and surprises. Rather than hash up traditional, expensive, and still quite impressive fare, the meal is construed to challenge the diners. Sturgeon masquerades in the shells of other creatures, in shapes and sizes where we expect to find meat, and hidden in pastries the contents of which are only revealed in a dramatic flourish of crust-breaking.

This is not to say that medieval banquets did not feature their own "subtleties"—peacocks resewn into their feathers spewing flames and such, but here the dishes are meant less to dazzle with mere spectacle than to get the diners thinking, conjuring associations, considering the many novel variations on a theme. Sixteenth-century poetry exploits the very same aesthetic approach—familiar classical topoi, somehow shifted or viewed from a new unexpected angle. Standard metaphors are reconfigured, repeated in various guises, always with the intention of showing off the creator's inventive wit. Not surprisingly, many of Rossetti's banquets also feature a theme, perhaps Hercules, Venus, or Orpheus, both impersonated by actors, depicted in sugar sculpture, and referred to in the food itself. A Turkish-themed banquet refers to the name of the principal guest—Signor Conte Hippolito Turchi.[6]

One might go so far as to suggest that even the textures, the variety and contrast of the individual dishes, and even the flavors themselves denote a particularly mannerist approach to food. Mannerism is the period in art history roughly following the work of Michelangelo, early in the sixteenth century and extending through his followers all the way to the century's end. It is characterized by witty transformations of the human body, elongation or twisted serpentine double *contrapposto* poses. The depiction of space and lighting is also not rationally organized. Figures crowd the surface and focus appears to give way to ornamentation, sharp contrasts, and decorative surface for its own sake. It is first and foremost a style about style itself.

The banquets described in dining literature appear to appeal to the very same aesthetic values. Soft and finely pounded dishes to one side, fried crisp morsels on the other, unctuous sauced dishes here, and charred morsels there. The same preoccupation with color and textural contrasts appears in the painting of the period. A marble-like complexion peers beneath a lush damask, or rippling muscles bulge beneath the sheerest pastel silk. Everything is suffused with a sweetness, in the case of cookery literally, and presented with dramatic poise, garnished and embellished to provide the maximum visual effect, even threatening a total lack of focus with attention to a profusion of intricate detail.

Perhaps the analysis of an individual recipe would clarify this manner-ist aesthetic, apparent not only in the presentation of an entire menu but within each cooked dish as well. Bartolomeo Scappi's *Opera* is without doubt the most extensive cookbook of this period, appearing in 1570 a decade before Rossetti, but recording meals served several decades before. Scappi and Rossetti were contemporaries, and Scappi offers a number of sturgeon recipes that match Rossetti's exactly—in fact, there is an even greater variety. One in particular seems a close match and illustrates this approach to flavor and texture contrasts, as well as dramatic presentation. It is found in book 3, recipe 15, and describes How to Make Stuffed Sturgeon Rolls, cooked on a spit or stewed.[7] The term he uses is *polpette,* which often refers to meatballs as we use that term, but here takes the chopped fish stuffing as the name for the entire dish. This treatment is normally called *brisavoli,* and Scappi uses that term as well when they are braised.

First, ten pounds of sturgeon from both the belly and the side are taken, and the lean meat cut into slices a palm wide, three fingers across, and one finger deep. These are then pounded twice with the flat side of a knife and sprinkled with fennel, salt, and pepper and brushed with a bit of verjuice—the sour juice of unripe grapes. The rest of the meat is then cut up finely with a knife to form a filling, flavored with two ounces of cinnamon, nutmeg, and cloves beaten together, along with four ounces of clear verjuice, half a pound of sugar, saffron, and enough salt, six ounces of currants (tiny raisins rather than ribes), and a handful of beaten herbs such as mint, marjoram, pimpernel, and wild thyme. This mixture is then stuffed into cutlets forming meat rolls in the shape of calzone, which implies little crescents. These are then skewered with bay leaves or sage between each and cooked quickly next to a hot flame to prevent them from falling apart or drying out. The juice that falls from them into a dripping pan (which indicates that they are cooked not directly above the fire but on spits beside it) is mixed with verjuice and sugar and served as a sauce. There are further variations, but this one seems closest to the dish mentioned by Rossetti.

The contrast of flavors and textures is most apparent in this dish. Sweetness from a great deal of sugar contrasted with the sour verjuice, the aromatic spices and herbs, as well as salt indicate that Scappi is aiming for a polyphony of flavors or a polysipid effect. The greater the concatenation of tastes discernible in the finished dish, the better. Rather than focusing on one flavor, accentuating it or heightening it with complementary seasonings, the goal here is for vibrant high notes each vying for attention. The textures too, in our mind perhaps discordant, here are calculated to offer a variety of sensory experiences in each mouthful, the soft chopped interior punctuated with raisins, yet surrounded by a firm roasted exterior and a smooth sauce. Then there is the matter of presentation, each little crescent of fish its own self-contained package, dainty and small enough to be eaten in a few bites.

One must also consider the sheer volume that would be produced by this one recipe. Estimating the total weight of ingredients at more than eleven pounds four ounces, and given each roll weighing about three ounces, that yields about sixty individual servings, which is roughly the number of guests at a good-sized banquet. Multiply that number by some thirty dishes and there are veritable mountains of food. Copiousness itself and variety is the message. Exactly as in mannerist arts and literature, the panoply of forms crowded onto the canvas, stuffed into the narrative, or piled onto the banquet table is itself an aesthetic ideal. And each variation on the theme highlights the author's creative talent. Not only the painter or writer but the cook too becomes a heroic master over raw untamed nature. In the end the message is one of artifice, or artificiality in the original positive sense of this word.

The comparisons between painting and cooking leap out when thinking of specific mannerist paintings. Consider Pontormo's *Deposition* in the Chiesa di Santa Felicita in Florence, in which a swirling mass of figures in vibrant pinks and blues floats in space as if recently stirred up in a huge cocktail glass. The bodies artificially poised on the edge of elegant toes defy gravity, filling practically every inch of the painting's surface. Profusion itself and attention to detail in every interlocking limb is much the same as Scappi's riot of tastes and textures, not haphazardly thrown together, but carefully counterbalanced to lead the eye, or in this case the tongue, around the full gamut of flavors.

Bronzino's celebrated *Allegory of Love* in Britain's National Gallery also provides an apt counterpart to late-Renaissance cookery. Here the topic, intentionally obscure it seems, unfolds only as the viewer peers within the recesses of the vibrant blue curtain. A sweet girl bearing a honeycomb is found to be connected to a slithering serpentine tail. A face writhing in agony, discarded masks, not to mention Venus and

Cupid twisted into anatomically impossible poses, are all juxtaposed to the brilliant marble-like shimmer of human flesh. Apart from the obvious theatrical references, and subtle hints about duplicity and the passage of time, it is the artist's frenetic powers of invention that are the real subject here, as well as surprise and marvels and deliciously perverse innuendoes. Technical virtuosity and style, so rarefied that only the greatest connoisseur can begin to unravel its meaning, makes the painting accessible only to the most cultured few. The viewer who "gets it," much like the diner who can discern the mayhem on every plate, thus stands apart as the true man of culture.

If these individual paintings may be compared to a recipe, then Michelangelo's Sistine Chapel ceiling perhaps provides the best comparison to the entire mannerist banquet. Though it was painted early in the century it does set the stage for mannerist taste for succeeding generations. Not coincidentally, steam from Scappi's kitchen may very well have wafted through the chapel. They were both in Rome from the late 1530s, though Scappi began to work for Popes Pius IV and Pius V only when Michelangelo was very old. But there are definitely several years in the late 1550s and 1560s when they were both in Rome. It is not inconceivable that they appreciated each other's labors. It is known for certain that Scappi cooked for Cardinal Pietro Bembo, who might be considered the greatest of mannerist authors. For the moment though, begin by thinking of the overall structure of the Sistine ceiling. It is highly programmatic, the nine central panels progressing chronologically through Creation as recounted in Genesis and ending with the Drunkenness of Noah. Stationed between each panel and perched along the trompe l'oeil architecture are the *ignudi,* each twisted into a unique pose. The trick here, of intentionally blurring the lines between solid architecture and the painted, is not unlike the ingenious devices employed by the cook—disguised foods and, especially, multiple variations on a single theme. Each of these bodies exhibits the skill and ingenuity of the artist in the same way a single ingredient prepared in dozens of ways displays the cook's skill.

The tonality of these frescos, especially after restoration, includes vibrant lavender, peach, and pastel greens and blues. These colors are placed in proximity on the garments of the prophets and sibyls, intentionally highlighting their contrast, again much the same way spices and flavors are juxtaposed rather than melded in late-Renaissance cooking. Michelangelo often uses iridescent shifts of color, particularly on silk, not only to please the eye but to delineate form and body mass and to suggest movement and tension. The effect is to call attention to a figure that would otherwise be lost or unreadable. Again, flavor combinations function in a similar fashion. They pique the palate, preventing it from becoming jaded or worn out. A succession of similar flavors from a variety of comparable meats or fowl would eventually become indistinguishable, but when highlighted by sour, salty, sweet notes, they become distinct and more easily discerned. By comparison, in polyphonic music, dissonance and modulation of volume and timbre serve to keep the ear awake and well-attuned.

There are also comparisons that can be made regarding composition and arrangement of space. Michelangelo's picture frame is crowded with forms facing every possible direction, so densely packed with ingredients that the variety and copiousness can easily be compared with the broad range of foodstuffs and composed dishes gracing the banquet table. Even their arrangement into balanced compartments reflects the same aesthetic approach to organization of what would otherwise be an unreadable mass of material. Still, the emphasis is on the parts rather than the whole, which cannot be digested all at once. If we imagine the entire ceiling to be a kind of banquet table, then the contrasts between large and small frames, bronze medallions, and marble pilasters are arranged precisely as the *scalco* would set the table. Two similar dishes, say two roasts or boiled dishes, were never placed side by side. Large central platters would be surrounded by smaller dishes, accented by vases, small condiment bowls, and other accoutrements, all symmetrically arranged in balanced groupings. .

Furthermore, although there are many placards explaining who the figures are, and the central biblical narrative would have been understood by most viewers, one cannot help feel that as a whole the ceiling could only be appreciated by cognoscenti, and of course those with strong necks. The prophets and sibyls, as well as the ancestors of Jesus, and other ancillary scenes all foreshadow events in the life of Jesus and the Final Judgment. Only a sophisticated viewer would have understood the way all parts are linked thematically. The subtle ways the stories resonate off each other function just as the succession of dishes in the banquet refers to other dishes or conjures associations in the mind of the diner. For example, in the banquets with running themes, sugar sculptures, foods or preparations that pun a guest's name, and even more subtle associations make the meal a complex narrative with many layers.

Also characteristic of mannerist style, celebrated both in painting and on the plate, is the conscious conquering of difficulty. The artist must fit the scenes and figures into an impossible series of planes, some of which are flat, others concave or triangular, some extensions of the architecture on which the bodies rest, and some painted faux marble putti, serving as supports themselves. The fresco technique, painted on wet plaster and often above the artist's head, is itself a Herculean accomplishment. The cook's triumph also lies in his ability to master numerous difficult techniques, and in the case of the sturgeon dinner mentioned above, using one ingredient. Although these mannerist feats are not explicitly competitive, they do nonetheless pit the artist against the raw material. The more difficult the challenges, the greater the skill of one who can overcome them. In all these cases, it is the performance and style that impresses the audience most, the decorations heaped on even superfluously, serving no other purpose than their own delicious beauty.

Before proceeding along these lines, a certain objection must be addressed. There are definitely taste preferences that run through the arts, and obviously we are dealing with the very same individuals eating, looking, and reading. It would be surprising not to find aesthetic similarities between various media. But how then can we account for the fact that Renaissance cooking is not from our vantage point radically distinct from medieval cooking, while in the arts there were major transformations between the fourteenth and sixteenth centuries? One can easily find similar juxtapositions of flavor and texture, ingenious tricks like the four and twenty blackbirds baked in a pie, and lavish presentations of huge amounts of food. What then makes these characteristics particularly mannerist? And why are these banquets aesthetically parallel to sixteenth-century arts, but not medieval ones if they are similar?

One possibility is that changes in taste regarding food change more slowly than visual tastes. We find many medieval recipes repeated in Renaissance cookbooks. They were sometimes placed there intentionally by the author, or often stuffed into a text by the publisher. Some recipes can be found in cookbooks spanning several centuries. *Blancmange* is a good example. A combination of pounded capon, almonds, rose water, rice starch, and sugar, it is repeated straight through the seventeenth century. No artist continued in the Gothic style by that time. Perhaps courtiers expected to find these traditional favorites alongside the novelties, and so they are reprinted though do not really represent Renaissance taste.

In fact, *blancmange,* and similar recipes using spices, rose water, verjuice, and almond milk are typical of Renaissance taste, as they were of medieval. In cooking as well as the arts, standard subjects do not disappear overnight, nor do forms of representation. The shift is always gradual and often takes centuries. Mannerism is not, in fact, as is sometimes stated, a conscious denial of early and high Renaissance values, imaginary contorted and elongated bodies replacing anatomically correct ones, illogical space supplanting the clear mathematical perspective of earlier artists, and crowded neurotic surfaces taking the place of harmonious balanced compositions with focus. Mannerists considered their work the logical culmination of Renaissance style, its perfection. So too can sixteenth-century culinary art be considered the natural progression of earlier cooking styles. There are major changes, to be sure. The use of precise measurements and cooking times is new. Attention to the quality of ingredients in season is new. Even some basic taste preferences shift. By the sixteenth century, for example, sugar and cinnamon become practically universal flavorings for every kind of dish. But late-Renaissance cooking is not an entirely new, self-consciously revolutionary style. Nor could one really claim such a thing for La Varenne in the seventeenth century. Cooks and *scalchi* inherited as much from their predecessors as they invented anew. But this is not to say that these are not distinct styles, paralleling those periods recognized by art historians, even though they are not conscious "movements" with a clear manifesto.

There is also the plain fact, then as now, that a cookbook author strives to please his audience, and this is often accomplished through breadth of coverage. There is no doubt that Scappi wanted to include absolutely every possible recipe he could think of, and of course most of them he cannot claim to have "invented" in any real sense. A number of his recipes are actually the first of their kind in print, but they too may merely have been called something else in older cookbooks. This is true of cookbooks to this day. For example, if we were analyzing one of Julia Child's classics as indicative of taste in the latter half of the twentieth century, would we be uncomfortable that some recipes are scarcely different than those found a century before? A basic pot roast is pretty much the same whenever it appears. We would look closely to find changes in ingredients, tools, or techniques, and modes of presentation. These would constitute the key elements that make the style unique. In the case of sixteenth-century cookbooks it is precisely these features that are novel: new ingredients—some from the New World, and more detailed attention to their preparation, more sophisticated techniques, a panoply of new tools—and lastly, a new way of dining. All these features will be explored in the chapters that follow.

Just as there was a gradual transition from Renaissance to mannerist taste, we must also ask if there was a comparable shift from mannerism to the baroque. There does exist a certain sobriety, particularly in Rome in the latter half of the sixteenth century and in the wake of the Council of Trent. Among its objectives was to impart a sense of decorum to religious art, nudes, and perverse compositions being seen as scarcely appropriate to bolster the faith. To that end, there was an effort to inspire works that would appeal to the emotion of spectators. Regarding incipient prudery, in this time Michelangelo's naked bodies in the Last Judgment were painted over with cloths, as was his naked Christ Risen statue given a metal loincloth. One can imagine a similar disjuncture in the career of Scappi himself, trained in the lavish style of dining fashionable since the era of Leo X, but near the end of his life made personal chef to Pope (Saint) Pius V, who was renowned for his abstemious diet. This may be why Scappi's work was published in Venice. The tenor of the papal court had indeed sobered. But this new tone, and particularly the energy and dynamism to grab and hold spectators, did not find its perfect expression until the next century in the baroque. Only then did a style emerge featuring emotional intensity, with lighting effects that heighten the central drama and are calculated to strengthen the faith of observers drawn into the picture frame by careful composition.

Because the scope of this study covers both mannerism and the baroque, can banquets of the seventeenth century be shown to reflect this new aesthetic in the same way artists like Caravaggio rejected what they considered the twisted artificiality of their predecessors? That is, does the focus on naturalism, emotional intensity, and dramatic unity somehow have counterparts in the realm of gastronomy? This comparison would be clear enough if we looked at French cookbooks after the mid seventeenth century and the gradual replacement of spiced, sweet-and-sour flavor preferences with stock reductions and flavors meant to focus and accentuate the main ingredient. The proliferation of unctuous roux and butter-based sauces might even be compared to the indulgent voluptuousness of artists like Rubens. But we have a good half century to account for, the first half of the seventeenth century, which coincides with the advent of the baroque.

The comparison to painting in the early seventeenth century is perhaps misleading, especially to the singular genius of Caravaggio, because there is no comparable intensification and simplification in the other arts. It can be said that there is a certain dramatic unity and heightened emotionalism in media such as architecture and the decorative

arts—perhaps the closest relatives to cookery. For example, the baroque
facade has a certain movement and focus lacking in those of the sixteenth
century: dramatic staircases, soaring towers, energetic curved rather
than static straight lines, and resplendent ornaments all lead the eye
to a central focal point. This style appears in Rome in the first decades
of the seventeenth century with Carlo Maderno, and thereafter a few
figures dominate: Gianlorenzo Bernini, Borromini (Francesco Castello),
and Pietro da Cortona. The aim in baroque art, and especially in altars
and ceilings, is to draw the viewer with intense and often grandiose out-
pourings of emotion. Thus we have putti spilling about, sunbursts and
clouds, grand staged settings that rivet the attention of spectators who
are able at once to grasp the meaning and intent of the whole composition. Rather than distracting the viewer with their elegant beauty, as in
mannerist works, the decorative motifs themselves are all subordinated
to and point with energy and thrust to the unified whole, which is the
hallmark of baroque taste. Perhaps the most familiar of works in this
spirit are the huge curved colonnades designed by Bernini in the grand
piazza in front of St. Peter's. Better yet is the massive bronze *baldac-*
chino in the center of the church, begun in the mid 1620s. The twisting
columns covered with foliage and putti, the grand canopy topped with
gesturing figures, everything draws the viewer's attention heavenward,
and ravishes the senses.

How could this aesthetic possibly have a culinary equivalent? In the earliest works of the seventeenth century also produced in Rome, such as the
books by Cesare Evitascandalo, we find few changes from the preceding
century. This probably reflects the fact that most of the events described
took place years before, the book on carving having been composed in
the 1570s. By 1609, when the *Libro Dello Scalco* is printed, there is not
yet much hint of the baroque aesthetic. But in Vittorio Lancelotti's *Lo*
Scalco Prattico, published in 1627, though it recorded banquets stretch-
ing back twenty years, it is clear that something had begun to change.
Rather than a profusion of dishes placed on the table and each vying for
attention, there is a definite streamlining of the banquet. First there is
a reduction in the number of dishes, from twelve or sixteen down to a
mere six or even three. But there is also a further elaboration of each.
Before, where one simple sauce or garnish sufficed, we are now given
multiple garnishes—the aesthetic equivalent of architectural baubles,
all intended to heighten and focus the attention on the main ingredient.
This is much like the attention to lavish ingredients used in baroque

architecture: colored marble, and especially gold and silver, used both in decoration of buildings and food.

Also interesting is that the former delight with copious and diverse ingredients—as many species as possible—now gives way to an almost narrow attention to capon and veal and a few other favorites. Wild foods have been significantly demoted, and only thrushes seem to appear with as great a frequency as before. One might also say that there is a definite focus. There is still far too much food for mortals to consume, and it is still served on a monumental scale, but meats and fish no longer appear together. Nor do foods of sharply contrasting ingredients or cooking methods. This gives the meal a certain thrust and logical progression that was lacking before. The central dishes presented in each course are huge *tableaux vivantes* of one main ingredient surrounded by a profusion of garnishes drawn from a fairly narrow repertoire. One might say the same of baroque ornament in general. The same volutes, solomonic columns, curved pediments, and soaring domes appear on everything. The language of ornament has become vibrant, elaborate, and energetic. In cooking it is shredded salami or prosciutto, pastry stars or toast points, and then truffles, eggs, lemon, sweetbreads or marrow, and sometimes vegetables like cardoons or fruit. These few garnishes appear on practically every dish, usually together.

For example, there is a banquet described by Lancelotti, thrown for the ambassador of Spain in 1611 on the Monday of Carnival. To be sure, this was a day to indulge, but each dish appeared in a single serving, so this was presumably a small retinue. Other banquets require multiples of four for each dish. The structure is somewhat different than in the preceding century. In this case a cold course of five dishes arrives first, then a hot course of six, a second cold course of two, a second hot course of four, and so on. Each course alternates with a cold course and is relatively small, with only the final sixth cold course of fruits, vegetables, cheeses, and confections offering some variety. Notice that each successive course is smaller and simpler, in a sense drawing the diner toward the final climax of desserts without becoming monotonous or repetitive. In any case, there is also much greater focus within each course. What is strange is that most of the dishes are made of either veal or capon or turkey. White meats take center stage. It is not, as with Rossetti, a challenge to create many inventions with one ingredient, but to put those few items in center stage, the extras only reminding the diner where to look and drawing the attention to the main action.

The details of each recipe are equally fascinating. Lancelotti offers complete descriptive menus rather than cooking directions, but the final dish and its composition is nonetheless very clear. The first cold course consists of a veal pie in the form of a shield bearing the arms of the king, which is nothing new. There is a sugar-glazed ham surrounded by pastry baskets, with pistachio pastry stars touched up with gold and silver. Next is a roasted turkey, larded with candied citron, the ends of which are gold and silver, as are the sugar pastry wings, neck and tail. There are some confections like candied citron, marzipan, and the like, as well as cream and butter. The vast profusion, a kind of counterpoint, of dishes in mannerist banquets gives way to just a few, upon which diners can focus.

In the first hot course there is boiled capon with couscous garnished with marrow, slices of salted pork loin, egg yolks, prosciutto, and butter. These are among the new standard garnishes. Then follows larded and roasted sweetbreads of veal, stuffed, with a bastard sauce (based on Malmsey wine) surrounded by gilded and fried Spanish biscuits—a plate for each guest. Also served are little pastries of veal morsels, sweetbreads, prosciutto, lemon juice, and gilded sugar paste. There are also two soups, or more precisely a soup and *minestra,* the former made of capon, salame, parmigiano, marrow, fried provatura cheese with veal and capon broth, then the whole baked in an oven and garnished with candied egg yolks. The *minestra* is simple sweetbreads in capon broth with egg yolks, cream, and bread slices served in individual bowls. Notice how the capon takes the spotlight, while the sweetbreads in small plates and pastries accent it but do not vie for attention. They are smaller in size and complexity. The same is true of the soups, one grand, the other simpler and smaller. This is the same kind of compositional subordination, movement, and energy found in baroque decorative arts, the garnishes serving the same function as putti, swags, and the like.[8]

The subsequent courses are equally fascinating. The second credenza course consists of an egg and sugar sculpture composition with a pastry crown, garlands, marzipan rosettes, and gold and silver touches. There is no complete description of the final result, but one can easily imagine a dramatic composition not unlike the baroque fountains in Rome. There is also the curious invention of gelatin columns filled with little birds and fish suspended within as if alive. These are the theatrical frames to the central set piece. The second hot course includes some remarkable inventions as well. Boiled pigeons are covered with a sweetbread soup, cardoon slices, cockscombs, and testicles—which will become a standard ornament throughout the century—livers, prunes, and slices of salted pork loin, all over bread, in individual porcelain plates with sugar covers. There are also roasted thrushes and an egg *crostata,* and at the center is a kind of grand lasagne casserole. Between the sheets of dough cooked in broth are slices of capon breast, skin, and fresh provatura cheese fried in butter and parmigiano. The whole thing is baked in an oven, presumably until melted and bubbling, and presented with a sugar cover touched with gold.

Without lingering on the details of the subsequent courses, a few items are worthy of mention: dueling marzipan Germans in the third credenza course, as well as a little scene of dancing rustics molded out of butter. The third course from the kitchen includes another dramatic centerpiece of a rose-shaped arrangement of pastry, each section filled with eggs, *blancmange,* and quince, or royal pastry and candied citron. What is interesting is that the next cold course includes only two dishes, as does the fourth hot course. By the fifth cold course there are only olives, grapes, and sugar eagles. The fifth hot course is a little bigger, with pheasants, *blancmange,* roasted turkey pullets, and an English pie. Only in the sixth course finale is there a range of fruits, artichokes, pastries, cheeses, and olives. At the end the guests retire to another apartment to watch the *palio,* or horse race, as it passes by, during which they can munch on confections.

The structure of this meal may seem anything but a progression of flavors, according to our modern palates. Every course contains sweet and savory items. There is, nonetheless, a certain progression that leads the diner through a series of bold surprises relieved by relative calm reminiscent of the structure of baroque facades and altars. Unlike the sharp contrasts in unending succession in mannerist banquets, we begin to see not only a concentration on the main dish in each course, but a certain calculated movement and energy that leads logically to a climax.

By mid century the baroque culinary aesthetic is even more apparent, and it spreads outside Italy. This happens at the same time that Rubens, Velasquez, and Poussin perfect the baroque in painting. By the time of Bartolomeo Stefani writing in Mantua in the 1660s, or of Robert May and William Rabisha in England, baroque taste is firmly in place. The flavor combinations began to shift from sweet and spicy contrasts to butter, marrow, and fats taking a central role. There appears a profusion of vegetable and fruit garnishes, anchovies, and oranges associated with the Mediterranean, and even ambergris and musk are used extensively. Equally important is that the presentation of every individual dish is a baroque tableau.

May's recipes are the best example of the tendency to use the baroque language of ornament on what are native traditions. Basic straightforward English preparations are cooked and served in a way that is entirely baroque. This is much the way baroque art was adopted in the reign of Charles I, survived among the Catholic nobility for whom May cooked, and then resurfaced in the Restoration. One need only think of Christopher Wren's towering spires, which are essentially traditional church structures with baroque ornament and organization, to understand May's recipes. Take for example a recipe for roast shoulder of mutton garnished with oysters.[9] The oysters are first parboiled, washed with white wine, and seasoned with nutmeg and salt. Then they are stuffed into the mutton, which is larded with anchovies and roasted while being basted with wine. Meanwhile the garnishes are prepared: artichoke bottoms with butter, marrow bones and oysters flavored with gravy, orange juice, and musk or ambergris. A gravy is also made from the drippings flavored with onion and thyme, and everything arranged together in a dish, further embellished with lemon slices. The final effect is a basic and very English roast, but its form and the ingredients are in line with the international aesthetic current in the mid seventeenth century. It also has a decisive energy and thrust and focal point that are comparable to Wren's churches. The garnishes complement and support the roast but do not detract from its central role in the finished dish.

By borrowing terminology and critical tools employed by other disciplines, this thread of discourse has begun to suggest some of the ways food might be discussed. Cooking is certainly an art form informed by the same values that influence other artistic media. But it is also a craft, one that involves managing a large staff, utilizing specialized equipment, and of course procuring choice ingredients. How all these factors came together, and the techniques used to bring them to perfection, is the most interesting part of this story. Most of the chapters that follow will be concerned with ingredients, cooking techniques, and the business of putting together a banquet, as well as the way events came together in courts across Europe and what it meant to those who sponsored a meal and those who enjoyed it.

CHAPTER 2

An Introduction to
Ingredients and Wild Food

Several fundamental shifts in the European economy in the early modern period had a pronounced effect on elite taste. The growth of market gardening and the dairy industry, as well as general specialization of food production and trade, all influenced major changes in the status of several food groups. Dairy products received attention as never before, especially butter, as did fruits and vegetables as centrally featured items on elite menus. Sugar was transformed from one spice among many to the key signature flavor of the entire cuisine. The range of wild foods commonly consumed also narrowed significantly as more land was brought under cultivation and increasingly devoted to crops destined for wider markets.

This is not to suggest that taste is inevitably determined by purely material forces. A certain amount of caprice always informs elite fashion. It would be equally simplistic to suggest that it is merely social emulation that causes culinary styles to trickle down from above, or that cost and rarity are the sole factors influencing whether an article of commerce can be perceived as prestigious. The relatively rare potato attracted practically no attention, while comparatively cheap fresh green peas enjoyed a vogue in the sixteenth and seventeenth centuries. Cost did play a central role in food choice though, as some products were simply beyond the buying power of anyone but the wealthiest diners.

Apart from those luxury items unavailable to the general populace, the attention lavished on relatively common ingredients in elite cuisine merits wider consideration. Perhaps these foods merely appeared with greater frequency in the marketplace and were bound to appear more often in elite cookery, of course prepared with complex techniques. A chef hoping to exhibit his skills would not hesitate to employ the broadest range of ingredients, and apart from a few items or methods of preparation that would have been readily associated with the lower classes, such as dried beans, why not transform relatively ordinary foods into fantastic dishes?

This would make sense except that many ingredients were presented without any fuss, and sometimes in their pristine state. Fruits and vegetables, for example, were often afforded care we would not expect to find until the twentieth century. It may have been the quality and perfection of the produce itself that warranted such respect. In the minds of Renaissance gourmands, the masses enjoyed their bruised and misshapen vegetables by tossing them into the monollaic soup pot, but only the cognoscenti would appreciate the barely cooked stalks of slender asparagus dressed with nothing but a drizzle of melted butter. That is, simplicity itself can become exclusive when the ingredients are superb, and the fruit or vegetable can stand out among other complex and strongly flavored dishes.

Yet the question remains, why would certain simple ingredients suddenly appear in elite cookbooks and menus? The answer must be sought in the economic shifts mentioned above. The sheer availability and range of domestic foodstuffs prompted chefs to invent new recipes and experiment with new ways to present what were otherwise ordinary foods, even if it meant seeking out perfect specimens and presenting them relatively unadorned. This was probably the case for many relatively new vegetables—cauliflower, "red" carrots, even spinach. There was an absolute craze for artichokes and cardoons.

It is probably not coincidental that gardening itself became a popular pastime among the leisured classes. Tending orchard fruits and maintaining elegant raised vegetable beds became a noble recreation. It should not be surprising then that these foods themselves became worthy objects of attention. Selective breeding for certain desirable traits in both plants and animals was beginning to become a fitting rival to hunting for food as the ideal noble pursuit. Hunting became more of a "sport," while gardening was seen as a genteel preoccupation, as well as something that affords delight to all the senses, the mind, and even the stomach.

The original impetus for this alternate noble pursuit might even have something to do with in the revival of classical culture. The ancient Romans were extraordinary farmers, and almost all agronomic literature of the early modern period pays homage to Cato, Columella, and Varro.[1] Massimo Montanari has suggested that gaining sustenance from the forest, hunting, and eating wild animals was essentially a Germanic value, while farming, eating domestic animals, and taming nature was the inheritance of classical culture.[2] This is a simplification of his argument, but it does help explain how early modern Europeans inherited one cultural ideal and reinvigorated another that was diametrically opposed. It also explains how the same people traipsing off into mock chivalric battle could preoccupy themselves with learning Ciceronian Latin. This is not to suggest that ancient cooking was in any meaningful way revived, though scholars were truly fascinated with it after the rediscovery of Apicius, but maybe that European society in the sixteenth and seventeenth centuries was growing closer again to the ideals of civilization rooted in ancient Rome.

Changes in the European domestic economy of course played their part, along with this invigorated sense of the nobility of landed wealth and country pursuits. These influenced shifts in elite taste and attitudes toward many ingredients. So too did broader global changes, though not in the way one might expect. The full impact of New World foods such as tomatoes, maize, peppers, and potatoes was not to be felt until centuries after their discovery. A few items made their way onto elite banquet tables, most notably turkey, but most new items were used, if at all, by commoners. Some items gained a foothold in particular regions, such as maize in northern Italy or potatoes in Ireland, but New World foods were usually absent from noble menus.

The products of colonial plantation economies, however, played a central and starring role in late-Renaissance cuisine. Sugar is the most obvious example, as are certain spices, cinnamon above all. Then at the end of the period covered by this book, there appear the new caffeinated beverages, chocolate, coffee, and tea. All three, along with tobacco, another plantation crop, would offer serious competition for traditional alcoholic beverages. These were commodities resulting from an entirely new mode of production, for the most part unheard of until the sixteenth century: the colonial slave economy combined with mercantile rivalry between competing nation-states. Such foods, if they can be called that, were not exotic expensive luxuries from the far ends of the earth, but ubiquitous bulky items grown, processed, and consumed by Europeans, at the incredible cost of indigenous peoples displaced around the world, not to mention Africans sold into slavery.

There remained exotic ingredients in recipe books, musk and amber being perhaps the strangest, that are found in few other cuisines in history. They were principally used as perfumes. The former is a glandular secretion from a central Asian deer, the latter (ambergris, not the petrified resin) is spewed from the intestines of whales and was found on tropical beaches. Equally important are flower waters and other aromatics, which generally replaced the much broader range of spices used in medieval cookery. Many ingredients common in medieval recipes, such as grains of paradise, galangal, and cubebs, had disappeared from cooking almost entirely. Coriander and anise, especially in comfits, became popular. Ginger disappears from Italian cookbooks, though it lingers elsewhere. It seems that only major changes in global trade can adequately account for these culinary changes. It also appears that certain items became popular merely because they were widely available for the first time. Almonds, a staple of medieval and Renaissance cuisine, vied for attention with pistachios and pine nuts. Other garnishes such as candied citron, raisins of Corinth (or, as we call them, currants) and other dried fruits were also among the favorite new garnishes. Most were imported from the Middle East. But we also find cockscombs and bone marrow in baroque cooking, hardly rare or expensive but for some reason popular. So too were caviar and truffles, though there is little indication that these had yet become super-luxury items shipped across the continent.

No discussion of the trade in foodstuffs can ignore the difficult question of seasonality. To what extent were the limitations of the seasons overcome with technology, and did diners appreciate food at the peak of seasonal perfection? In hindsight and in an era of global trade in even the most basic foods—thanks to food technologies such as refrigeration, canning, and dehydration—we naturally assume today that all menus in the past were utterly and inescapably dependent on the seasonality of produce. Apart from a few preserved and perhaps imported items, most food had to be consumed fresh. Among elite diners there definitely was a preference for fresh meat, fowl, and fish, though there was a place for prosciutto and parmigiano, pickled birds from Cyprus, herring from the North Sea, and eventually anchovies, which became a major flavoring agent by the eighteenth century. Still, most of the food consumed by the wealthy was fresh.

It is clear, moreover, that cookbooks and culinary literature, most notably Bartolomeo Scappi's *Opera,* devoted a good deal of energy discussing how to choose the best ingredients according to season. This is especially important for wild animals and plants; a particular fish or certain fruit may only be available for a limited time. Scappi goes further in describing the optimal time of year to eat certain foods, and he often specifies where to find them. That is, one might be able to find certain wildfowl through much of the year, but they are at their best for a few months in fall, when fattened, and from cool mountaintops with brisk, clean, and circulating air. Dietary authors also discussed such considerations, though from the perspective of health rather than taste.

We might then assume that Renaissance chefs made a virtue of necessity and made the best of seasonal limitations, offering the right foods appropriately seasoned and in the right quantity and proportions for each month. Indeed, many printed menu books were arranged by month, and we can tell exactly what was served any time of year. The most obvious differences are Lenten or lean meals versus meat-based meals. There is a certain seasonal logic to these, as Lent occurs in the last months of winter and early spring, when stored meat would be running low and fish and preserved vegetables, perhaps beans, would provide a good substitute. This can, however, only have been a major consideration for poorer or rural diners, not for the wealthy, among whom stockfish, old sausages, and dried beans were often associated with the poor.

The menus reveal that for all the lip service paid to seasonality, there was little variation apart from the fast days. Salads appear any time of year, and even fruits we would not expect to find outside a narrow range of dates nonetheless show up, presumably brought up from storage. Certain dishes we might consider light and appropriate summer fare were served in winter, and conversely heavy soups and rich stodgy foods appear in summer too. There is practically no variation in seasoning, and some foods were served year-round. Credenza courses almost always contain salads and cold pastries, cured meats, and cheeses to start. The closing "fruit course" always contains items such as grapes and pears, truffles, nuts and olives, artichokes, and asparagus. Obviously, grapes in spring and asparagus in fall would have been impossible, but it does seem that if something was unavailable a comparable item would be substituted. How items like spring fava beans and cherries can appear with autumn pears remains a mystery.[3] There is no indication that any of these were preserved. Sweets hardly ever vary, nor do the basic meats. In every season there are roasts, boiled meats and fowl, pies, soups, and so forth. The type of meat might change slightly from season to season, but veal seems to have been available practically year-round, as were domestic fowl.

In fact, it may be the very idea of overcoming seasonal variability that commends the use of domestic animals, vegetables, and fruits that can either be forced out of season, preserved in cold cellars or ice houses, or reduced to conserves. Rather than an appreciation for seasonality, Renaissance menus reveal a desire to ignore nature's dictates whenever possible, through artifice or merely by importing foods from further afield. Obviously, trade in perishable food across the equator could not happen for a few centuries, but fruit out of season, especially early, titillated Renaissance diners' palates even more than it does the jaded modern supermarket shopper who today expects such things.

Bending nature to the whims of man's desires more closely approaches the late-Renaissance attitude toward produce, and in the end it seems that discussion of seasonality in cookbooks is merely meant as a buying guide, describing what one is likely to find in the market and offering some tips to make the best choices. Our recent aesthetic to eat local produce and only at the height of its season would have struck the Renaissance diner as extremely odd, particularly because eating foods out of season fetched from all around the world was a lot more impressive, and something only the wealthiest could afford to do.

Each of the chapters that follow examines in greater detail the changing status of a major food group or type of ingredient. Though the taste preferences will still appear very different from our own, the gradual progression toward modern cuisine will seem logical and not an abrupt switch from medieval spicy, sweet-and-sour preferences to the salt- and butter-based haute cuisine of the late seventeenth through twentieth centuries.[4] In most cases it was not a sudden invention or conceptual breakthrough but rather the greater availability of certain ingredients and their gradual migration into elite dining, where they remain today.

Wild Food: The Call of the Domestic

In the late Middle Ages wild foods were among the most esteemed items on banquet menus, primarily game and wildfowl but also fish, wild fruits, and vegetables. By the eighteenth century we find domesticated meats, especially veal and even beef, cooped and fattened capons, and cultivated vegetables as the focus of elegant dining. Some species had disappeared altogether from the dining room, many wildfowl and sea mammals in particular, but also smaller four-footed creatures. Something had changed during the intervening centuries. Among the factors that may have influenced this turn of fortune, ultimately causing the range of wild foods to diminish, were a growing population, shrinking acreage of uncultivated land, and the growth of cattle rearing. There may also have been a deeper cultural and intellectual shift that relegated a few wild animals to exclusive hunting, and all other wild species to marginalization, as control over nature, taming, and even, to paraphrase Francis Bacon, bending her to our will became the conceptual ideal.

There are economic reasons why the general food supply would have been more dependent on production of domesticated species. A rising demand for food resulting from demographic pressure can only have been met by increasing output and cultivating or grazing more land. There was also a greater percentage of the population living in cities, and more legal restrictions on hunting and collecting food in the wild. Ultimately there was a more dependable supply of cultivated plants and domesticated animals, particularly in northern Europe. For wildfowl the reduction of nesting grounds because of agricultural sprawl imperiled their reproductive cycles. These factors cannot be discounted, but there are other equally interesting cultural reasons for a shift. The change in mentality may have been triggered by material factors, or one could say conversely that a new relationship to nature and the willingness to subdue and master it for the benefit of humans is what ultimately led to the economic and social changes. This is a matter of ideological chicken or material egg. Whichever, there was a reduction of the number and variety of wild foods normally consumed by Europeans between the late Middle Ages and the eighteenth century. For some reason people came to prefer domestic animals and plants to wild ones.

Ingredients and Wild Food

This was also the case among elite diners, though certain wild species never lost popularity. It is nonetheless true that chefs and their patrons consciously chose whiter and lighter meats, blander vegetables, and generally more soft and delicate foods in smaller cuts over what they increasingly saw as rough food unperfected by art. Veal and capon were the rising stars in sixteenth- and seventeenth-century cooking. For many, to consume dark, rough, and gamy food was, in a sense, to become wild and uncultivated. This may itself have been an exciting diversion from the normal order of courtly behavior, not only running wild in the forest on the hunt and satisfying one's primal urges but sating the taste for blood. It seems that such a desire would only be pronounced in a culture where such food was somewhat of a transgression of the norm. This may explain why some hunted wild animals, boar and venison in particular, remained popular while others disappeared entirely.

Of course, in many places only the landed nobility were allowed to hunt venison; that had always been the case. Thus the de-emphasis on game may owe to the broadening audience of cookbooks, increasingly written for urban elites or, later, even bourgeois readers. These books would have necessarily offered fewer recipes for game. This is apparent, for example, in the mid-sixteenth-century French cookbooks.[5] Although venison and boar are briefly covered, there is also a recipe for mock venison made with mutton, red wine, and bouillon.[6] This might be taken as an indication that readers could not normally obtain wild game. The social class of the intended reader thus played a major role in the frequency of recipes for wild foods. For the cookbooks examined here in the sixteenth and seventeenth centuries, the audience is still primarily courtly or landed gentry, people with access to untamed land and thus venison, but in particular, wildfowl remain predominant.

Apart from the cookbooks and banquet management guides, there are also references to wild food in other types of culinary literature, most notably natural histories, dietary literature, and herbals. Expectedly, agricultural texts are relatively silent on the topic. These sources often reveal those species that were once common but have fallen from favor on elite tables. The authors also wrote primarily as outsiders and usually for an academic audience, and were interested in relaying facts rather than impressing with elaborate recipes and descriptions of banquets. Thus sometimes wild food that was once esteemed and had since gone out of fashion can only be found in this type of food literature.

Beginning with cookbooks, medieval sources show that people enjoyed an extraordinary range of wild species. Hunting was a favorite pastime of the leisured classes, and various species of deer (roebuck, fallow deer, and red deer), boar, and wildfowl were served and even offered as presents to relatives or to gain political favor. Patronage networks were sustained by presents of this sort. Professional hunters were also employed to bring in fresh game and were often kept permanently employed on noble estates. From late-medieval menus, in England for example, we learn that venison with frumenty (boiled whole grain) was a regular centrally featured item, as were swans, herons, cranes, and the stereotypical boar's head.[7] At royal weddings and affairs of state such items were absolutely necessary. These were often served simply roasted or, according to cookbooks such as the French *Viandier,* venison was parboiled, larded, and then simmered in wine, or set in a pastry shell with plenty of spices and perhaps served with a cinnamon-based sauce.[8] In fourteenth-century English manuscripts roe deer or boar is parboiled, chopped into pieces, and boiled in water and wine, thickened with bread and blood, spiced, and then finished off with vinegar and raisins.[9] In Italy Maestro Martino Rossi offers a civet of venison that is parboiled with vinegar, fried, and served with a sauce of raisins, almonds, bread, wine, cinnamon, ginger, and onion.[10] All these were typical medieval flavor combinations.

In the end though, there are not that many recipes for game in medieval cookbooks. Although the stereotype of the huge beast turning on a spit at every medieval feast is certainly overplayed, when a large animal was killed there would have been a desire to present it intact to show it off. This may account for the paucity of recipes, especially when compared to the lowly chicken, which a chef would not hesitate to pound, reshape, and disguise. Because roasting and simmering were fairly simple procedures, a professional chef would not need a recipe.[11] Keeping in mind that medieval cookbooks were always written for professionals in a kind of culinary shorthand and rarely give explicit measurements or detailed instructions, this may be why simple venison recipes rarely appear. It does not reflect a lack of popularity.

The relative status of venison, which then meant any hunted large wild mammal, not just deer, did not change significantly from the late medieval period into the sixteenth century. In fact it may have increased in prestige after becoming rarer and increasingly confined to enclosed parks. Recipes abound straight through the seventeenth century, especially where owning land remained the economic and cultural ideal, that is, practically everywhere in western Europe.

But game animals were only one part of the entire category of wild foods. A few wild foods were associated with the lowest classes, gathered only by those at the margins of subsistence or during famine. Hence we find reference to vetches, darnel, and lupines, normally considered weeds among grains, eaten by starving peasants. In some places there was a stigma against eating chestnuts, especially putting them into bread as was done in the Cevennes. Surprisingly, few wild foods were explicitly associated with poverty, and at the start of the early modern period it is clear that there was no particular aversion to wild foods. A remarkably wide variety of these were eaten, especially wildfowl and fish, which were among the most desirable and frequently offered menu items.

Many small wild animals were also considered viable food. References to such creatures can be found throughout cookbooks of the period; they absolutely abound in the dietary literature. Hare and rabbit are always mentioned, but so too are hedgehog and fox, especially those that have been fattened up on autumn grapes. The Paduan physician Antonio Gazius includes in his list of wild meats, even though he generally disapproves of them, wild donkeys, mountain goats, and gazelles, which are best cooked in oil to temper their heat.[12] Melchior Sebizius describes how bears are usually prepared: they are skinned, hung to tenderize, salted, and seasoned with fennel, cinnamon, and cloves and served as an appetizer.[13] Martino of Como preferred them in pies, and Scappi admits that though uncommon, he has cooked them. The limbs roasted are the best part.

Dormice, as we know, were a favorite among ancient Romans, but their descendants centuries later also enjoyed them. Messisbugo and others included dormice on their menus.[14] Bruyerin says that in the Auvergne people eat squirrels, and Poles serve them at banquets.[15] Porcupines were used in pâtés or roasted on a spit larded and stuck with cloves.[16] Sebizius commends the musky fragrant odor of the flesh of marten (a weasel-like creature), and definitely prefers it to fox.[17] In the Alps marmots were roasted or made into a black broth based on their own blood. Badgers (*Taxus*) are mentioned as food in the dietary guide of Michele Savonarola, and Conrad Gesner says they are cooked with pears. Beaver tail was also served in more elegant dinners, especially for Lent,[18] because "*Carnem comede Pontificos est concessum,*" that is, because always in water, this part of the animal could be considered fish.

One particularly perverse fashion among elites involved removing the unborn fetus of a deer and cooking it. "This was invented either by gluttonous men or to be something elegant, not because it's pleasant or healthy, but uncommon and acquired at a high price," claimed Domenico Sala.[19] Petrus Castellanus attests to the same fashion and adds that young stags' horns have also become popular as delicacies on noble tables, just when they begin to poke through. Normally they were boiled and the soft interior removed and served, or they were grated and boiled to make hartshorn jelly.[20] Most of these references come from seventeenth-century dietary works, and they usually condemn practices they found aberrant or unhealthy. They do suggest, however, that these wild foods were disappearing or were only eaten in extremely remote places or by courtly gluttons with jaded palates and a taste for the perverse. They do not appear at all in elite banquets by the seventeenth century, but had in earlier cookbooks. That is, in the course of these centuries small furry wild creatures went from viable, if rare, menu items to strange and perverse foods.

The diminution of wildfowl species is even clearer. The range of wildfowl presented on elite tables in the late Middle Ages and sixteenth century was simply staggering. There were wild geese and ducks and many waterfowl such as cranes, swans, storks, and herons. Sebizius says, "Truly Princes and Magnates love to hunt them."[21] The lists of small wildfowl regularly served are seemingly endless. The familiar pheasant, partridge, and wild doves appear, and even starlings, quail, fig-peckers, sparrows, and tiny thrushes. Snipes would be roasted whole with guts intact, which were later squeezed out on toast.[22] By the seventeenth century fewer and fewer species were eaten, particularly the waterfowl. Swan's flesh was found to be dark and malodorous, and even wild ducks and teals were thought to taste like the pond muck they consumed. The preference shifted toward whiter and lighter-fleshed fowl, which could include pheasant but was more likely capon or turkey.

Wild herbs were another set of common ingredients in this cuisine. The term usually referred to anything not classified as a garden vegetable (*olera*) and included wild greens, cresses, skirrets (*Sium sisarum*), samphire (*Crithmum maritimum*), Eringoes (Sea holly roots), water caltrops, nettles (whose red spring buds went into pottage),[23] mallows (*Malva sylvestris*), and wild onions. It also included herbs in our sense of the word, as culinary seasonings. It is difficult to tell when an herb was grown in a garden, but authors do sometimes specify wild thyme, or note where a certain herb can be found, denoting that it would not be in the kitchen garden. Scappi often specifies wild asparagus.[24] Salvatore Massonio says that one can gather laver or cress growing wild in rivers and springs. Both can be used in rustic salads or chopped in a pesto.[25] The use of herbs is not as important as it would become in subsequent centuries, but chefs did use parsley and mint extensively, as well as flowers such as fennel, elder, borage, and violets. Myrtle and bay could also have been collected wild. Wild thistles were used as a curdling agent for making cheese in place of rennet, and Englishman Thomas Cogan recommends blessed thistle leaves in the morning, on bread and butter.[26] He also suggests many wild herbs for medicinal as well as culinary uses — the root of the herb avens was used in stew, and although it turns it black, the taste is reminiscent of cloves.[27]

Gathering wild herbs for a salad seems to have been common among all social classes. Cardano mentions rustics and women gathering wild endive (*condrilla*) and sow thistle. These were not eaten out of desperation but for pleasure. He also mentions mallow shoots as a first course. Naturally, noblemen would have their servants do the actual gathering, sometimes with grave results. Cardano mentions a case he saw of a Bolognese nobleman whose female servant accidentally put hemlock in a tart instead of parsley. The following night, the nobleman was dead.[28] It is difficult to determine precisely when Europeans became so frightened of such mistakes that they turned away from gathering potentially poisonous wild herbs, but clearly warnings like this would have helped dissuade people from doing so.

Massonio in his book on salads mentions the *mescolanza rustica,* which he explains is a popular wild salad among noblemen, so called either because the people who usually eat it are rustics or because the herbs themselves are rustic or wild.[29] The impetus to eat such things was much like dressing up as shepherds and playing at pastoral, piping and dancing among the woodland nymphs and other such nonsense. Eating rustic wild foods was one part of this whole diversion.

With the popularity and availability of sugar, honey went almost completely out of fashion in sixteenth-century cooking. Not that honey was truly a wild product, but the relationship of these two sweeteners is revealing. It appears, though, that once sugar became ubiquitous and was used among ordinary people, honey regained a certain vogue, especially in seventeenth-century England, where it was made into mead. Rarity of honey may have had something to do with this. Apparently many monastic beekeeping operations disappeared during the Reformation, and beekeeping became one of those noble rustic pastimes, perhaps following Virgil's *Georgics,* the fourth book of which is about the topic. Among authors such as Kenelm Digby, recipes for mead and quasi-medicinal drinks, much like the ancient Hippocratic concoctions, were passed around and published as a nobleman's personal invention. At any rate, the rarity of a wild food, or in this case a managed one because the honey itself was not taken from wild bees, can bring it into fashion.

Collecting wild fruit was also considered noble. Cultivating fruit was of course a popular pastime, but only those with substantial stretches of wasteland could march off into the forest for a rustic picnic, Bacchic revel, or a day picking berries. Wild fruits including cornel cherries, sorb apples, service berries, mespila, arbutus (strawberry tree), *uva ursi, uva crispa,* and especially tiny wild strawberries were all very fashionable. Vaccinia (whortleberries), along with the others, were gathered and usually made into conserves, syrups, or *sapori,* which were sauces used as condiments. There is no way to tell who actually did the dirty work of making these confections. Though recipe books are addressed to elite readers, the audience could have left the messy job of collecting and cooking to servants. In any case, there was something titillating and daring about eating such wild foods, precisely because in the course of the early modern period they became increasingly out of the ordinary. Most meals would be made up of domestic plants and animals, and for those cooped up at court and in the city, the rustic diversion on one's own estate or villa suburbana provided a pleasant but ultimately safe way to escape into the wild.

Without doubt the largest category of wild foods was fish. Nearly all fish had to be wild, with the exception of a few species that could be raised in ponds—eels and freshwater carp, for example—although these were probably caught wild and then stocked in ponds rather than bred in captivity as hatchlings. Of course, most fish are still wild. What makes this cuisine so different is the incredible variety of fish that were eaten. In fact, many cookbooks and practically all dietary guides spend a great deal of energy just straightening out the various names for fish, whether ancient or alternate names in dialect.

In the late Middle Ages and into the Renaissance, dolphins and whales were consumed and were considered fish. At some point thereafter they disappeared from elegant tables entirely. It may be that their numbers dwindled in European waters and they became too difficult to bring home fresh. Cogan says of porpuis [*sic*], "Although for rareness they bee esteemed of great estates."[30] It seems unlikely that some sudden realization that these are intelligent mammals had anything to do with a growing aversion. Many other intelligent mammals were eaten happily. But the fact remains that sea mammals did disappear from elite tables during the early modern period.

We must not forget other aquatic creatures that were among the dainties served at noble tables. Frogs, often eaten whole, turtles—which grew in popularity once they were brought back from the Caribbean—as well as snails must also be in the list of wild foods.

Admittedly, many of the stranger wild foods appeared rarely in elite cookbooks. Nonetheless, given the high proportion of recipes for wild birds and fish, it is undeniable that wild foods played a major role in aristocratic cuisine in the sixteenth century. For example, in the summary of all foods that can be used in banquets, divided by lean and meat days, Domenico Romoli lists 169 recipes based on wild ingredients out of 301 specifically for lean days, which includes every main dish without meat, any pie, pastry, soup, or pasta based on fish, vegetables, or fruit. Of those recipes containing meat, 68 of 360 are based on wild ingredients.[31] These numbers are based on the primary ingredient, and it is assumed that fish are captured and fruits are usually cultivated, unless specified. For many items it is specified, as with *oche salvatiche* (wild goose) or *piccioni casalenghi* (domestic pigeon). Mushrooms and truffles were necessarily wild; the cultivation of mushrooms was still in its infancy. There are some items whose source cannot be determined, so these numbers cannot be precise. Nonetheless, wild foods account for more than half of the dishes eaten in Lent and about a fifth of meals on meat days. The proportion among meats seems to be the result of a wide variety of dishes made from specific parts of domestic animals, such as veal head, liver, tongue, and so forth.

Bartolomeo Scappi was a bit more enthusiastic about wild foods. His fish recipes are, again, mostly wild, but he also offers far more recipes based on wildfowl. With more than one thousand recipes in his cookbook, a statistical analysis would be impractical. Suffice to say, Scappi had no aversion at all to the idea of wild food. There are about ten wild boar recipes, about twice the number for deer of various types, a handful of recipes specifying wild duck, four for porcupine, and even a recipe for guinea pig.[32]

Rossetti, in his list of all possible dishes for banquets, offers three boar recipes, eleven for deer, fourteen for crane, twenty-six for hare, thirty-five for wild duck (which he specifies, along with a recipe for their tongues smoked),[33] fifty-seven for pheasant and partridge together, and four for guinea pig: roasted, in a fricassee, baked in an oven, grilled, and with French mustard. Mountain goat he says to cook like mutton (*castrato*).[34] On the other hand, peacocks did not interest him much—cook it like turkey or serve it resewn into its feathers, but that is a dish more antique than modern, he insists.[35] Among wild foods sturgeon takes precedence, with no less than 202 recipes based on the flesh, milt, liver, or caviar.[36]

In the early seventeenth century (though written earlier) Cesare Evitascandalo's enthusiasm for game is nearly as strong as his predecessors'. Although the actual menus he presents rarely specify game, he does have separate entries for many wild species. Rabbits are stuffed with fruits and roasted or stewed with the same, placed in a pie, either hot or cold, cooked or alive. The latter was an old trick, though how the rabbits jumping around the table could rouse laughter time and time again one can only guess.[37] Although the medical advice Evitascandalo includes is rarely favorable toward wild animals, he still includes, along with fourteen ways to cook boar and nine for hare, entries for dormouse, which sounds enticing stuffed with chestnuts, pine nuts and spices, or roasted and served on toast.[38] There are also dishes featuring porcupine, hedgehog, and guinea pig. As usual, wildfowl and fish are given prominence.

In Spain, Francisco Martínez Montiño's *Arte de Cocina* (1611), while heavily dependent on domestic meats such as mutton, kid, sucking pig, ham, and chicken also makes extensive use of wild foods. Hare and rabbit are presented in numerous guises. Boar appears whole or in pieces roasted. The head is made into headcheese, the flesh put into empanadas and other pastries.[39] Venison is served just as many ways: roasted, its horns on a plate, breadcrumbs (*migas*) fried in venison fat, empanadas, salted, and even a version of venison jerky or *tasajos*.[40]

Lancelot de Casteau, also writing in the early seventeenth century in Liege, has a *Heuspot de venaison* made from boar or stag, which is essentially the medieval standby of meat in a sauce of toast, pepper, nutmeg, sugar, and cinnamon with red wine and onions fried in butter, all boiled together.[41] Even his English pie is made of goat or lamb or a piece of fat venison, which is offered as an alternative to the standard ingredient.[42] The rest of the cookbook is almost completely dependent on veal, beef, pork, and other domestic species, as would be expected from a highly urban audience. It is only at the grandest banquet served for the entry of the Prince-Archbishop in 1557 that a variety of venison, boar, hare, cranes, swans, and other such wild foods appear with frequency.[43] This seems to be more of a historical curiosity for his audience, though, and not something they would be likely to cook, judging from the actual recipes in the book.

Ingredients and Wild Food

Gradually, recipes for game diminish, and by the latter half of the seventeenth century the dominance of domestic species is apparent in most cookbooks. Some wild foods retain their noble status, but it appears that chefs and their readers were less inclined to cook or serve them. Bartolomeo Stefani in the latter seventeenth century says of wild boar that "the meat of this animal is very much appreciated by grand Lords, and of this are made various dishes."[44] These words imply that his readers would not only be excluded in this category of grand lords, but that they would be unlikely to have the opportunity to cook such animals. He does give a recipe for wild boar salami, though, just in case. Of deer he says that they are rarely found in Italy and proceeds to describe how they are prepared in England. This supports the idea that game was merely overhunted. (Though, if this is the case, deer have returned in numbers today.) Hares he says go into many dishes: cold pastries, gelatin, fricassee, but he seems more interested in the fur and how many cooks appreciate it to keep warm in cold weather.[45]

At about this same time, Venantio Mattei offers menus of meals he planned for the Rospigliosi in Rome through the 1660s. His first, a meal in January for twenty noble ladies and gentlemen, provides good evidence that although wild foods had not disappeared entirely, there were fewer offered. The banquet in five courses included sixty-six separate dishes (requiring eighteen covered platters, one hundred large plates, and four hundred small round ones) mostly made up of veal and kid, capon, pigeon, or turkey, or sturgeon and other fish. Wild foods appear occasionally—perhaps thrushes as a garnish to fried sweetbreads—but few dishes feature wild food. In the first course there is hare in a black broth made of prunes, chicken livers, crushed biscuits, and pear syrup, served in little marzipan baskets touched with sugar glazing and gold— the eighth of fourteen dishes in that course. In the second course there is a whole roast pheasant, and also roasted larks and thrushes. Some of these appear in the next course as well. The fourth course is all fish, presumably wild. Lastly came the fruit course, including vegetables, conserves, olives, cheeses, and truffles. Nowhere are venison or boar, though we know the former were hard to find according to Stefani's testimony.[46]

The French authors of the latter seventeenth century are a little more ambivalent. In La Varenne there are a good number of recipes for wild food, and this may, ironically, betray his conservatism. Teal, larks, and woodcocks appear. Even heron is still present. There are several recipes for boar and a few for stag, fawn, and roebuck liver.[47] These dishes are usually simply roasted. He no doubt had the opportunity to cook such animals for his patron, the Marquis d'Uxelles, and anticipated that other chefs working for similar patrons would too. In other French cookbooks of the latter seventeenth century, wild game plays a smaller and smaller role. Pierre De Lune offers several recipes for stag deer and roe, as well as three for roasted boar at the beginning of his *Le Cuisiner* of 1656, and then a few pâtés,[48] but they are not mentioned elsewhere in the cookbook.[49] By 1674 in L. S. R., wildfowl are still present according to season, but far more dependable chicken, lamb, suckling pig, veal, and even beef are the mainstays. Boar's head, served cold as in La Varenne, is still there among *entremets*[50] and a recipe for young boar (*marcassin*),[51] but otherwise he has no interest in venison whatsoever. Again, whether this has to do with a broader and more bourgeois audience or the increasing rarity of wild game cannot be determined, but it does appear that a cultural preference for domestic food also plays a role.

Cookbooks in their aim to be as comprehensive as possible continue to include wild ingredients, especially the aristocratic deer and boar and wildfowl. It is clear, though, that the proportion of these foods had diminished and appeared in menus with less frequency. There may be underlying cultural reasons for the shift, one of which is clearly discernible in the dietary literature. The relative merit of domestic versus wild meat was a standard topic. Many authors contended that exercise and fresh air rids an animal's body of superfluous humidity and thus makes it leaner, more digestible, and ultimately better for you. This was the standard Galenic view, that wild meats may be a little tougher but ultimately more nourishing. In the early sixteenth century this would have been considered medical orthodoxy.

Interestingly, in preceding centuries the opposite view usually held sway. For example, Antonio Gazius in the late fifteenth century, using Arab authorities, insisted that wild animals are too gross, which here implies dense and dark-fleshed, and therefore generate melancholy. Domestic animals taste better and are more nourishing. Their internal heat is tempered by being well fed, getting a moderate amount of exercise, and leading a relatively easy life. The same is true of fowl: "The domestic nourish more and are more tempered and generate better blood."[52] Perhaps this reflects the classical ideal internalized among medieval Arab authors long before it had been in Europe.

In any case, by the early modern period, although lip service is paid to Galen and the Greeks, it is clear that game has diminished in physicians' estimation. Castellanus remarks that lamb and kid are easier to digest and preferable to deer and hare. Rather than any specific medical reasoning, the preference for lighter, whiter, and softer foods appears to be more a cultural shift than any major theoretical reappraisal. It appears that somehow people lost interest in gamy tastes. Castellanus, speaking of the roe deer, says that "the odor especially and noxious flavor of the woods causes nausea, such that it is hardly able to please unless cooked with artifice and condiments to remove the persistent wildness."[53] In England Thomas Cogan exclaims, "A wonder it is to see howe much this unwholesome flesh is desired of all folkes. In so much that many men rashly will venture their credite, yea and sometime their lives too, to steale venison." He also goes so far as to criticize nobles for wasting so much land for deer parks. "I could wish (saving the pleasure of honourable and worshipfull men) that there were no Parkes nor Forestes in England. For a great parte of the best pasture in this Realme is consumed with Deer, which might otherwise be better employed for a common-wealth."[54] Of course, over the next few centuries his prayers would be answered as more and more land came under cultivation.

It appears that physicians in general came to prefer lighter, whiter, and more easily digested meats, and this was paralleled in culinary literature. Perhaps physicians influenced elite taste in some way, or more likely the two developed in the same direction together. A cultural shift seems to play some part in the gradual disappearance of wild species in both genres.

Keith Thomas has argued that the reduction of wild bird species for food in England, although partly owing to the reduction of wild space and extinction, has as much to do with the custom of keeping birds for pets. Italians never lost the taste for small birds though, and perhaps keeping them as pets was never so widespread as it was in England. Keeping small furred mammals as pets was common in both places and may have some connection to the acquired aversion to eating similar wild animals. This is clearly the case in modern times.[55] It seems unlikely that concern for animal welfare played any major role in the diminishing use of wild foods per se. At least such sentiments are extremely rare in culinary literature, and were normally expressed by vegetarians, whose aversion was to killing in general, not just wild creatures.

If anything, the preference for domestic foods began at a time when most people had less familiarity, domestically or otherwise, with animals rather than more. Fewer people would have had direct experience of untamed space, and it is interesting and odd that it is precisely when killing and eating wild animals becomes less common that human beings begin to grow fond of wild nature for its own sake. Beginning in the eighteenth century, many begin planning gardens to look uncultivated. In other words, romanticizing nature in its wild state, an idea that emerged at the close of the early modern period, may be linked directly with ceasing to use wild nature as a food resource. Only when one stops eating such foods can the idea develop of preserving them for their own sake. Presumably, seasoned hunters have no such conceptions of nature. It is the urbane outsider who prefers to dote on swans rather than serve them up.

CHAPTER 3

Dairy

It would be safe to say that the use of butter and dairy products was fairly limited in medieval aristocratic dining. These products certainly existed and were used at many levels of society, in some places as staples in the diet, particularly in the north. The exact impact of Lenten restrictions on dairy products in elite cuisine is difficult to discern, but it is true that for perhaps as much as a third of the calendar year such products were forbidden, or consumed only with special dispensation from the church. Court records might reveal how often such restrictions were violated, which is well beyond the scope of this study, but it is not impossible to imagine that in northern Europe, the Alps, and in places where dairy cattle predominated, it must have been difficult to forbear using dairy products. Some cities actually bought official dispensations. At the very least, the ban on butter and dairy products was a bone of contention in the Reformation era, when humanists and reformers complained about having to purchase oil for fast days, while butter and other animal fats were relatively abundant.

The sudden interest in butter as a cooking medium, and perhaps most importantly in pastry, does not seem to have any direct tie to the Reformation, particularly because their popularity in elite cuisine began in Italy around the mid fifteenth century. Maestro Martino is credited with the introduction of the butter-based and edible pie crust to literate audiences in the first printed cookbook, Platina's *De honesta voluptate,* which contained Martino's recipes.

Apart from mere whim or fashion, it seems likely that the prevalence of dairy products and increased economic incentive to raise dairy cattle

{ 45 }

at the beginning of the early modern era would have influenced the appearance of milk, cream, and butter in cookery. Improved transport, combined with significant population growth, meant that relatively perishable products could be assured of a market. This process happened through most of Europe, first in the Netherlands and northern Italy, then in France and England. Put simply, if in extremely exaggerated form, population density and the growth of cities favored highly capitalized enterprises. Rather than rent out a number of small plots to tenants and leave them to their own devices using subsistence farming, landowners were encouraged to manage their land directly and hire workers, who were abundant and affordable. Profits from selling foodstuffs or meat, or leather and wool in the case of sheep farming, were much more promising than collecting rents from an increasingly impoverished peasantry. Large-scale dairies could focus and specialize their operations, particularly in places where there was abundant pasture, or even where fodder crops such as alfalfa or clover could be planted just for animals. That is, it was more profitable to invest in dairy and new agricultural techniques and reap profits directly than to try to collect rent and services in kind from a poor family owning only the odd cow and a broken plow.

It would be a mistake to suggest that there is some direct causal connection between the economic incentive to raise cattle and the prevalence of dairy products in European cuisine, but there is no doubt that cooks were suddenly inventing new recipes. Their use, especially, of butter is perhaps the cooks' greatest legacy to the art of cookery, right down to the present. In some cases it even comes to rival the traditional adipatry—oil in Italy or pork fat through most of Europe. Butter also becomes a flavoring agent in its own right. There was also a new willingness to experiment with milk and cream, and a new appreciation for white and unctuous dishes based no longer on almond milk, but cow's milk. A wide variety of cheese recipes equally suggests a creative and innovative kitchen using what was not a totally new but certainly a fashionable product.

Through the medieval period milk was typically made into cheese, and in Italy commerce in hard aged cheeses was thriving well before the early modern period. Pantaleon de Confienza's *Summa lacticiniorum* (*Treatise on Dairy Products*) is one of the most extensive discussions of cheese ever written, and dates to the mid fifteenth century. It names dozens of varieties and describes them in detail. Naturally, such products could be shipped long distances and were already firmly "branded" and associated with place names, not only parmigiano for Parma, but placentia or placentini for Piacenza (which most authors considered the best),[1] lodigiano for Lodi, or more generically fromage de Milan, as it was sometimes called in French cookbooks. All these are merely lumped into the Grana Padano category today. In the mid sixteenth century there was even a detailed treatise on Swiss cheese making written by Jacob Biffront and appended to the *Ars Magirica* written by Iodoco Willich. The author states "so much is cheese and butter celebrated among us that great quantities . . . are exported throughout Italy and German regions."[2] He also insists that Swiss cheeses age well, just like placentini.

The use of cheese in cookery focuses primarily on such hard cheeses, but softer varieties also make their way into recipes, normally local varieties. Cheese figures into dishes in ways that are innovative and appear to be totally new. What we would call rice puddings were standard fixtures for a long time, but Messisbugo offers a recipe that begins with a pound of rice or farro, a primitive relative of wheat, boiled in broth. Next, two pounds of grated hard cheese and ten egg yolks are mixed and stirred into the rice with pepper and saffron and cooked until it comes together.[3] It is served with sugar and cinnamon, as indeed most cheese recipes are in the sixteenth century. The end result would be a thick and rich mixture somewhat like the medieval rice pudding, but approaching a modern risotto.

It is interesting that there is no particular social stigma against eating cheese, even hard cheese, which according to many dietary writers is not only difficult to digest but is best left for laborers with powerful stomachs. Clearly, elite diners did not heed this advice. Messisbugo, for example, offers a simple but apparently popular cheese frittata that was at the time called "*fritte a Scartozzo.*" The technique is absolutely flawless. Two eggs are beaten with salt and a little water. This is placed in a pan of hot butter, and just as it begins to bubble, grated cheese and pepper are thrown in, along with a tender sprig of rosemary. Lastly, it is folded over with a spatula and presented three per serving plate, of course sprinkled with sugar.[4]

Messisbugo was no less enthused about other dairy products, and he offers instructions on preparing cream in various forms: *mantigilia*—a kind of butter made from goat's milk in the skin of a kid, presumably of Spanish origin—as well as other kinds of butter including vermicelli, which is sweetened, scented with rose water, and pressed through a syringe into long strings.[5] His most interesting dairy recipe is a *crema alla francese* used to fill tart shells. It is essentially a flan of milk, eggs, and sugar with a little flour.[6] Similar recipes appear in contemporary French cookbooks of the era. The *Livre fort excellent* contains both *dariolles* based on cream and *flantz,* which use bread to make them a little firmer.[7] Clearly, the appreciation for the taste of dairy products was a compelling new fashion in courts throughout Europe.

Scappi reveals perhaps the most extensive dairy repertoire in these centuries, and even offers an illustration of a separate cool kitchen devoted solely to milk products, where a churn is being used to make *latte mele.* Another man whisks a bowl that appears to be set in a larger bowl chilled with ice to make "snow," and a third is pouring something from a large skin, perhaps the *mantequilla* mentioned above. Although Scappi mentions the snow in his first chapter[8] and that it should be made in a cool place, there is no recipe. Nonetheless, it was one of the most popular dishes of the mid sixteenth century, probably the same as what was called in Latin *lactis spuma,* or milk foam. The physician Girolamo Cardano claimed that it was especially popular at banquets in Milan.[9] There is a recipe in the English *A Proper Newe Booke of Cokerye.*[10] It is made of beaten egg whites with cream, rose water, and sugar added and then beaten until snow rises on the top, which in this case is then passed through a colander to replicate snow. The *Livre fort excellent* also contains a recipe for *neige contrefaict,* though uniquely it also contains one or two drams of rice flour.[11] In the next century Ludovico Nonnius attests to its continued popularity, associating *spumosum lac* (foamy milk) with the ancient *aphrogala* mentioned only by Galen. In any case, he claims that now it is eaten daily in sumptuous meals and is vulgarly called "snow."[12]

Scappi also uses milk in a variety of cooked dishes. There is an intriguing soup commonly called *Ongaresca* (meaning Hungarian). It is made of six pounds of milk, twenty eggs, salt, saffron, cinnamon, and a pound and a half of sugar, which is cooked in a kind of *bain marie* until solid, and served either hot or cold. Interestingly, Scappi also suggests that it can be made without saffron or cinnamon if you want it white, which appears to be something desired in itself. The variation on the common dish appears to indicate the ways that not only Scappi is experimenting, but the ways tastes are changing. The variation includes orange juice and rose water, making it both tart and aromatic.[13] Sixteenth-century French sources, on the other hand, insist that milk-based soups must never contain sour flavors. In the *Livre fort excellent,* in a *potaige cretonne* with chicken or veal or a *laict cretonne* including just bouillon, the absence of vinegar or verjus is perhaps a fear of curdling the milk, but also it seems an appreciation for the unsullied taste of the milk.[14]

As for cheese in the Italian sources, there are literally dozens of recipes in the *Opera,* and Scappi is particular about the origin and type called for.

He distinguishes between aged and fresh, animals, and city of origin, and even names many varieties.[15] There is cascio cavallo, pecorino, ricotta, marzolino, parmigiano, provatura, mozzarella, as well as cheese from the Romagna, Liguria, and Sardinia. Cheeses, of course, always appeared on the credenza, and Scappi lists many varieties,[16] along with junkets, creams, fresh butter, ricotta, and mozzarella, as well as milk snow. It is in his recipes that Scappi makes the most interesting use of cheese, though.

Consider the Genosese *gattafura,* offered in two versions.[17] It is made by pounding fresh cheese (struccoli), provatura (today the term refers to a fresh cow's milk cheese), or a sharp provaggiole. One recipe mixes this with beet greens and mint, and the combination is spread on a thin sheet of pastry dough, sprinkled with olive oil, and covered with another thin sheet and baked. The second version uses parboiled and beaten onions. The dough itself is made of flour, water, and oil, though he says you can also use butter. It is cooked on a sheet in the oven or in an earthenware *testa,* a kind of covered casserole set in the coals. The result, as one can imagine, is a thin, crisp cracker, something between a double-crusted pizza and a tart of pastry dough filled with a simple savory cheese filling.

Cheese is also often used in stuffings for meat or fowl.[18] One version calls for a pound of grated aged cheese to six ounces of creamy cheese along with walnuts, breadcrumbs, broth and beef marrow or butter, raisins, spices, and eggs. Another version uses sweetbreads and gooseberries or whole unripe grapes, and yet another ground almonds and goat's milk. The last version is perhaps most interesting of all and includes four chopped raw capons' breasts, a pound of pork fat, two pounds of parboiled pork belly, one pound of grated aged cheese, one pound of fresh cheese, two ounces of spices, one-half pound raisins, six ounces of truffles, six eggs, salt, sugar, and saffron.

It is clear that by the mid sixteenth century, cheese and dairy products had become a major item on banquet menus. This trend was replicated outside Italy and into the next century as well. In England the popularity of cream seems sudden. *A Proper Newe Booke of Cokerye* has the "snow" mentioned above, but it also makes use of dairy products in recipes—milk and cream rather than almond milk are used to make a *Blewe manger,*[19] and a custard uses a quart of cream.[20] Comparable recipes can be found in Scappi and elsewhere. A proliferation of dairy-based desserts now appeared in English cookbooks as well: trifles, fools, creams, and flummeries, all of which used milk. To these were subsequently added syllabubs and dairy-based caudles and other mantequated drinks floating with butter.[21] Thomas Dawson has a version of a "leach," which is a standard "sliced" medieval dish, but here it is "white" and made with milk, isinglass (a gelatin obtained from fish), sugar, and rose water.[22] A new appreciation for dairy products led English cooks to experiment with recipes such as these. Dawson's trifle is basically just heated cream with sugar, ginger, and rose water.

There were, of course, dairy cattle in medieval England, and it was well known that ordinary people commonly ate cheese and butter. But the proliferation of dairy products in elite dining was new. Milk in particular was considered a dangerous and corruptible substance, and it is quite possible that the prevalence of milk in cooking is good evidence that aristocratic diners ignored their physicians' warnings.

The sixteenth-century French cookbooks also use dairy products in interesting new ways. The use of butter and milk, particularly in sauces, is dramatically new. There are some descendants of the strange medieval solid concoctions, such as *laict gras larde,* which is exactly what it sounds like: rich milk, lardons, and egg yolks cooked together, left to cool, pressed under a weight, then sliced and fried the next day with spices or sugar.[23] "Fried Cream" is perhaps more indicative of this era, consisting of cream, butter, fresh bread crumbs, egg yolks, and sugar (without spices).[24] A good proportion of the recipes throughout the book use butter as the cooking medium. The Lenten dishes that appear toward the end of the book offer the option of olive oil, but recipes appearing earlier are cooked and even flavored with butter. If anything in this cookbook anticipates developments of the coming centuries, even without a proper roux, it is dishes that have butter-based sauces. Fish, for example, such as pike or salmon are cooked in butter and something sour like verjus or orange. The roasted salmon incorporates the pan juices, is deglazed with vinegar and verjus, colored with parsley and "white powder" (a mixture of sugar and ginger), and served with orange juice. With the exception of the powder, this might be mistaken for a modern recipe.[25]

The milk-based sauces in the *Livre fort excellent* are even more indicative of this shift toward dairy. For example, for capons there is an *Abremont* sauce of milk, bouillon, and starch (or the older use of bread crumb) with "white powder" and a bit of saffron, and thickened in the end with eggs.[26] A similar *dodine blanche* is made from the drippings of roasted waterfowl and milk with cooked egg yolks, a little sugar, salt, and parsley, plus marjoram if desired.[27] In another version specifically for duck, fried onions are added and the entire mixture is sieved.[28] The dodine was a common dish in the middle ages, and the printed Viandier has several versions, but here it seems to have become exclusively a white milk-based sauce.[29] As in other European sources of this century, there also appear flans, milk-based soups, vegetables such as peas cooked in milk, and butter. Whatever the reason, it is clear that the publisher of the French cookbooks believed that his readers had both the interest in cooking such dishes and the ability to acquire the ingredients. And most interestingly, whiteness itself derived from dairy products becomes a culturally laden symbol of good taste.

In the seventeenth century this trend continues and intensifies. English cookbooks absolutely abound in recipes using cream. In Rabisha, for example, there is a curious cabbage cream made of three gallons of milk boiled with a "pottle" of cream, and set into milk pans overnight. The clots of cream are then poured over half heads of cabbage and between the leaves, and it is finally sprinkled with cinnamon, sugar, and rose water.[30] Cream also finds its way into fruit dishes with raspberries, currants, or apples, or with grains such as barley or rice. Judging from the few menus Rabisha offers, these were not yet considered dessert items. They could normally be found among banqueting dishes, which indeed was a kind of dessert course in England, but here custards and creams appears in ordinary second courses right alongside vegetables, fowls, flesh, and fish. A flesh day in summer features a custard in the first course, and in the second a dish of cream, as well as green codlings (apples) and cream among thirty other dishes including ingredients such as anchovies, artichokes, peas, turbot, bacon, sturgeon, rabbits, tongue, and so forth.[31] The point is, white dairy-based products had become a standard feature in elegant menus.

In seventeenth-century Spain, Maceras has a simple milk tart, thickened with flour and eggs, that is both savory and sweet. Salt and mint (*yerva buena*) but also half a pound of sugar are included.[32] Otherwise he rarely uses milk—except with rice, which is a medieval standby. This is somewhat surprising, given the source of the cookbook, based on the author's experience as college cook. One might expect that cow's milk was relatively cheap in Spain, but it may be that the concentration on sheep farming, and the power of the *mesta* (a kind of aristocratic syndicate protecting grazing rights) and the incentive to make sheep's milk into cheese, made fresh milk comparatively rare. Judging by contemporary comments, Spain was also, by the seventeenth century, experiencing a demographic slump, which would mean that economically the impetus toward dairy enterprises was less appealing, because there was a smaller market.

Nonetheless, at the royal court, dairy products can be found. Montiño makes use of butter to a degree that we would not expect in a Spanish cookbook, and he even calls for it on "fish" days. Pork fat is still more typical for "meat" days. He does have a handful of dishes in which milk is the predominant ingredient or is so named in the recipe title. An *ojaldre con leche* is milk, butter, and flour cooked into a dough, with eggs and more butter and sugar stirred in. Thus far it looks like a sweet choux paste, but it is then cooked in an oven much like a flat wafer and can be filled with fruit.[33] The term *hojaldre* today refers to a kind of puff pastry used for empanadas, sometimes fried, but this is clearly an ancestor. Montiño's other dairy recipes include a *pan de leche,* eggs poached in milk, and *bunuelos* of fresh cheese.[34] There is also a typically Spanish flan that he calls *pasteles de leche.*[35] Spanish authors do then make some use of dairy products, but they have not become a major ingredient in a variety of savory dishes. Dairy is mostly used in sweet and what we would consider dessert dishes.

It is in the seventeenth-century Italian sources and then to a greater extent in French sources that we find dairy products being used in totally new ways. The extensive use of cheese, particularly on the credenza at the start of a meal and at the end with fruit, was still firmly in place at Italian banquets. The story of ice cream's development from mountains of ice festooned with fruit and flavored ices, traceable from Antonio Frugoli through Antonio Latini late in the century, has been aptly told by Elizabeth David.[36] So too has the story of the development of ice-cream-making technology using saltpeter, which began with sixteenth-century experiments and ended with ice cream on every eighteenth-century table. The increasing use of dairy products in cooking is less well known, though.

There is a distinct possibility that the appearance of milk in new contexts is in some way related to the gradual breakdown of humoral physiology and the sway it may have exerted over the culinary imagination. This is not to contend that recipes were once informed by medical logic and were now suddenly freed, but it does seem likely that there were certain combinations diners thought inherently repulsive that ultimately derive from medical theory. Once that medical theory began to lose sway, they became "good to think," as it were. The most obvious example of this is milk with fish. According to physicians well into the early modern period, both are inherently corruptible products that increase cold phlegmatic humors. In combination, they can be poisonous. As people began to take such ideas less seriously and followed their own experience, we find milk as well as cheese included in fish dishes. The popularity of smooth creamy textures and flavors induced chefs to experiment, perhaps not in ways we would find palatable or even related to the cream sauces that would develop in the following centuries, but innovations nonetheless.

In Vittorio Lancellotti's *scalco* guide—not exactly a cookbook, but detailed enough that one can get an explicit sense of how the dishes are prepared—there is a banquet served in August 1612.[37] The first cold course is nothing out of the ordinary, except perhaps that there is a soup made with *pane di Spagna* (sponge cake) and cream, strawberries, sugar, and snow—presumably the whipped dairy version of the last century. Then in the first course from the kitchen there appears a dish of red mullets, parboiled and cleaned, then poached in a combination of milk, butter, rose water, and sugar. The fish are then plated with butter, sugar, sponge cake, and lemon juice. To the milk poaching liquid, egg whites are added with *pignocata* (a pine nut biscuit), which is then poured over the fish and then placed in an oven to set. Cooked egg yolks adorn the plate with more sponge cake. Clearly the preference for sweetness and aroma still predominates, but the arrival of a dish consisting primarily of fish and a milk-based sauce is a good indication that tastes were shifting and medical opinion had been completely abandoned. Nor is this an isolated example. In the next course a soup of sturgeon in a cream- and egg yolk–based broth appears. In the next course there are little gnocchi made with milk, flour, and bread, cooked in milk. Milk and dairy are featured in several other offerings, including a beautiful lasagna of fried provatura dripping with butter, and especially in the last cold course, which includes cream tarts, *latte mele,* and a variety of cheeses. It was the Italian baroque authors who first worked dairy products into a wide variety of main dishes.

It is interesting that during Lent, dairy products are not included, and that pine nut milk usually takes their place. For example, it is the broth base for a soup of artichokes, fresh peas, and sturgeon milt as well as several other soups and pastries where cow's milk would be expected.[38] In periods of no dietary restrictions, the cook can really experiment, and dairy products appear in savory dishes with flesh as well. Lancelotti's *zuppe reali* includes capon breast, grated salame, crumbled cooked egg yolks, cheese fried in butter, mouthfuls of marrow, and cream cooked in an oven. Should this not satisfy the baroque predilection for perversity, the soup is garnished with gilded testicles and cream-filled flaky pastries and covered in a gilded sugar paste lid.[39] Butter and cream are also used in large veal meatballs, along with marzipan, biscuits, and spices. The meatballs are breaded, fried, and seethed in a creamy meat broth (sweetened, of course), with lemon, rose water, and garnished with cake.[40] Such combinations of meat and cream are still rare in Lancelotti, though, and there is nothing yet resembling a cream-based sauce, but this does come close.

A few years later Giovanni Battista Crisci's *Lucerna de Corteggiani* (1634) offers menus brimming with dairy products. We find curds of sheep's milk sprinkled with sugar, plus goat ricotta (also sweetened), parmigiano gnocchetti, and caciocavallo cheese, and milk "snow" adorning fruits and even fennel.[41]

In mid century, the fashion for creamy dishes increased. Vasselli, for example often served creamy soups in the first hot course.[42] One such is a *minestra* made of minutely chopped pheasant flesh with cream and sugar. Each diner gets his own plate.[43] Later in the century Stefani in Mantua uses cream in equally surprising ways. His brain fritters are held together with a batter of eggs, grated cheese, cream, crushed biscuits, and flour. They are fried in butter and sprinkled with sugar.[44] Brains are also served cut into pieces, sautéed, and served in a soup of capon broth, herbs, egg yolks, and cream.[45] A "most exquisite" soup is made from partridges in a creamy broth with the usual sweet and aromatic flavorings.[46] There is also an intriguing polenta of rice made of rice flour cooked with milk and butter, formed into little mouthfuls with a spoon, and flavored with parmigiano, rose water, butter, and cinnamon.[47] Even stranger is a capon skin tart made with eggs and cream.[48]

Health concerns had apparently not been totally excised from cookbooks, but merely changed form in strange ways. Stefani's pheasant breast soup includes chopped roast pheasant pounded with melon seeds, amber, and mostaccioli biscuits, and the whole is interestingly "tempered" with cream. The word has come to mean moistened and made smooth and has completely lost its original medicinal meaning, which is to balance opposing flavors. This mixture is passed through a sieve, to which chopped pheasant, pistachios, egg yolk, sugar, the juice of two lemons, biscuits, and cinnamon are added. Despite the cream, and even stranger the lemon juice, Stefani claims this is good for cold stomachs and for those with little natural heat, which is standard and very old medical advice.[49] At any rate, cream and milk are frequently used ingredients by the late seventeenth century, finding their way into a great proportion of Stefani's recipes and often featured as the primary ingredient in various "creams."[50]

It is, not surprisingly, in classical French cuisine that the dairy finally takes a major role. La Varenne is perhaps less revolutionary in this regard than one might expect. Most important, his breakthrough invention (or at least the first published reference to) roux, a cooked flour and fat thickener for sauces, is made with lard rather than butter.[51] Butter is often suggested as a variant cooking medium but definitely subordinate to lard in meat dishes. With fish dishes, however, butter is the preferred cooking medium and flavoring ingredient.

Some meats and vegetables in La Varenne are cooked in a combination of broth, wine, and butter, as with a recipe for stewed pullets,[52] or butter is used to flavor cauliflower[53] or asparagus in a white sauce of butter and egg yolks.[54] A variant of the asparagus recipe includes cream.[55] Other vegetables such as pumpkin are cooked in milk and butter.[56] So too are mushrooms fried in butter, parsley, and green onions and finished with cream.[57] Many egg dishes are made with milk or cream, including omelets, and one recipe includes cheese.[58] There are also tarts based on cream, such as the *fran-gipanne,* a cream tourte,[59] and a potage of milk thickened with egg yolks, bread, and sugar.[60] It is difficult to tell if these recipes mark a dramatic departure from culinary practice a century earlier. Dairy products are still a staple in the kitchen and are called for far more frequently, but they do not seem to be used in any new fashion, with the exception of sauces for fish. Yet even here the real novelty is the use of aromatics, wine, and herbs in place of spices; milk and cream are rarely found in La Varenne's fish dishes. This perhaps demonstrates a lingering cultural antipathy toward a combination long considered dangerous in medical circles. On the other hand it is absolutely clear that there is no restriction against using milk or butter during Lent, because many dishes specifically designed for lean days include them. At the end of the book are recipes that specifically exclude eggs, as these appear to have still been forbidden.

Though the French cookbooks of the latter seventeenth and eighteenth centuries are beyond the scope of this study, both butter and cream retained a prominent place in French haute cuisine. Milk would be used in a variety of sauces, the béchamel being the newest, but there followed many others as well. Without doubt the shift from spicy and sour sauces to fat-based had taken place. This was, however, a gradual development spanning the late fifteenth century to the eighteenth.

Dairy

CHAPTER 4

Spices and Garnishes

The paradigmatic shift in European cookery is normally explained in the following bold terms. Medieval taste preferences depended heavily on spices such as pepper, ginger, cinnamon, and cloves as well as some exotic species that have since disappeared from Western tables, such as grains of paradise (malaguetta pepper), cubebs and long pepper, galangal, and spikenard. Combined with sweet-and-sour sauces thickened with bread, almond milk, verjuice, and a number of striking flavors, medieval cuisine was essentially one of sharp contrasts and complex spice mixtures. Various explanations have been brought forth to explain this culinary structure: the prestige of serving extremely expensive spices fetched from around the world, a medicinal logic of combining foods to counteract their potentially harmful humoral qualities, as well as less-convincing notions about covering the taste of tainted meat—an idea, one hopes, that has long been put to rest.

The shift in flavor preference came about as a result of medical theory losing its grip on the minds of chefs, spices arriving in greater quantities following the discovery of a direct trade route to Asia by the Portuguese (thereby becoming less exclusive and a less-potent symbol of wealth and status), and, finally, a new culinary aesthetic that depended on accentuating and concentrating the flavor of the main ingredient. Distinction of taste no longer depended on the quantity of food served or the exotic seasoning but on meticulous preparation, careful blending of flavors and reductions, and, more importantly, the invention of new techniques such as roux-thickened stocks, butter-based sauces, and a preference for salty flavors over spiced ones. Judicious use of native herbs gradually replaced the medieval spice larder as well. Though La Varenne is no longer given sole credit for these innovations, and in many ways his preferences were still very traditional, his work is still regarded as a turning point that ushered in French haute cuisine.

There is some truth to the basic outline of this shift, but it ignores the intervening centuries of development, roughly between the fifteenth and late seventeenth centuries. Clear contrasts are easy to see given this time span, much as they are comparing Giotto with Rembrandt, or Roger Bacon with Isaac Newton. But the shift is only sharply apparent in hindsight. Some of Bacon's procedures we could easily call scientific, and some of Newton's ruminations on angels we would not hesitate to call essentially backward and medieval, given our knowledge of how science would develop. As with science and art, culinary culture also developed slowly and never in one clearly discernible direction. This is not merely to say that spices gradually went out of fashion over the course of these centuries, but the development was in no way progressive or a straight path. Tendencies we might see as throwbacks (sweet-and-sour sauces, for example) linger well after they should, and indeed into the present if we think of barbecue sauces, and techniques we might consider revolutionary sometimes appear long before we expect them. The bouquet garni is present in sixteenth-century England, for example.

Moreover, the shift in flavor preferences was not simply a transformation from a highly spiced, sweet-and-sour to a more concentrated and subtly sauced and salty cuisine. Certain spices came in and out of fashion, the role of sugar changed more subtly and not everywhere at the same time, and new garnishes played a much more important role in culinary evolution than is usually recognized. Some of these changes have been outlined and even statistically verified. Flandrin noted several important changes in early modern cookbooks — the gradual disappearance of the more exotic spices, for example. Beyond mentioning that these changes took place, little explanation has been offered. What do these changes in taste preference mean and what triggered them?

The simple availability of certain spices could certainly have been a factor. It has often been noted that the changing fortunes of eastern trading partners, and sometimes war with the Ottoman Empire, could suspend shipments of a particular spice indefinitely. A cookbook author would naturally hesitate to recommend an item none of his readers could find. It appears that the disappearance of grains of paradise from the west coast of Africa may simply have been the result of intentional trade protection, keeping a cheap and supposedly inferior product off the market to prevent competition with the more expensive commodity, in this case black pepper from India. The very fact that some spices remained popular while others from similar sources were less favored argues against this simple solution. Why nutmeg would hold on to a place in European cuisine into the eighteenth century while cloves were marginalized cannot be explained in terms of supply, because both arrived from similar sources via the same suppliers: first the Venetians via Arab middlemen, then the Portuguese, and finally the Dutch by the seventeenth century.

There must be another cultural reason for the change in taste preference. It becomes clearer if we examine exactly which spices were employed, where, and when. The late-medieval palate, practically everywhere in western Europe among courtly diners, favored spices that should be recognized first and foremost as hot, that is, flavors that sting in the mouth. In fact, our use of the term *hot* in this sense comes directly from the humoral sense of the term — not physical temperature, but the effect on the tongue and body. These are primarily spices that burn — freshly ground pepper and grains sear the tongue in quantity, ginger is "hot i' the mouth," and cloves actually have a numbing effect. This, it seems, was what most thrilled medieval diners. They craved the intense sensation, the daring but ultimately safe burn that every devoted chili-head of modern times knows well.

This flavor preference has been for the most part obscured by two persistent ideas among culinary historians. First, there is the notion that spices were used in small quantities, in ways that would really appeal to modern palates. Not only would it be unseemly to be sparing with the very item with which you were trying to impress your guests, but the aesthetic effect is totally lost with the application of a subtle sprinkling of spice. As with Indian food, the intention is not to overwhelm or mask flavors but to layer intense sensations to create powerful and complex combinations. In fact, both northern Indian and medieval cuisine have a common ancestor in Persian cuisine as it spread with Islam. Spices were used in dense complementary clusters and in ways such that small hints of flavor would become superfluous. Smooth pounded foods, highly seasoned morsels, and piquant sauces should, again, remind us of Indian food. Of course, everything had to be digitescible (eaten with the fingers) as well.

Because medieval cookbooks rarely mention spice quantities, the assertion that they used spices liberally is ultimately impossible to prove. Even if we could travel back in time to taste their dishes there is no way to be sure that what we find spicy they would too. But it is certain that when quantities of spice are suggested in Renaissance cookbooks, and subtlety does become a goal in itself, it is a mistake to assume that medieval chefs had the same preferences. This would be akin to extrapolating medieval painting techniques from a treatise by Leonardo. In any event, the spices used in the Middle Ages were for the most part "hot," and there is no persuasive reason to think that they applied them with a light hand.

It has also been assumed that spices, in whatever quantity used, must have been stale and flavorless after the long journey from Asia, sometimes taking two years from harvest to soup bowl. Of course there is no assurance that the spices we find on grocery shelves are any fresher, and it would be a mistake to assert that spices must have been old and tasteless. Very old spices do indeed lose much of their punch, especially when they are pre-ground, but this seems to be more characteristic of modern cookery, in which spices are used infrequently, are left in glass jars for years, and are used mostly in cookies and rarely ground from whole spices. There is a world of difference between ground cinnamon (actually cassia) or ground cardamom and the bite from the same spices freshly pounded in a mortar. It is not too fanciful to suggest that the latter is what medieval diners were really looking for, and that their typical spice mixtures were not ground and mixed long in advance but probably just enough for a few weeks and what could be kept conveniently in a small pouch or container.

Without lingering on the details of the medieval spice repertoire, suffice to say that it was extensive. A large proportion of dishes, not yet divided into savory and sweet, employed pepper, ginger and galangal root, cloves, nutmeg and mace, cinnamon and cassia, as well as cassia buds, grains of paradise, cardamom, long pepper and cubebs, spikenard, southernwood (*abrotonum*), and saffron, beloved especially for its bright golden hue. Color was one of the preoccupations of medieval chefs, and they tinted many dishes, green with parsley for example or red with sandalwood. We might even call it chromorexia, a hunger for brightly colored foods. As for spices, they were almost always used in complex combinations or along with herbs, mustard, or garlic, and often accompanied by sugar or *sapa* (boiled down grape must) and with a sour agent such as vinegar or verjuice.

As we pass into the fifteenth century, spices by no means disappear. Nor did they vanish in the following centuries, but the profile of the flavors most frequently used changed. Cubebs, long pepper, and mace practically disappeared. They could still be obtained. Apothecaries carried them, as pharmaceutical recipes clearly attest. In fact, alternative medicine shops are one of the few places to find cubebs today. But cooks were no longer very interested in them. The same is true of other spices such as spikenard and galangal.

Even into the sixteenth century, spices were called for in generally the same percentage of recipes as before, in at least three quarters in most cookbooks, but the range of spices had diminished considerably. Most important, cinnamon and sugar had come to dominate the entire cuisine. In a nutshell, the preference for hot spices was replaced with sweet and aromatic spices, along with rose water, musk, and ambergris. Sour dishes still appeared, as did old standbys based on almond milk and gelatins, but with less frequency. Orange or lemon juice often steps in for verjuice or vinegar. Increasingly, garnitures such as candied citron, raisins, and nuts proliferate. Again, lightness, delicacy, sweetness, and perfume gradually replaced the sharp and complex spice combinations of previous centuries. Contrasting flavors and textures are still the desired result, but rarely the dense clusters of many hot spices and thoroughly pounded ingredients.

These trends, as well as the precise quantities of spices, are found in the recipes offered by Messisbugo. Take, for example, one of his typical pies made with a flaky pastry (*sfogliata*) composed of a pound of flour, two ounces of rose water, six ounces of butter, four eggs, and two ounces of sugar. In one version this delightful crust is placed in a pan and sprinkled with two ounces of sugar, one-fourth ounce of canella, two ounces of raisins, and a half pound of finely chopped proscuitto. The pie is then filled with veal's eyeballs, or lacking these, sweetbreads or *tettine* (udders).[1] Successive layers have more sugar, raisins, and cinnamon, along with pine nuts, orange juice, and butter. The last top leaf or layer is anointed with more butter and sprinkled with three more ounces of sugar. It is clear that despite this seeming incongruity of flavors to our minds (not to mention the eyeballs), this was an overwhelmingly sweet and unctuous dish. Canella (cinnamon) is used quite sparingly, only one-half ounce, compared to nine ounces of sugar in total, including the crust and the fillings. Most important, no other spices are used.

In some recipes, Messisbugo does use pepper, ginger, cloves, and saffron, but that is virtually the entire range of spices he employs. His recipe for meatballs in sauce is one example that uses all of these.[2] It consists of chopped meat rolled into balls, fried, and then simmered in a sauce including raisins, toast soaked in vinegar, parsley, and honey or sugar and the above spices. If anything, this is a traditional recipe, and in fact this combination is used elsewhere formulaically. It also appears in a *brodo lardiero* (rich broth)[3] and is closely related to the traditional and medieval cameline sauce,[4] which here includes one pound of raisins, vinegar-soaked toast, a carafe of red wine, a pound of honey more or less to taste, an ounce of canella, one-half ounce of pepper, one-half ounce of ginger, and one-fourth ounce of cloves, all cooked down with raisins and served over meat, fish, or poultry. This sauce is an old standard, no doubt included so the cook might satisfy his prince's craving for comfort food. But most recipes in the book are quite different and use only canella and sugar, perhaps with fennel or "a bit of saffron." Hot spices have been for the most part marginalized, or are presented in traditional recipes.

Most important, sugar comes to dominate everything. Take, for example, a recipe calling for three pounds of pike, boiled, cleaned, and pounded in a mortar with a pound of almonds, parsley, and herbs. This is then "distempered" or moistened with fish broth and passed through a sieve. The procedure so far is nothing novel. Then nine ounces of sugar are added, one ounce of canella, six ounces of raisins, and one-fourth ounce of rose water and the mixture is cooked in a tart with more sugar on top. The final dish would weigh roughly five pounds, one-fifth of which is sugar or sweet raisins. Clearly sweetness and aromatic perfume was the ultimate flavor sensation sought here.[5]

Scappi offers a comparable approach to spices, but is more direct about their use. Toward the beginning of the first book, he specifies that spices should be used no more than a year old, and the fresher the better their aroma. Significantly, it is the aroma he is most concerned with. He also adds that if you care to use a premixed spice combination for a variety of dishes, it should be made in one-pound batches of $4^1/_2$ ounces of cinnamon, two of cloves, one of ginger, one of nutmeg, one-half of grains of paradise, one-half of saffron, and one ounce of sugar.[6] That this adds up to $10^1/_2$ ounces is perhaps irrelevant, but it does seem that Scappi offers this as something his readers might want (and it does have direct ancestors in the Middle Ages), and that he calls for in a handful of recipes. On the whole, however, Scappi's recipes are relatively light on spices. Ginger is mentioned rarely in the book, grains nowhere else. Scappi, when he does specify spices, uses far fewer than this combination demands. He also uses some subtle and aromatic spices that were little used in medieval kitchens, such as coriander and fennel pollen. Like Messisbugo though to a lesser extent, there is dependence on sugar and cinnamon. Pepper appears frequently, as does saffron, but the number of dishes that call for spice mixtures has significantly diminished. This may be related to Scappi's general appreciation for the quality of ingredients in season, unhampered by what he may have considered complex flavors normally associated with medieval cuisine.

Not that these would seem simple and austere flavors according to our palates, but it seems significant that small fowl, for example, are usually seasoned merely with salt and fennel. Sometimes they are served with sugar and orange juice, as with fried quails,[7] are sometimes larded, and in the case of pheasant, peacock, and turkey, the fat is stuck in with cloves.[8] In general, Scappi prefers such flavors relatively simple and straightforward. Spices are used more frequently and in more complex combinations on heavier meats, such as beef or boar,[9] but less so on lighter meats like veal or fish. In the end, Scappi's recipes are certainly more heavily spiced than most cuisines we would be familiar with, and he uses cinnamon, cloves, nutmeg, and saffron in places completely alien to modern European cookery. Nonetheless, his recipes, if indeed any generalizations can be made about such an enormous collection, reflect the general trend toward sweetness, aroma, and bright citrus flavors over the dark, thick, heavily spiced and vinegar-laden sauces of previous centuries.

Much the same can be said of the slightly earlier cookbook of Domenico Romoli, writing in Florence. Spices have in no way disappeared, but there are usually sweeter types like fennel, sugar, and canella, the darker spices being reserved for darker meats. Take for example the handful of recipe he offers for veal's brains. A so-called German version includes many spices stewed with wine and verjuice, and appears to be an older recipe—which he nonetheless mentions will be "more noble" with sugar and canella sprinkled on top. The other versions, as he says, are more delicate, and include pepper and saffron, and are perhaps gilded with egg yolks or fried, but he always mentions not to forget the sugar and canella.[10] These have obviously become the most important flavorings.

France in the sixteenth century remained somewhat conservative in the use of spices. There is not the same shift toward cinnamon and sugar, though sugar itself is given greater prominence. Judging from the *Livre fort excellent* of the 1540s, a convenient spice mix, either *menu epices* or *pouldre blanche,* was kept on hand for seasoning most dishes. Individual spices—often canella or ginger—are sometimes called for in recipes, but rarely a spice mixture specifically suited for an individual dish. Such is the case with a galantine flavored with canella, ginger, nutmeg, grains of paradise, and galingale, though the author insists that nutmeg should predominate.[11] This recipe is most likely an adaptation of a medieval standby. For most recipes, readers are offered a convenient spice mixture, and exact measurements of each ingredient are supplied. Most frequently used is a mixture of four drams of ginger, four of canella, two of round pepper, one of long pepper, two of nutmeg, one of cloves, one of grains of paradise, one of mace, and one of galingale, all reduced to a powder.[12] In total this equals seventeen drams, or just about an ounce, which is about one-third the standard in spice bottles used today.

The author also mentions that each of these spice mixes can be kept for six weeks or a month. Not only was freshness obviously a major concern, hence mixing in small quantities, but one might extrapolate a rough estimate of the quantity used in a typical meal. If the cook went through a mere ounce in a month for all the recipes calling for this mixture, it would necessarily have been a tiny soupçon per dish. On the other hand, he merely states that it can be kept this long without corrupting, not that this would be enough to season a month's worth of food.

In any case, this combination and the roughly similar though less complicated one that follows, which the author admits is inferior, are still thoroughly medieval in structure and effect. Much the same can be said of this cookbook itself in its Gothic typeface, and also the chateaux being built by François I at exactly the same time, though these have at least a veneer of Renaissance influence. Of spices, in whatever quantity they were used, their presence signifies that cuisine in France had not made quite the same shift toward cinnamon and sugar as was evident in Italy. In fact, the major difference between these two countries is the persistent use of ginger in France. The "white powder" called for in numerous recipes is merely powdered ginger with a bit of starch, and is used in all white soups and sauces.[13] This is not to say, however, that there are not significant changes in the use of spices in sixteenth-century French cuisine. Their combination with herbs and aromatics such as onion seems to point in a new direction. One must also not forget that there are a number of recipes in this cookbook that warn not to use too many spices,[14] and many that call for none at all. For example, a *capilotaste*—relative of the *capirotada* that is in nearly every cookbook of the sixteenth and seventeenth centuries—here is a tower of bread soaked in beef bouillon, layered with chopped partridge and garlic, and some added cheese as well, but no spices.[15] There are many reasons why this cookbook does mark a departure from medieval cuisine, but the use of spices does not appear to be among them.

On the question of sugar, the French cookbooks do tend to be in line with trends elsewhere. In the *Livre fort excellent,* the majority of recipes in the first part of the cookbook specify adding before service a "grant foyson de sucre"—a great deal of sugar. These are, significantly, savory dishes such as boiled capon, a white sauce, an omelet filled with croutons, or fried trout.[16] For the most part, these are "light" and white foods. Though sugar does not become ubiquitous as in Italian sources of the same period, the preference for sweetened lighter fare does appear in both. The author makes concessions to personal taste as well, specifying in a recipe for cream of fresh peas made with white wine, white bread, and clarified butter that some people do not sweeten it at all, suggesting that the normal practice, and perhaps fashion, dictates otherwise.

English cookbooks of the sixteenth century at first seem to lag behind in the shifting use of spices and sugar. In *A Proper Newe Booke of Cokerye*, we find sugar in familiar places, certainly among pies and custards and in "blewe manger" but not often in savory dishes. Stewed capons and white broths, for example, are served unsweetened.[17] Meats are regularly seasoned with salt. The spices used are typically cinnamon and ginger; in a few recipes cloves, mace, or saffron appear, but most recipes call for salt and pepper and perhaps some vinegar as seasoning. Both the range and frequency of spices called for has diminished, though. This is also true of *The Good Huswifes Handmaide,* in which herbs, salt, and pepper are at hand for a good proportion of meat and vegetable recipes. There are recipes for sweet boiled capon or capon in white broth quite similar to those in the French sources, and sugar is used in many savory dishes. The author rarely uses a dense cluster of spices as found in cuisine of previous centuries, and many recipes call for no spices whatsoever. Even in places we would expect to find spices, they are absent, as in a Hodgepot, made with mutton neck and beef rump boiled. The flavorings are onions, marigold flowers (to make it yellow), and parsley chopped not too finely. Only pepper and a little vinegar are added.[18]

There are two possible reasons for the relative scarcity of spices. Ostensibly, these sources are in line with continental trends, at least in the use of native herbs over exotic spices. But this may merely reflect that these small inexpensive manuals were meant for households that would not or could not squander a great deal of money on expensive flavorings. Unlike the courtly cookbooks of the Middle Ages and those of the baroque era, designed specifically with ostentation in mind, these English sources appear to target an audience of "middling sorts," and it might be a mistake to assume that they reflect the evolution of elite taste. Unfortunately they are the only cookbooks of the era, and only at the end of the century and in the next do we find courtly cookbooks fully in line with European developments.

The cookbook of Thomas Dawson, printed at the end of the sixteenth century, in many respects descended from the early ones. It also reflects simple, homegrown tastes. When spices are called for, often in combination with raisins or dates, they are usually cinnamon, ginger, and pepper. Sometimes mace, nutmeg, or cloves are included. But there are still many recipes that use herbs such as parsley, rosemary, or thyme and no spices. In general though, Dawson does expect that his readers will have spices to use, and of course we know there was still a great demand for them in the marketplace, as witnessed by the many efforts to found trading companies or by the many fruitless efforts to discover the northwest passage to Asia over the top or through North America. If anything, the spices in Dawson reflect that increasing numbers of people could afford spices, though significantly, many of the spices familiar in the medieval kitchen are now absent, and a typical spice mixture consists of pepper, cinnamon, and ginger in combination with either mace, cloves, or nutmeg, essentially the Christmas spice blend with which we are familiar.

In the seventeenth century the use of spices in European cookbooks diminished further. Though influenced by the preceding generation's international style, Lancelot de Casteau uses far fewer spices than his predecessors. Herbs and citrus have begun to replace them and, significantly, butter has become a flavoring agent in its own right, which is not surprising given the provenance of this book in the Low Countries. In his first recipes we find rosemary, marjoram, chopped mint, orange juice, or slices of salted lemon. Some recipes, mostly stews or *heuspots* (hot-pot, a typical Netherlandish dish), still contain the medieval spice combinations: nutmeg, ginger, cinnamon, saffron, and sugar. These are no doubt traditional favorites. There are newer alternatives, though, such as a veal stew made with broth, salted lemon, mint, marjoram, and a bit of verjuice or wine.[19] There are also several variations on the medieval *blancmanger,* none of which contain spices.[20] It may be that such simple recipes had always existed in common households that could not afford spices, but that they now appear in an elite cookbook shows that tastes were becoming simpler, that the appreciation for uncomplicated flavors and delicacy was beginning to replace dense and complex flavor combinations. Typically Lancelot offers a complex older recipe, like one for hashed carp and salmon in a stew with spices and fruit, but then follows it with an alternative that uses just water, wine, and herbs.[21] Similarly a sturgeon *en adobe,* which suggests a variation on a Spanish adobo, involves roasting then fricasseeing the fish in butter or olive oil, then simmering in vinegar and wine with lemon, saffron, pepper, bay, rosemary, and marjoram leaves, pounded radish, and a little handful of coriander—which implies fresh leaves rather than seeds.[22] Other fish, or even capon, go in the same sauce. In terms of technique the sauce is nothing novel, but the seasonings are definitely on the path of evolution away from medieval spices and sugar and toward classical haute cuisine.

In Spain the development of cuisine was somewhat different. Domingo Hernadez de Maceras, cooking for a college refectory, represents a level of cooking somewhat beneath that of nobles and the royal court. This may explain his apparent conservatism, or perhaps that fashions had not yet changed among his audience. The majority of his recipes merely call for "spices," often along with parsley and mint. This suggests that the use of spices, as well as what might be considered elite cuisine of the preceding generations, still appealed to people slightly down the social ladder—if not quite middle classes, certainly the aspiring professional classes. It is not entirely clear who his audience might be, though some comments suggest it is professional chefs working in noble households. For example, a meat in green sauce recipe suggests garlic "if your Lord eats it."[23] In any case, the recipes are still largely medieval in structure, thickened with bread and verjuice or vinegar, presented in thick homogenous concoctions often combined with eggs. Again, spices are usually unspecified, though one recipe explains that six *maravedis* of "common spices" include cloves, pepper, and saffron all pounded together. Another includes ginger and cinnamon as well.[24] There is, in fact, scarcely a recipe that does not call for spices.

At the royal court of Spain, tastes were quite different. The only logical explanation must be that if people somewhat down the social hierarchy could afford spices and chefs to present complex concoctions, the court would have to find sophistication and elegance in some other form. By comparison, the dishes of Montiño, first published in 1611, are direct and in their own way as novel as those of Lancelot. The author also insists in the prologue that many of the recipes are of his own invention, and the book contains absolutely nothing that he has not personally prepared. Presumably this sales pitch was directed both at Maceras, with his antiquated recipes, as well as Diego Granado, who pilfered most of his cookbook from Scappi and the medieval Robert of Nola. From the start, the sparing use of spices is apparent. For roast fowl, he says that the peacock can be stuck with cloves, but some people do not use it. With capon, he insists it should not be used. The flavorings, much like in Italy at the same time, consist merely of a sprinkling of sugar and cinnamon with lemon, though he also suggests a sauce based on pomegranates.[25] A leg of lamb is seasoned merely with salt and "nothing else thrown on."[26] There are still many recipes that call for "all the spices," but Montiño will often suggest a tiny bit of pepper or cinnamon or just "a little spice."[27] Spices do not seem to impress as much any more. Even though they are still included in a significant proportion of the recipes, mint, marjoram, oregano, cilantro, and a variety of other herbs, often with onions and lemons or oranges, appear to be gradually taking their place. He even suggests in one recipe calling for mint, cilantro, marjoram, and a little bit of parsley that if you happen not to have fresh, dried and ground will serve.[28] What this suggests is that herbs were becoming an indispensable part of the kitchen in all seasons.

Spices and Garnishes

The Italian sources of the seventeenth century still use spices, but the trend toward sweetness and aroma, as well as the tendency to garnish, recounted below, began to dominate the recipes. In Stefani, for example, nutmeg is still present, and the ubiquitous cinnamon and sugar, though not perhaps as prevalent as in the preceding century. But the obsession has shifted to musk and ambergris, mastic, and anything perfumed, such as citron flower water, jasmine water, and the old standby, rose water. Juniper also makes an appearance in sauces and syrups,[29] as do flowers such as elderberry (*sambuco*).[30]

This fashion is directly paralleled in English sources, particularly Robert May. Spices are still used, especially nutmeg, but aromatics have become the real star attractions. Anchovies, capers, olives, pine nuts, lemon, and orange and other Mediterranean flavors appear as never before. Native mushrooms and onions and a whole new range of garnishes have replaced the dense spice mixes. No longer are ingredients pounded together and sieved, thickened with bread and vinegar, but rather the diversity of ingredients is left to be seen, and sometimes the spices are whole. Most important, they are used lightly as seasonings. A recipe for Olio of Sturgeon with other fishes gives a good indication of this aesthetic. Sturgeon and eel are minced with herbs, grated bread, egg yolks, salt, nutmeg, and pepper, along with gooseberries, grapes, or barberries. These are rolled into little balls. Then filleted fish in pieces is seasoned with pepper, nutmeg, and salt, as are shellfish. "Season them as the other fishes lightly with the same spices," May specifies. Boiled potatoes, skirrets, artichokes, and chestnuts are added and also seasoned. More egg yolks, "large mace," and more fruit left whole come next, and everything is placed in a pie with bay leaves and whole cloves, and the pie filled with butter and orange juice. It is also garnished with lemon slices.[31] Although spices are still present, their use has changed completely, and that they are left whole is clearly so the diner knows they are there along with the other ingredients. Garnishes have also taken center stage.

Garnishes

Among the most significant innovations of the early modern period is the systematic use of garnishes. The term is defined here as an edible adornment to a dish designed to offer a texture, flavor, or most important, color and form that contrasts with the primary ingredient. It should be noted that this is a different sense of the word than is used in French cuisine today. According to Laroussse, a garnish can be simple or composite, but "always blends with the flavor of the basic dish and sauce (if there is one) . . . to achieve overall harmony of shapes and colors pleasing to the eye."[32] This aesthetic could easily refer to painting or music in the classical era. Garnishes in the sixteenth and seventeenth centuries, although they may seem redundant and repetitive to the modern palate, were designed to offer counterpoints, identifiable nodes of ornament in a stock decorative vocabulary. Much as putti and cloudbursts in religious paintings and balustrades and urns in architecture serve as standard and requisite embellishments, the garnishes on a plate become indispensable markers of refined taste. Most important, they slowly replace the mélange of spices that dominated late-medieval cuisine.

Medieval cooks also used a wide variety of contrasting ingredients, but these were normally pounded and sieved into smooth combination, melding each component into a complex whole. Stamegnosis, understanding how to achieve smooth textures with a sieve, was one of their major preoccupations. This had all changed by the latter sixteenth and seventeenth centuries. Garnishes were more often added to the plate at the last minute and were left not quite as side dishes but as integral, distinct parts of the varied composition. Such garnishes were usually rare and expensive and sometimes intentionally odd, and usually accompanied every dish in staggering and repetitive profusion, particularly in the baroque era. Truffles, usually whole and cooked, are one garnish that has survived into modern times, although today they are usually served raw and shaved. Sliced lemons appeared beneath dozens of recipes as a foundation, rather than a few thin slices under a piece of fish or vegetable. Then there are garnishes of bone marrow, cockscombs and testicles, asparagus tips and artichoke bottoms, fruits such as gooseberries or unripe grapes, pistachios and pine nuts, and, most curiously, candied citron, capers, and anchovies. Often all these appeared together. Their purpose was at once visual, textural, and savory, and obviously there was still nothing unusual about combining sweet and savory with salty and sour, or fruits and vegetables with flesh.

Garnishes do begin to appear in the late Middle Ages, as does the word itself in a culinary sense. In English the verb originally means merely decoration, usually of pewter wares or clothing. The Viandier is clearly obsessed with the color of sauces, and for most recipes even specifies particular shades, but really calls for nothing like a garnish. The closest the author comes is a capon dish, a form of *blancmange,* with toasted almonds on one half and pomegranate seeds on the other, and sugar sprinkled over.[33] Martino and his contemporaries were also familiar with pomegranate seeds decorating a dish, and they too appreciated vibrant colors, notably greens and reds, and gilding. They rarely took pains, though, to build presentations upward, studded with many distinct ingredients for lavish effect. Ingredients contrasted in flavor, but these were normally thoroughly incorporated into the main ingredients. Nuts are the best example. Almonds were pounded smooth or were added in the form of almond milk. In the seventeenth century, by contrast, pistachios become more popular, but they are normally sprinkled over a dish or around it to add a decorative flourish.

The development of the garnish in the early modern period generally follows the use of precise measurements, detailed cooking instructions, and suggestions for presentation. Messisbugo is fairly novel in this regard. His flaky pastry, *sflogliata,* is filled with a variety of ingredients that are kept distinct, whether prosciutto, pigeons, or other items layered with raisins, pine nuts, and other embellishments. Atop one is a garnish, added after cooking, of comfits made of canella or anise seed.[34] Following a recipe for *torteletti* (what we would call tortellini) filled with beet greens and cheese, he notes that these can be served on their own or on capon, duck, or pigeon.[35] Normally his dishes are sprinkled with sugar and cinnamon, sometimes along with grated cheese, but a *pastello* is clearly adorned for decorative effect. It can be made of any kind of meat in a pastry shell, and adorned with lemon slices, wisps of fresh fennel fronds, unripe grapes, or sour black cherries (*marena*).[36] Another *pastello* for Lent is made of artichokes with smoked *meggia* (Ferrarese dialect for smoked mullet) or sliced *botargo* (salted dried whole fish roe).[37] The overall effect is to create a dish studded with whole items of contrasting color, shape, and flavor—in effect, rudimentary garnishes. Elsewhere egg yolks, fruits, or raisins and pine nuts are used to the same effect.

It is perhaps significant that Domenico Romoli, when he begins to discuss recipes, speaks of two separate verbs for the cook's activities.[38] There is *cuocere* (to cook) and *condire,* which means to add seasoning or to pickle. In the medical literature it usually means adding spices or flavors meant to balance a dish humorally. Here, however, the term is beginning to suggest foods that accompany others—garnishes as well as sauces or condiments, as we use the term for ketchup and mustard. For a variety of fried livers and organ meats, he reminds readers not to forget slices of orange, lemon, or citron.[39] The boiled veal's head is adorned with flowers and herbs,[40] and this would normally be the most fantastically garnished dish in cookbooks through the next century. Interesting garnishes also appear on simpler dishes. A pork loin is cooked with onions and quince, which are strewn on top when served hot.[41] There is also partridge covered with cabbage and garnished with a slice of prosciutto, accompanied by a garlicky bastard sauce (made with sweet wine) or sweet mustard.[42] Increasingly, dishes are composed of several main ingredients and are plated with decorative intent.

With Scappi, although he does not usually specify garnishes, smaller items do sometimes decorate a plate. More frequently, however, he notes at the end of a recipe to serve a main ingredient such as cow's udder, liver, or beef spleen "con alcuni saporetti sopra" or "servire alcuni saporetti in piatti."[43] Literally translated, *saporetti* would be "little tastes." The term refers not to garnishes but to little bowls filled with various sauces, which each diner can dip into at will, or which are poured over different parts of the dish for decorative effect.[44] In a small section in Book VI, Scappi describes these little sauces, most of which are made from fruits or nuts and are sweet. In texture they appear to be more like jams or chutneys. They are not really sauces in our sense of the word. A raisin sauce, for example, includes pounded raisins, mostaccioli biscuits, marzipan, and sugar ground, strained, and moistened with vinegar and orange juice. Another is made from boiled-down pomegranate wine and sugar.[45] A similar one is based on orange. These are definitely quite thick. The red currant sauce is put aside in a jar until it sets, and Scappi says it is really more of a jelly. Technically, we should label these condiments, functioning the same way a mint sauce or even ketchup would be used, but because they are used to adorn the plate, they function more as garnishes. They are thick, syrupy, and cold, much like honey, which serves as a sapor when clarified.[46] These characteristics distinguish such concoctions from a proper sauce, or *salza.*

As for garnishes in the modern sense of the word, it is more difficult to tell what Scappi's plates looked like. There is usually something sprinkled on top of the dish—sugar and cinnamon, fennel pollen, or a chopped herb. Sometimes there will be adjunct dainties, as with a stuffed suckling calf's head served surrounded with slices of ham or sausages and some *sapori*.[47] Other recipes suggest that the garnishes might be slices of lemon or lime, fruits such as gooseberries, or spring onions. There is not yet the wild variety of standard garnishes as found in the next century.

The same is true of Rossetti's *scalco* guide, though here we get a greater impression of a plate's appearance. They are sometimes adorned with fried sage or rosemary leaves, which are often gilded. Biscuits are sometimes called for around the edge of a plate, or a fish is encircled in caviar or *bottargo,* or a fowl with prosciutto or tongue.[48] Often called for are slices of lemon or citron, or pitted olives.[49] There is not yet a conscious combination of a main dish with extraneous smaller items, the signature of the baroque plate.

In the seventeenth-century Italian sources, such garnishes adorn every plate. The repertoire is fairly standard and includes most of the highly valued vegetables that would previously have appeared separately on their own plates. Lancelotti's *scalco* guide of 1627 gives the most vivid descriptions of how a plate would be organized. For the word *garnish* he uses the term *regalando,* meaning to present. Frugoli also calls garnishes *regale,* as a noun.[50] The decorations typically consist of biscuits, marzipan or fried bread, candied citron, nuts, asparagus tips or artichoke hearts, grated salami, prosciutto or tiny mouthfuls of sweetbreads or egg yolks—and often many of these together.[51] The effect is of dazzling contrasts of color, texture, and flavor. It is also as if many of the items previously found on the credenza or in the final "fruit" course have become adornments for every plate. Even broths are similarly arranged. For example, Lancelotti describes a *minestrina* of artichokes, pigeon meat, chunks of sweetbreads, veal rolls, chicken crests and livers, aromatic herbs, slices of prosciutto, and a broth of egg yolks and lemon juice, with garnished fried asparagus. Each lordly diner received his own plate.[52]

Judging from the other Italian *scalco* guides, the fashion for elaborate garnishes became obligatory in courts throughout the peninsula. Vasselli in Bologna sprinkles mostaccioli crumbs everywhere, and pistachios and pine nuts proliferate, along with aromatic musk and amber, citron peels, and of course sugar on practically everything. Mattei a little later in the century goes even further. In one banquet is the by now traditional veal head, boned and stuffed with eggs, capers, pine nuts, truffles, candied citron and prunes, and bacon. Here, it is also garnished with an *oglia podrida* of boiled capons, pigeons, small birds, sweetbreads, stuffed cabbage, chickpeas, lentils and chestnuts, heads of garlic, whole truffles, and spices.[53] Again, the variety and contrast with the main ingredient, studded with jewel-like morsels of every description, creates the dramatic effect these baroque presentations are striving for. A French bisque is similarly regaled with pigeons, biscuits, sweetbreads, asparagus, prunes, marrow, cockscombs, testicles, and pistachios.[54]

The fashion for baroque garnishes appears to originate in Italy and spreads from there to the rest of Europe. The early seventeenth–century sources in French and Spanish such as Lancelot and Montiño were written before this influence was felt, or at least we are not given much detailed information about garnishes aside from lemon slices, chopped mint, or toast and the like.

By the middle of the seventeenth century, particularly in English sources like May and Rabisha, the influence is evident, and precisely the same oddments show up on the plate. In fact, despite their obvious debt to Continental cuisine, the garnishes seem to be thrown haphazardly onto what are still very basic and traditional English dishes. In Robert May, a stuffed and boiled swan or other wildfowl is combined with stewed oysters, artichoke bottoms, marrow, gooseberries, sliced lemon, barberries, mace, and grated bread and doused with butter. The dish as presented contains fowl, fish, beef, fruit, vegetable, dairy, starch, and spice. This combination did not seem in the least incongruous, but rather elegant and decorative.[55]

La Varenne is also fond of garnishing the plate, and his English translator in the seventeenth century uses the term *garnish* in the sense of decorative presentation. For example, in a recipe for frog's legs boned and shaped to look like cherries, they are served in a broth on bread with hashed carp, lemon, and pomegranate.[56] As a rule, though, the preference for a wild variety of ingredients cannot be found in the French sources, which look positively tame compared to the English and Italian. The author recommends that you garnish with whatever you see fit, or with something simple like capers, parsnips, or perhaps chestnuts.[57] That is, as in the arts, the flamboyant baroque style became increasingly cool, detached, and calmer in late-seventeenth-century France. This can clearly be seen in Versailles. The reduction of garnishes from a staggering array of contrasting ingredients to perhaps one decorative element can be considered one of the important developments in French classical cuisine.

CHAPTER 5

Vegetables and Fruit

It is a common assumption that in the past, the diet of the wealthy consisted first and foremost of meat. Bourgeois households consumed less meat. Peasants, laborers, and the poor ate a tiny amount of meat, perhaps only on special occasions or to flavor the soup pot. The proportion of meat in the diet bore a direct relationship to one's social class, and those on the bottom of the hierarchy naturally spent the greatest part of their household income on basic starchy staples and ordinary vegetables. When they could get their hands on meat it was usually either an inferior cut, offal, or something preserved. There is some validity to this impression. The majority of recipes in cookbooks are for meat (and diners were visceravores at every level of society as well), along with pastries, which often contained meat. These were certainly the most complex part of a cook's repertoire. Naturally, cookbook authors were most interested in writing about the expensive and elegant foods. Vegetables were given a minor role by default, because they were seen as less versatile, and being comparatively inexpensive, less impressive.

To jump from these basic premises to the idea that elite people in the past ate mostly meat and few vegetables would be a great error, though. So too would the assumption that vegetables were somehow seen as lowly and degrading, not only because eaten by common peasants, but because they are at the bottom of the food chain, close to or within the earth, and therefore inferior to higher animals and birds as food.[1] By this logic, truffles should have been the worst of all foods. In fact, physicians referred to them as the excrements of the earth. This did nothing to deter elite diners from lavishing the most ardent attention on them. Nor did elites neglect such vegetables as cabbage, turnips, carrots, and beets, and other base foods. That is, the wealthy harbored no such conceptions about the ideological place of ingredients in the great chain of being. Nor were they worried about any social stigma attached to lowly vegetables. People in the middle classes may have had fears of debasement, of being mistaken for a peasant, but rarely nobles, it seems.

In a word, vegetables were crucial to the ideal elite meal, and they were given leading roles, especially during Lent. Even at other times of the year, certain courses were always structured around vegetables both raw and cooked. To be sure, banquet managers, chefs, and perhaps most importantly the *credenzieri* who arranged the salads and cold courses had their favorites. These particular vegetables were not, as might be expected, always the most expensive or rare, though. They were the most intensively cultivated, the product of a thriving network of market gardeners. The most prized vegetables were grown on small, carefully managed plots on noble estates or bought from farmers engaged in commercially oriented agriculture. Unlike in peasant farming, which was devoted primarily to bulky crops like wheat, beans, and other foods that could be stored, vegetables were increasingly supplied by capitalized specialists growing exclusively for the market. This kind of agriculture developed most successfully around cities and in the most heavily urbanized areas, such as northern Italy and the Netherlands. In more remote places the same kind of agriculture could develop on the noble estate for private consumption, or in some cases such produce was intended to be sold for profit in regional markets.

For many people of the leisured class, growing fruits and vegetables became a hobby, and just as today there was a certain amount of pride in presenting guests with the perfect specimen from one's own garden, even if it was servants who did the dirty work. As part of the entire Renaissance obsession with gardens, ordered nature, botanical rarities, and experimentation, it only made sense for vegetables to receive new attention.

An offering of a few intensely cultivated vegetables became absolutely requisite on the finest tables. They were used in recipes, and practically everything found its way into a pie at some point, but vegetables were often presented simply in a separate course devoted almost entirely to them. Artichokes and cardoons (the stalky relative in the same family) were without doubt the most highly esteemed. It is perhaps the comparatively seasonless nature of their growth that made them regular favorites. That is, there are both spring and fall crops, and artichokes can be eaten at any stage of growth, large or small. Unlike fruits, which ripen all at once, artichokes would have been available much of the year, and they do appear in banquet menus in most seasons. Asparagus is exclusively a spring crop, but it ranks right next to artichokes as a vegetable of choice. Close behind were fennel, broccoli, and cauliflower. What was then called *cavoli fiori*, "flowers of cabbage," was perhaps sometimes just that, something closer to broccolini than our modern cauliflower. When the plant is described, some authors, such as Vasselli, mention its umbrella shape and suggest it should be peeled, which would clearly be impossible for modern white cauliflower heads.[2] Others such as Stefani, however, mention many compact buttons connected to a united foot, which is certainly modern cauliflower.[3] These two authors were nearly contemporary, so it does not appear to be changing usage over time. In any case, there were many available brassica forms, just as there are today.

Alongside all these were salads, usually composed of lettuce, endive, chicory, and other leafy greens, as well as herbs and flowers. Perhaps strange to our minds is that salads usually appeared in the first course cold, but vegetables were normally served in the penultimate "fruit" course right before the confections. That is, vegetables were not usually considered *contorni*, or side dishes, to accompany the main dish but were gastronomically linked with grapes, nuts, truffles, olives, and other "fruits" and cheese in a course normally devoid of meat or fish (though sometimes oysters were included.) It was as if a certain botanical logic took precedence over a sense of gustatory balance, as we conceive of it. In grand banquets and dinners, the meal always closes with confections, but domestic meals, simpler in structure, usually conclude with the fruit course—including vegetables. Thus conceptually vegetables were given a certain prominence rarely afforded when they appear on the side of the plate as an afterthought, as in much modern cookery.

When vegetables were included in hot main courses prepared by the cook, they were either the central focus in a pastry, egg dish, or soup or were added to a complex dish as a garnish. This was increasingly the case in baroque cuisine. In the sixteenth century vegetables often appeared as main dishes in their own right. For example, in an all-vegetable meal organized by Rossetti,[4] the first course consisted of seventeen cold dishes—mostly salads, fried mushrooms, stuffed artichokes, and a cold fruit soup. The hot course that followed shows the panoply of main courses featuring vegetables: artichoke pastries, spinach in a sauce, tiny fresh fava beans with fried leeks, broccoli with orange, red chickpeas, fennel soup, tender shoots (*coresini*—a word of Venetian dialect) of white cabbage, fried. In other courses, different preparations of the same vegetables appear, as does a parsnip pie, along with fritters, stuffed vegetables, grilled vegetables, and so forth. Clearly there was nothing degrading about eating lowly vegetables. Artichokes appear in several guises in every course, including the fruit course.

The best-known treatise about vegetables was written in 1614 by Giacomo Castelvetro, a protestant Italian in England. It was called *Breve racconto di tutte le radici, di tutte l'erbe e di tutti i frutti che crudi o cotti in Italia si mangiano* (Brief account of all the roots, herbs and fruits, both raw and cooked, eaten in Italy). It was written either to inspire his new neighbors with a love for greens, or was purely nostalgic.[5] Castelvetro's account includes many of the same favorites as in cookbooks—asparagus, broccoli, and artichokes, which he says can be either eaten raw, boiled in broth, baked in pastries, or grilled and preserved in oil. There are also various sprouts, of hops or mallows, or roots such as rapunzel (*Campanula rapunculus*—a bland but crunchy white root. The leaves of the plant can also be eaten, if one recalls the fairy tale). Castelvetro also mentions legumes and a wide variety of salad greens. Strangely, he even has a salad he calls an *olla podrida,* presumably because it is composed of a hodgepodge of ingredients: herbs, endive, chicory, radishes, raisins, olives, capers, slices of tongue, citron, lemon, green onions, and so forth.

On the topic of salad there was actually a much more comprehensive source, written by Salvatore Massonio and published in 1627, called *Archidipno overo dell'insalata.* The title reveals the important place of salads—it is a made-up Greek work meaning "to start" (*archi*) and "dinner" (*deipnon*). The book discusses the properties of every ingredient that can go into a salad. Interestingly, Massonio sometimes notes that the quality of ingredients differs according to social class. The salt you find in taverns and rustic inns is grayer than on better tables.[6] Lettuce is eaten by country folk, but they normally put it into soup.[7] The rich prefer their peas cooked with prosciutto,[8] and they also like borage and rosemary flower salads.[9]

Contrary to current fashion, salads were always eaten at the start of a meal, intended to stimulate the appetite, though Massonio tells us that there were some who, in imitation of ancient practices, ate them at the end.[10] A salad was also considerably more broadly defined than today and could include cold fowl, pickled fish, pastries, prosciutto, and salami or tongue, but interestingly not fruits, including olives, nuts, and vegetables like artichokes and fennel, which came in the fruit course just before dessert. But other vegetables could show up cooked or raw in a salad, including parsnips or carrots, the former of which were preserved as a "compost," which was essentially light pickling in vinegar, sugar, and spices.[11] There are also beets, which are used cooked and sliced in salads, or, among the Germans especially, pickled.[12] Massonio also describes a salad made from cabbage thinly sliced like pasta and seasoned with vinegar, oil, salt, pepper, and cooked grape must (*sapa*)—a rather enticing coleslaw.[13] Among the great variety of herbs and leafy greens, he explains that though fava beans are not used often in a salad, "some people will eat the first sprouts, when they are tender, right when the plant begins to raise its stem, being just a short point above the ground."[14] This constitutes no less than a deep and almost poetic reverence for vegetables.

It was not merely the Italians who doted on greens. Salads were eaten elsewhere in Europe as the fashion for things Italian caught on, particularly in the late seventeenth and early eighteenth centuries. John Evelyn's *Acetaria* is probably the best-known book about salad, and having traveled in Italy during the civil wars, he knew about its customs first hand. But Evelyn did not associate salads exclusively with Italy. He notes that "the more frugal Italians and French, to this day, accept and gather ogni verdure, anything that's green and tender, to the very tops of nettles; so as every hedge affords a salad."[15] He also mentions that Italians make a "sallet of scalions, cives, and chibbols only season'd with oyl and pepper; and an honest laborious country-man, with good bread, salt and a little parsley, will make a contented meal with a roasted onion."[16] Evelyn also remarks that Italians enjoy pimpernel and artichokes, and that their rule in dressing salads is to season judiciously with oil, vinegar, and salt alone.[17] Although the work is primarily intended to show off the author's classical erudition, it is testimony that salads were appreciated in England by the end of the seventeenth century.

Vegetables also feature prominently in cooked recipes in a profusion that sometimes puts modern cookbooks to shame. Scappi, as usual, offers the greatest variety. For the lowly cabbage and all its relatives he has the following recipes. There is a soup of *caulo torsuto* (kohlrabi), as well as one each for cauliflower and Brussels sprouts and three others for regular cabbage varieties.[18] There is also *minestra* of cabbage alla Romanseca, in which cabbage is parboiled in broth then beaten with a knife, after which it is placed in a casserole with melted lard and fried quickly with some pepper and cinnamon. Then broth with yellow cervelat sausages is added, and it is served hot, with cheese on top.[19] Cabbage leaves are also stuffed. Kohlrabi appears in a pie,[20] and Bolognese or Milanese cabbage appears as an ingredient in dozens of recipes, such as a quail soup or eel soup.[21] Again, there is no lack of imagination or affection even for the commonest of vegetables, as well as their newer cousins. He even mentions that Milan cabbage is exported to France, and French cookbook authors do indeed refer to it by that name.

Scappi also offers several eggplant recipes, a vegetable notably reviled by physicians as dangerous. One involves peeling and slicing the eggplant, soaking for a half hour, parboiling, and then lining an oiled casserole with the slices, along with mint, marjoram, pimpernel, chopped parsley, fennel fronds, and garlic. On top he adds pepper, cinnamon, and cloves with enough salt, a bit of verjuice, and sugar. The casserole is then baked. It is a vegetarian meal meant for Lent, but on other days it can be made with butter and slices of cheese on top.[22] He also has recipes for stuffed eggplant, fried eggplant with garlic and a hazelnut sauce or green sauce, and eggplant soup with almond milk and verjuice.[23]

Without lingering on these magnificent recipes, suffice to say that Scappi, particularly in his recipes for Lent, lets vegetables truly star. They are not necessarily simple recipes presented without adornment, nor do they preserve pristine vegetal flavors, but they are recipes that with minor adjustments have withstood the test of time. Perhaps most important, there is scarcely any vegetable Scappi hesitates to use in a thoughtful and creative way.

The Spanish are no less enthusiastic about vegetables, partly because they too were interested in providing recipes for Lent. But there is also genuine creativity. Not surprisingly, Maceras often served vegetables in his college refectory. His third book is devoted to recipes based on such vegetables as spinach, truffles, lettuce, asparagus, gourds, carrots, and eggplant. His spinach recipe involves blanching and squeezing out the leaves, then cooking in a pot or casserole with oil and garlic, raisins and honey.[24] According to Montiño, calabashes can be made into "the best dishes of the entire year" when parboiled, fried, and then combined with chicken or pigeon in a pottage.[25] So enthusiastic is he that he offers nine separate recipes, including several stuffed calabash recipes both for Lent and meat days, baked with cheese and eggs, fried, and made into soups. One in particular he claims is not really for dainty people, but rather for private meals when one does not want to fuss too much. It is simply calabash in a casserole with onions and butter or oil, with spices, sugar or honey, hot water, bread crumbs, and egg.[26] It is not entirely certain to what vegetable the word *calabaça* actually refers in the seventeenth century. Today it always designates a pumpkin or some other variety of New

World cucurbit. No other American plant appears in Spanish cookbooks for some time, though it is certainly possible that these could be true pumpkins. More likely, however, they were edible gourds (*Lagenaria*) that may have originated in Africa. Just like the word *phaseolus* was applied to New World beans indiscriminately, it seems that the old word *calabash* (deriving from Arabic, as do most Spanish food words) was also used for anything pumpkin-like, and eventually the gourds were replaced by New World species without any change of name.

Cookbooks in French, again with the interest in Lent, also offer many vegetable recipes. The *Livre fort excellent,* apart from using onions as a flavoring throughout, also offers salads, artichokes,[27] herbs — even ones dried for use through the winter.[28] There are also several recipes for cucumbers, normally cooked, and a curious cucumbrance that the author calls *cocombre contrefaict* made of sausage meat shaped into a long cylinder, poached, and painted green with egg yolk and wheat juice.[29] Lancelot in the next century offers a cauliflower pottage with sausages, perhaps a chicken or pigeon, or roast mutton and a bit of mint.[30] He also includes several vegetable tarts based on spinach, herbs, eggs, and cheese, clearly the ancestors of quiches.[31] His tarts can be made of practically any vegetable. *Tourtes geneves* are made with onions fried in olive oil, saffron, and pepper. Another is made of pounded fava beans, and another of roasted turnips.

> To Make Turnip Tarts — Take the turnips and roast them on the fire, being cooked cut them in little long slices like one cuts tripe, then take 4 ounces of rich and tender cheese, mix 3 raw eggs with the cheese, $^1/_4$ ounce of canella, 2 ounces sugar, a bit of pepper, four ounces of melted butter, a bit of rose water, and make tarts like the others and serve thus.[32]

Lancelot even has a recipe for spinach ravioli, which he calls *raphioulles,* made with parboiled spinach chopped and pressed dry with mint, parmesan, butter, egg yolks, nutmeg, and canella.[33] Such recipes are good evidence not only of the interest in Italian food, but of vegetables in general. His recipes also reflect his local taste. For example, there is a perfectly workable recipe for cucumber pickles.[34]

In northern Europe, Lenten restrictions would not have made the focus on vegetables as important, nor would all of them grow easily, but there still seems to have been an interest in them among food writers. Marx Rumpolt lists fifty different kinds of salad based on endive, white and green cabbage, rapunzel, hops, asparagus, chicory, capers, citron, artichokes, various lettuces, and other vegetables popular among elites throughout Europe. There are also particularly German ones, like the red cabbage salads and a peeled cucumber salad with fennel and cumin. For some reason he thinks cauliflower is a Spanish salad. There is a definite and pronounced interest in vegetables here.[35]

The sixteenth-century English sources are not quite as enthusiastic about vegetables, though it may be that vegetables were merely served simply, and in short cookbooks were not considered complex enough for inclusion. The *Proper Newe Booke of Cokerye* has a simple spinach tart, as well as one for borage flowers, egg yolks, and curds or, oddly, apples. The tart can also be made with marigolds, primroses, or cowslips.[36] *The Good Huswifes Handmaide* also has relatively few vegetable recipes; when ingredients like spinach, carrots, or cabbage appear they are usually stewed with mutton.[37] Lettuce, endive, and borage are given the same treatment. The spinach tart differs from the previous only in including cream, but there is an excellent spinach fritter recipe. The spinach is blanched, cooled, and wrung out, chopped with the back of a knife, mixed with four egg whites and two yolks, bread crumbs, ginger, and cinnamon and then fried in butter and sprinkled with sugar.[38] The author also has three recipes for a peculiarly English dish, the tansy, which is essentially a green omelet. Tansy is a bitter green plant with fern-like leaves. These are mixed with parsley, borage or strawberry, and violet leaves, which are washed, beaten in a mortar, mixed with the eggs, and then strained. The result is fried in butter and seasoned with sugar and salt.[39] The English were not yet interested in the vegetables that were all the rage on the Continent, though Thomas Dawson does have a recipe for artichokes boiled in broth and then baked with marrow.[40] There are a few salads, but in general the craze for vegetables had not yet reached England in the sixteenth century.

By the seventeenth century it is clear that both in England and in France vegetables had become popular, warranting attention and recipes in their own right. This may have something to do with the fact that cookbooks were much longer and comprehensive, and patrons were interested in having even their vegetables presented in interesting new ways. Whatever the cause, presumably in part merely a matter of availability, cookbooks such as Murrell's in 1615, purporting to relay French recipes along with English, nonetheless offer only a few oddities such as pickled rosebuds, broom buds meant to be mock capers, purslane, and radishes. It seems that Murrell knew about Continental fashions for vegetables but could not yet acquire the goods. His salads, revealingly, are made of hop buds, mallows, and burdock root.[41] There is an interest by the early seventeenth century, but not yet, it seems, the ability to present the full range of vegetable dishes.

By the time we get to Robert May mid century it is evident that vegetables have come into their own, and again, the sheer size of May's book probably has something to do with this. Nonetheless, he serves grand baroque salads, artichoke pie, buttered cauliflower,[42] and asparagus. Recipes for carrot soup or artichokes, or even potatoes, skirrets, or parsnips are included.[43] There is also a section on "The best way of making all manner of Sallets,"[44] which shows that combinations of greens, cold meats, olives, mushrooms, capers, lemons, nuts, and raisins had come into fashion in England just as it did on the Continent. May, true to his roots, does include native plants too, including Alexander buds (*Smyrnium olustratum*), samphire, cresses, and even scurvy grass (*cochlearia*—a pungent green that grows near the seashore, not unlike a bitter cress in flavor). Perhaps most important, vegetables have become garnishes.

The interest in vegetables is also evident in contemporaneous French and Italian cookbooks. La Varenne has as much enthusiasm for artichokes as Scappi had a century earlier. In several elegant preparations, he presents the bottoms alone, either fried or boiled with a kind of hollandaise sauce made with butter, a drop of vinegar, nutmeg, and the yolk of an egg.[45] They are also pickled. Fresh green peas were also served in several soups, or garnished with lettuce and a touch of cream.[46] As in other cookbooks there are also recipes for asparagus, truffles, and an extensive interest in mushrooms—which would become one of the signature flavors of the haute cuisine to develop in the following century.

The Italian cookbooks, although perhaps not as innovative as the French, still sustain the interest in vegetables. In Vasselli (La Varenne's almost exact contemporary), the tendency toward elaboration and profusion of garnishes affects even the simplest of vegetables. For example, what promises to be a salad of lettuce turns out to be lettuce leaves blanched, carefully dried, arranged on a plate in the shape of a rose, star, or other capricious form, garnished with mint and raisins boiled in wine, and seasoned with oil and citron flower vinegar.[47] Lettuce was also, strangely enough, candied, and Italians still regularly seasoned it with sugar. Another recipe has whole lettuce heads wrapped in paper and roasted under the coals. This is not to suggest that they regularly ruined vegetables. Vasselli's admonitions about asparagus ring strangely modern. He warns that it should not be overcooked and should still have a little bite after being briefly boiled. Stefani some years later approaches vegetables in a similar way. Cardoons are carefully peeled and soaked so they remain white, after which they are cut up, boiled briefly, then seasoned with lemon, salt, pepper, and canella, then fried in butter with nutmeg, crushed pistachios, and sugar, and then seasoned again with spices before serving hot.[48] The procedure sounds like overkill, but for the relatively bland and potentially tough cardoon, it does yield a savory and complex dish. A similar recipe is given for celery, which was largely ignored by earlier authors. Stefani's recipes for *zucche ò zuccoli* (again, either gourds or squash) are equally interesting. They are peeled, sliced, and salted to drain. Then they are dipped in flour and fried in butter. They are then covered in a sauce made of pounded basil, fennel seed, cheese, some verjuice, sugar, egg yolks, and butter.[49] He offers several variations as well, some based on oil, but this one appears to be an odd cross between a pesto and a hollandaise.

Although the recipes for vegetables changed considerably through the sixteenth and seventeenth centuries, the same dozen or so remained favorites on elite tables. Contrary to the impression that noblemen only cared to eat meat, the culinary sophistication with which vegetables were treated suggests otherwise. What is notable in all these tracts, however, is the absence of New World vegetables. Potatoes appear in some English sources, and Jerusalem artichokes do as well, in La Varenne, for example. Some vegetables were introduced with scarcely any recognition that they came from the Americas — many bean varieties and squashes. But there is no mention of corn, peppers, or tomatoes in European cookbooks. They were certainly known to botanists by the mid sixteenth century, and were grown experimentally. That elite diners had no interest in them suggests that novelty in itself was not sufficient to recommend a new vegetable. That these were being grown and were available did not lead chefs to experiment with them, even though some clearly went out of their way to at least mention every food that could possibly be cooked. It is not until the end of the seventeenth century and then into the eighteenth that we find these New World vegetables in cookbooks.

Fruit

As with vegetables, the idea that European elites of the past would not eat fruit no longer needs refuting. It is also clear that despite physicians' warnings, fruits were eaten both cooked and raw and were among the most prized items on the banquet table. They were eventually given the spotlight in their own course, and while fruits were defined broadly and botanically, the culinary fruits were given prominence. One might even say that melons, pears, and peaches were among the quintessential foods associated with nobles. They were given such status that they were even elegantly carved tableside in midair, peeled in delicate curls, and proffered in elegant bite-sized shapes. The most cursory glimpse at sixteenth- and seventeenth-century still life painting reveals this era's obsession with fruits. Even if fruit was depicted as a symbol of decay, mortality, rebirth, or whatever, the sensual and almost erotic attention to the texture and glistening skin of ripe wet fruit gives some indication of how interested diners were in eating it.

Much of the confusion surrounding fruit consumption seems to be the result of cookbooks only offering recipes for cooked fruits. Hence pies proliferate, as do fruit sauces or dried fruits cooked along with meats and fowl. It is true that dried fruits were highly esteemed alongside exotic spices. It would be a mistake, however, to assume that elite diners in the sixteenth and seventeenth centuries avoided raw fruit. In fact, the strident warning of physicians that such foods risk corruption in the body may only have added to their appeal.

Compounded with the gastronomic interest in fruit and its prominence in the formal meal structure, fruits, because of their perishable nature, seasonality, and necessarily local provenance—that is, for all but the wealthiest of hosts—aroused an extraordinary appeal. In other words, fruits are special precisely because you cannot have them year round, nor do you often find a perfect, beautiful, and ripe specimen. And (unlike with most other foods) diners were greatly interested in the origin and cultivar of fruit, especially if it came from a renowned region or one's own estate. As with other foods in this period, the most highly esteemed fruits were the most perfumed and sweet. Such specimens were also the perfect symbol of the values this culture held most dear—preciosity, rarity, delicacy. Fruits also flaunt more than a hint of erotic suggestion, particularly with swollen, rubescent peaches about to pour forth unctuous juice, figs yearning to split from internal pressure, revealing seed-studded flesh, and melons ripe with anticipation before the fork plunges in. In the case of candied and conserved fruit, literally dripping with syrup, a suggestively sexual message probably could not be avoided.

From the early sixteenth century, it is clear that a profound interest in fruit is already in place. Messisbugo, in his introductory list of items required for a banquet, lists fruits both fresh and dry, cultivated and wild, along with many foods we no longer consider fruits, such as olives and artichokes. There are peaches, fresh and dried figs, melons, fresh and dried grapes, dates, wild azaroles, pears, apples, apricots of several kinds, quince, pomegranates, dried and fresh plums, blackberries, cherries, strawberries, sorb apples, medlars, and elsewhere are mentioned lemons and orange. Obviously, this is compiled long before tropical fruits would be known, but the variety available is still quite impressive, and several of these are even today little known outside Europe. Azaroles, sorb apples, and medlars are small, sour, and normally wild fruits that can sometimes be eaten raw if extremely ripe (or practically rotten, according to many authors) but are usually cooked into pies or made into jams. Messisbugo's banquet menus have not yet designated a separate fruit course; they often appear interspersed among other dishes at any point in the meal, as well as in the last course. What is interesting is his tendency to specify varieties of many fruits, such as bergamot pears, moscardine, or Caroelle, and *pere guaste,* which means spoiled pears. Apart from their placement in various banquets, we are not told much about fruit, though there are various recipes using them in tarts, fritters, and the like.

Scappi offers some scattered remarks about how dates will not last more than six months, while dried figs prunes and cherries last a year.[50] Instead of red grapes, he prefers white grapes with small or no seeds. It is in his recipes, though, that fruits are featured in truly surprising ways. He offers a melon soup in which the melon is cooked in butter or chicken fat, strained, and added to meat broth with gooseberries and unripe grapes, then thickened with beaten eggs and grated cheese.[51] Apples couple with onions in a sauce that is equally intriguing and worth translating in full:

> To make a sapore of apples and onions
>
> Take a pound of apples without peeling, but remove the seeds and core, and pound in a mortar with four ounces of large onions roasted beneath the coals and four cooked egg yolks, three ounces of fresh bread crumb soaked in rose vinegar and red wine. Then pound everything together, pass through a sieve, and place in a casserole with 4 ounces of orange juice and a bit of verjus, and cooked must, and a half pound of sugar. Cook and serve hot or cold to taste with sugar and cinnamon. If you like, in place of onions use cooked garlic cloves.[52]

Similar sauces are made of cherries, raisins, pomegranates, and red currants. Clearly, the sweet and sour flavor of fruit was considered an indispensable part of a well-set table. Diners would dip their meat into a variety of sauces, which seem to have been prepared ahead of time and kept in the larder. Scappi usually suggests how long these sauces will last—a few days, or sometimes longer if they resemble thickened jellies. For example, a black grape sauce is put into glass vessels or a glazed *albarello* (a pharmacist's jar) for keeping.[53]

It has been claimed that such *sapori,* syrups, and conserves were one of the major contributions of sixteenth-century Italian cuisine. In the case of medicinal fruit syrups, robs, and electuaries, this may be true. For culinary use there is a simultaneous outpouring of literature on the topic through most of Europe, although a fine line is usually not drawn between cuisine and medicine. Sour fruit syrups, classified as cold and dry, were used to treat fevers, but they were also added to hot and moist meats, perhaps to temper their humoral qualities, but also obviously for flavor and piquancy. Interestingly, some of the most familiar figures in sixteenth-century history wrote books on syrups and conserves— Michael Servetus, the first heretic to be burned in Calvinist Geneva, and Nostradamus, the renowned mystic. These works lie beyond the scope of this book, but they nonetheless demonstrate that there is an intense interest in fruit for a variety of purposes.

To return to Scappi, fruits figure in most cold credenza courses, but clearly according to seasonal availability. Like Messisbugo, he specifies varieties and contrasts methods of presentation. For example, for a garden collation served in Trastevere, south of the Vatican, Scappi serves raw fruit in the first cold course—palombine cherries, strawberries, conserved grapes, and citron with sugar, along with various salads and cold appetizers. In the second course, more fruit appears—*pere guaste* again, along with raw *pere moscarole,* and *pere riccarde* in pastries. Finally, in the last course are candied fruits such as melon, limes, citron, pears, peaches, and apricots. Cherries in syrup, quince jelly, a box of quince paste (*cotognata*—thicker in texture, in Spain called *membrillo,* in France *cotignac*), and a quince foccacia also appear. Clearly, the season, meal type, and location dictated a concentration on fruit in season, or even preserved from the year before, in the case of grapes.[54] The Italians were clearly crazy about fruit in any form.

In the list of items for the credenza, Scappi exhibits the range of familiar fruit varieties. There are five different varieties of raisins, pomegranates, quince, and sweet oranges—the kind that can be eaten out of hand, as well as the bitter Seville and a semisweet variety, citrons, two different limes, seven pear types, and three apples, plus other sorts.[55] In addition, he lists all varieties of fruit according to season, including cherries, straw-berries, apricots, plums, mulberries, melons, figs, azaroles, sorb apples, and medlars. These also find their way into tarts, fritters, and soups for invalids.[56] For these soperific concoctions, soups are made from pears, plums, prunes, dates, unripe grapes, or cherries and are served with a slice of bread in the bowl that defines the *zuppa*—or *sop*. One is tempted to suggest that fruit consumption was considerably greater in the sixteenth century than in our own day.

It is in Rossetti's *scalco* guide that we finally get an entire course called the fruit course, which would be standard thereafter in Italy. The course, which comes at the end of a meal but before the final dessert course (which contains conserved fruit), is composed normally of raw fruits, along with nuts, vegetables such as artichokes, truffles, and cheese. For dinner, the smaller evening meal, the fruit course concludes it, as is still the custom in much of Italy. Despite the incredible variety and abundance, diners were happy to eat what were relatively light foods, particularly fruit, at the end of a meal.

We know this was a custom throughout Europe, primarily because a medical controversy ignited over whether fruits should come at the start of a meal, in which case they might be forced prematurely into the veins before being digested, or at the end of a meal, where they might float on top of other foods, corrupting and sending noxious vapors up to the brain. Clearly, elite diners paid practically no attention whatsoever to these debates, and continued to eat fruit both ways. A corollary to this medical discussion was whether fruits such as peaches and melons should be consumed with or even cut up in wine. The wine was supposed to prevent the fruit from corrupting, though once again some physicians thought it would force the fruit through the system too quickly. In any case, diners went on eating fruit with wine, perhaps with no consider-ation of bodily harm.

Elsewhere in Europe, the sixteenth-century sources do not reveal nearly as much about fruit consumption, though again this should not be taken as evidence that fruit was in any way disdained. Without doubt the fashion for growing fruit trees, even citrus, in hothouses in more northerly climes shows that there was great interest among nobles. The cookbooks do not say much about fruit, though, as recipes focus overwhelmingly on meat, fowl, and fish. The *Livre fort excellent* offers a recipe for confect cherries or *griottes* (morello cherries),[57] and a fasci-nating quince recipe in which it is cooked in beef broth and red wine with cinnamon, cloves, and sugar, served with marrow on toast but little else.[58] This may owe to the fact that fruits were indeed served raw, and required no recipe or description. In fact, the book does list a few banquet menus, and here there is fruit. A salad of oranges appears in a first course,[59] and then a *papillon* of apples at the end. These are apples boiled in wine, sugar, and spices served cold and sliced.[60] There do not appear to be many fruits served mid meal among the soups, roasts, and other dishes, but the extremities of the meal do contain fruit. Fresh peaches and pears as well as pears in *hipocras* start one meal, along with almonds, junkets, and jellies.[61] Elsewhere, apricots are mentioned, as are strawberries and a few other fruits. There is neither the variety nor frequency of fruit served here, as in Italy.

The Spanish sources of the next century differ little from the French, but the first entry in Maceras lists fruits that should be served at the start of a meal, including cherries, citrus fruits, plums, figs, melons, and grapes.[62] There are also several quince recipes, one for candied citron, as well as a melon tart in which the slices are fried in suet, cooled, and sprinkled with sugar and a syrup made of white wine, cloves, and canella, with everything baked in a pastry shell with egg yolks. On meat days this tart can contain marrow.[63] Apart from these clues, the book contains practically no indication of how fruits were eaten. Montiño has a section at the end on conserves, including those made of apricot, plum, quince, and pears.[64] But he too gives scant information about how or in what context fruits were served. There is an apricot tart made with transparent leaves of dough basted with butter and arranged in several layers in a tart pan, with preserved apricots inside.[65] Montiño also suggests a startling way to serve conserved cherries, pears, apricots, and plums—on a plate with *huevos mexidos* (scrambled eggs, most likely with sugar) and *ojuelas,* a kind of fritter usually drizzled with honey.[66] The Spanish clearly had access to fresh fruit in season, but the cookbooks say little about how it was eaten.

Cookbooks in England, both in the sixteenth and seventeenth centuries, do include some details on fruit. The *Proper Newe Booke* has a few sample menus, but fruit only appears in those for "fyshe dayes" in the second course, and only figs, apples, raisins, and pears. There are several tarts for fruit, though—strawberry made with egg yolks, grated white bread, sugar, and butter and baked (without a crust, it seems). Similar ones are made of medlars, damson plums, and cherries.[67] The combination of eggs with fruit may strike us as odd, but even an applemoyse—a kind of apple sauce popular in the fifteenth century (the name suggests a Germanic origin; it sounds like apfelmus)—here includes whole eggs, damask water, sugar, and butter boiled together and served with biscuits, cinnamon, and ginger.[68] There are far more curious combinations in the *Good Huswifes Handmaide*. A pie for Lent mixes fruits and fish. The wardens here are a kind of pear.

> Take Eeles and flea them, and cut them from the bone, take Wardens and figs, & mince them together, and put to them cloves and mace, pepper, salt, and Saffron, and season all these together, and mingle it with great and small Raisons, Prunes and dates, cut it in small peeces, and so put it in the coffin, and let bake halfe an houre.[69]

For the English, one can understand the appeal of imported dried fruits, especially in winter, as this Lent recipe shows. But many native fruits were also baked, or put into various pies and other desserts. Baked peaches and apples and tarts of damson plums or pippins appear. The most interesting, though, is a recipe for baked oranges, which is essentially conserved orange peels baked in orange-shaped and saffron-colored pastry, with sugar and spices.[70] Thomas Dawson has many recipes for fruit preserves, as well. Marmalade is made of quince, now scented with musk and rose water.[71] Peach marmalade is cooked until stiff and imprinted with a mold and then dried by a fire.[72] Oranges are preserved whole in syrup, as are quinces and wardens. Melons or pumpkins are preserved with spices and honey. Suffice to say, these were the sorts of tasks any competent housewife was expected to master.

The English texts of the seventeenth century continue with this tradition of conserves and pies, and it appears this was the preferred way of eating fruit—or at least the authors do not reveal much about how fresh fruit was eaten. Gervase Markham offers many detailed recipes for pies and tarts, based on pippins, codlings (little green apples), wardens, and quince—all native fruit.[73] John Murrell scarcely mentions fruit at all in his menus, though he too has typical pies, including apple, gooseberry, and cherry.[74] As in Spain, fruit is combined with eggs in "Apple-puffes." These are minced apples with eggs, plus raisins, nutmeg, rose water, sugar, ginger, and spices dropped from a spoon into a frying pan and seasoned with orange or lemon juice on top.[75]

There is no dearth of fruit recipes in seventeenth-century Italian sources. Vasselli has sweet fruit sauces as before: a pomegranate julep and a thick sweet lemon sauce, which he specifies to "serve over roasts, or in plates whichever pleases you more."[76] There is also a pie of peaches and cheese.[77] Judging from the *scalco* literature of this period, fruits were still featured in a separate course, and were served in a variety of ways, including raw, in which case they were carved tableside. Everywhere in Europe, the fascination for fruit enjoyed fresh and in recipes continued unabated through the seventeenth century and into the next.

CHAPTER 6

Starches and Pasta

Despite the overwhelming dearth of recipes in the culinary litera-ture, starches—and above all, bread—formed the base of the European diet through the medieval and early modern periods. This was especially true among the less-well-off social strata, but even elite diners used thin slices of crustless bread, the trencher, as the base from which they ate food. Whether these were given away as a gesture of charity, thrown to dogs, or actually eaten after soaked with meat juices is not a question that can be answered definitively. Whatever became of these, one should not conclude that elite diners never ate bread, or rather sub-sisted solely on meat. Even after plates replace bread trenchers, bread and rolls are always on the table. Provisions of bread in elite households through the late Middle Ages and Renaissance were among the most important parts of the expenditure. The *scalco* literature attests to a well-stocked supply of bread for all meals. Fine white bread (or manchet, as it was called in England) or rolls were a requisite part of every banquet menu. The dietary literature delineates the quality of bread appropriate for delicate, or merely wealthy, stomachs, stating that it should always be made of the whitest and finest flour. It is also evident that bread, usually the soft inner crumb, was a primary ingredient in late-medieval cuisine, used as a thickener for sauces after being toasted and soaked in vinegar or some other liquid. However it got into their stomachs, elite diners consumed bread as a significant proportion of their diet.

In the sixteenth century, white bread was still the cultural ideal on elite tables. However, a significant shift occurred regarding the variety and forms the bread and, increasingly, pastry could take. Significantly, more and more of the starches presented were either butter-laden pastries or sweetened breads, which approach what we would now call cake. Sponge cake, marzipan, flaky leaves of dough, as well as other forms of starch such as ravioli—which are really another form of pastry, in cook's minds, boiled or fried rather than baked—became a new object of fascination. Bread itself was the object of experimentation, baked into puddings, placed under savory dishes as "sops," or toasted and anointed with butter or rich toppings in the form of crostini, *fettunta,* or, as they were called then, *panunto*—a word that Domenico Romoli took as his nickname.

The bread most esteemed would have been a light, sweet, and egg-laden batter, not unlike a brioche or challah. Messisbugo offers a recipe for nine-ounce, round *pani di latte.* The ingredients seem clear enough, but the proportions seem inexplicable and are obviously intended for dozens of breads. There are thirty-five pounds of flour, six pounds of sugar, seventy-five egg yolks, three pounds of rose water, six pounds of milk, six ounces of butter, and some salt.[1] After reducing and converting the recipe to cup measurements, it begins to make sense: for two loaves of roughly the same size, one would need one pound flour (about three cups), about one-third cup of sugar, two egg yolks, 1.3 ounces of rose water, a little more than one-fourth cup of milk, and a mere hint of butter. The liquid measurements probably need a little adjustment, but otherwise the recipe works well, even without Messisbugo's precaution to heat the yolks.

Pastries themselves were something fairly new, as well. To be sure, there were stiff, self-supporting pastry crusts made of rough flour intended to serve basically as disposable containers in which foods could be baked. These were not sliced, as we would a pie today. Usually they were broken open and the contents spooned out. The crust served as a way to keep the contents for a longer period without spoiling. Often whole animals were baked into pies, even creatures as large as a deer, bones and all. A liquid was often poured into a hole at the top of the pie to keep the contents moist, and then it was sealed to keep the air out. A pie recipe for oysters, still in their shells, is pretty good evidence that the crust was merely meant to be a container. That it could hold live birds or bunnies is further evidence that the "coffin," as it was called in England, was merely a container, even when the contents were still alive. Dutch still life paintings of pies glistening with dried fruit show clearly that the contents were scooped out as late as the seventeenth century, and that the dough was thick, supported its own weight, and was perhaps completely inedible.

The tart was another creature entirely. It consisted of a bottom shell only, and the contents were thus exposed to the heat of the oven and fused to the lower crust. In the case of a custard or fruit tart, or indeed any of the concoctions in these cookbooks, the crust was definitely meant to be eaten. There is still no complete consensus on the topic of when and how the edible pie crust developed, but the first recipes for butter-based crusts that were definitely meant to be eaten are found in Maestro Martino of Como in the mid fifteenth century. These were used both in tarts and in enclosed pies baked in a pie pan, the type with which we are familiar today. By the time we get to the sixteenth-century cookbooks, pies of all shapes and sizes and fillings were well known, and among those things most prized on the banquet table. Even decades before, Platina could complain that in this prosperous age people are no longer content with simple tarts of vegetables but want pies made from fowl.[2] In subsequent generations they wanted everything and anything in a pie: vegetables, meat, fish, eggs, or starches, with top crusts and without, folded as pasties, baked, fried, large and gilded, or as tiny mouthfuls. The sixteenth and seventeenth centuries might as well be called the Age of Pies.

It should also be remembered that pies were not standard fare for most people; they immediately signaled wealth and affluence for a simple reason. Large pies had to be baked in an oven. Keeping an oven warm after bread baking and then placing in pies or other baked goods was the usual procedure, the bricks retaining the heat for many hours after the coals and ashes were swept out. Their importance in banquets was that they could be served at room temperature and were often supplied by the *credenziero* rather than the cook. Thus they gave the kitchen brief respites during cold courses, often between the appearance of hot courses that would take up space on the fires. Also, there were almost always pies ready to be eaten whenever guests arrived at the table, a practice that gave the cooking staff time to begin final preparations for the first hot course. In this, the structure of the meal seems more dependent on the practical realities of serving a large number of people dozens of dishes, rather than on any gastronomic logic. Banquets begin with pies, cold meats, and such simply because there is no other convenient way to do it.

Smaller pies and pasties could also be fried, of course, and as Scappi suggests, they could even be cooked *sotto il testo*,[3] which means in an earthenware vessel. Normally, foods would be cooked slowly, or braised, in the *testa* —a vessel that had been in use since classical times. It consisted of a flat-bottomed clay bowl, sometimes with legs, and a concave, well-fitted lid with a handle. The *testa* was placed on a pile of hot coals, and then more coals were heaped on top. The technique should be familiar to any aficionado of cast-iron campfire cookery. The slow ambient heat would, ideally, cook the crust without burning, and seal in the contents without losing any moisture. For any family without a proper oven, this was probably the only way to make pies, because if exposed to direct flame, any crust containing fat would burn.

Whatever the method, elite diners were clearly crazy about pastries, and they were not only included in practically every course, but usually form a good percentage of the dishes as well. Before looking closely at the recipes themselves, it is significant to consider that when physicians criticize the eating habits of courtly gluttons, the food they most often associate with intemperate eating is pastry. There were naturally other practices they complained about, such as drinking chilled wine, or eating too many melons or foods composed of too many jumbled ingredients. But more than any other food it is pastry and pies that are associated with luxurious riotous dining. They are the quintessential *aristobroma*, or food fit for nobles. Most physicians thought pastries, pies, and similar junk foods were designed specifically to stimulate the appetite, or as they would call them, *irritamenta gulae*—gluttony inducements.[4] None considered that there were practical reasons for these to be served at the start of meals, much as snacks, or hors d'oeuvres. At any rate, despite medical warnings that such foods are indigestible and lead to an infinity of diseases, elite diners persisted in demanding them at banquets.

In addition to pies in the standard form, free standing, or in a pie pan, and tarts with only a bottom crust, there were also innumerable small pastries, pasties folded in half and decorated with a crimped edge, tiny fried ravioli, and then dozens of variations on little finger foods—tartlets and morsels encased in dough of many types. The standard pastry dough of the sixteenth century is a rather light and surprisingly delicate and crumbly mixture that has since become extinct. Most were made from fine white flour, rose water, egg yolks, water, and butter. There were also crusts made from marzipan, flaky multilayered pastries, or the *sfogliata*, as Messisbugo calls it, and several other doughy variations that range from soft biscuits to short crusts. The range of pastries discussed by Scappi is absolutely staggering; the entire fifth book of his *Opera* is entirely devoted to pastry.

Scappi offers both new and old forms for pies. For example, in his recipe for an ox tongue *pasticcio* (wrapped in pastry), he suggests using only coarse whole wheat flour with only the bran removed, and unsalted cold water. This type is intended to be kept for several days. Most important, this crust is not eaten. Only a variation with fat is intended to be eaten, but in this case it should be served hot from the oven or within an hour of baking.[5] These two variations not only show the basic differences in pastry-making techniques from medieval to modern times, but also the change in kitchen function. The earlier staff merely prepared the dish and kept it until someone was ready to eat it. The latter kitchen makes it to order, ideally right before the event.

In his recipe for sweetbreads in flaky pastry, Scappi reveals his long and extraordinary experience with pastry making. Here he specifies that a low-domed oven is best for flaky pastries, because you want more heat on top rather than the bottom so that the dough puffs up well. The dough itself is made from fine flour, egg yolks, and warm water—which apparently aids the expansion he is looking for—and just a little rendered lard. This is rolled out and brushed with more melted lard. The flat dough is then rolled up tightly into a log and sliced into two-finger-width rounds. Another bottom crust is made without fat and formed into a shell. The contents, including fruits such as gooseberries or raisins and spices, are heaped high into a mound, and the flaky pastry pieces line the sides all around, forming a kind of teepee. It is greased and then baked and brushed with grease using a feather, plus a few times more during baking, and finally sprinkled with sugar. He even suggests another variation as they make it in Rome, which looks good, but he insists does not taste as good. It is a stretched dough, essentially a filo or strudel, anointed with fat and folded to create many layers.[6]

Another common shape of pie Scappi uses is a kind of case, which can be made specifically for whatever shape the contents might be—a leg of some animal, a whole rabbit or guinea pig, ham or sausages, whatever—often with bones included and with stuffing. Frequently, a liquid is poured into the top after baking, and the pie sealed and kept until needed. Perhaps the oddest of these is a free-form pie containing a whole peacock or turkey laden with spices and pork fat and wrapped in pastry dough, with the head sticking out. The head is wrapped in parchment paper while baking to prevent burning.[7]

Among the panoply of pastry forms Scappi describes, there are *crostate*—shallow tarts with a decorative edging of crimped dough. There are torte made with an upper crust adorned with various devices. Some are made from strips of dough overlapping like Venetian blinds. There is even a flat pastry he refers to as a Neapolitan pizza, which is laden with almonds, pine nuts, and raisins pounded together, egg yolks, sugar, cinnamon, rose water, and crushed musk-scented cookies. Anything candied goes well on this, too. The designer pizzas of our own day are nothing strange compared to this.[8] Other pizzas are made dry with only sugar and rose water, and one contains parmesan cheese, sugar, rose water, and eggs worked into the dough.[9] A few are made with risen dough, and thus approach the modern pizza, if not in flavor than at least in structure, though they are laden with butter and again sprinkled with sugar.[10]

An entire section of Scappi's book on pastries includes "lean" variations based on fish or vegetables. Some of the most inventive include oysters, snails in a pastry shell, deboned frogs' legs, caviar, and every fish imaginable. Pies were one of the vehicles through which cooks could unleash their most imaginative inventions. How else can one explain this most extraordinary *crostata* made with the organ meats of turtles?

Starches and Pasta

> Take the liver without the gall bladder, and eggs without their shells, and for every pound of this, three ounces of salted eels' flesh cooked, pounded in a mortar, with an ounce of fine mostaccioli biscuits, fry the liver, and the eggs for a while with butter, then have the tart prepared with three leaves like those mentioned above, and crimped dough added around the edge, and above the leaves put mint, beaten marjoram, and raisins, pepper, cloves, sugar and canella, and put over that mixture the liver and eggs and pounded eel, tempered with orange juice or verjuice, and then a sprinkling of the same material on top that you put on the bottom, and a sprinkling of the same spices, cover the tart with two other similar leaves, and some shapes of flaky dough, and cook in the oven or in a testa, and serve with sugar and rose water on top.[11]

There are also variations offered using mushrooms, almonds, or olive oil instead of butter (for fast days) or turtle meat. This recipe not only gives a good impression of Scappi's style of writing but his open-ended attitude toward recipes. They are not meant to be followed religiously, to the letter. There are always variations, options according to personal taste, season, and available cooking equipment. In this respect, Scappi's recipes are liberating; they encourage the very sort of experimentation he himself has obviously enjoyed. Unlike most modern recipes, they empower the reader to be an active participant in the creative process, offering suggestions but never rigid directions. This, without doubt, is the sign of a masterful culinary mentor, or any teacher for that matter.

Many of Scappi's pastries are also fried, some of the pizzas included, and these constitute one of the largest categories of food enjoyed by the papal court: fritters. Like other pastries, they are almost always sweet but could contain practically any ingredient—flesh, fowl, fish, fruit, or vegetable. Elder flowers make their way into fritters, as do cheeses and even chickpeas and chestnuts. They can be formed into balls, little rings, or dough fitted into a mold and fried, and in numerous other shapes. When pressed from a syringe into hot oil, they form the direct ancestor of the funnel cake.[12] Elegant diners appear to have been most excited by, if not addicted to, what we would today call junk food. These are for the most part glorified doughnuts. Not only candy in the form of sugar sculptures and comfits, but fried pastries and greasy snack foods were among the most elegant creations cooks could devise.

What is perhaps most interesting about these confections is that they were considered anything but desserts. In the menus recorded by Giovanni Rossetti, they appear with rigorous consistency in the first cold course placed on the credenza, regardless of the ingredients. We might expect to find cold meat pies and other savories as starters, even with their sugar sprinklings. But fruit pies and creamy flans appear too. They show up in subsequent cold courses as well, in the middle of the banquet. Or as in the case of his "German"-style service, in which large platters arrive adorned with many dishes in each course, pastries appear in every single course. For example, in one banquet for Lucrezia d'Este, there are boar pasties in the first course. Veal liver pasties appear in the second, cream pie in the third, fritters of *genestrata* in the fourth, jujube and pistachio *retortoli* in the fifth, and so on.[13] In other words, pastries were considered merely one entire genre of food—like roasts and boiled foods—regardless of their main ingredient. Rather than a procession of courses from one type of ingredient to another, each course progresses either by cooking method or contains every cooking method in each course. Thus pastries can appear anywhere in a menu, but ironically not with the fruits, which are fresh or cooked and served with nuts, olives, and so forth. Nor are pastries served at the end of large banquets with sugar-based confections or fruits. For this reason apple pie, for example, can show up virtually anywhere in a meal, but practically never at the end as a dessert.

It must be said that the sophisticated level to which the Italians raise the pastry maker's art is unmatched elsewhere in Europe in this period. The English, despite their vaunted association with meat pies and pasties, offer fewer varieties, but there are nonetheless interesting innovations. English cookbook authors also appear to have known about Continental developments. The author of *A Proper Newe Booke of Cookerye* describes making "pyes" of mutton or beef, which had been made there for centuries, but offers the option of using "paest royall" made from butter and egg yolks.[14] The directions are not entirely clear because they also say "take the fattest of the broth of powdered beyfe." If this is put into the pastry to temper it—this is essentially fat from a boiled corned beef—then it is clearly something different than used in Italy. Even without it, the essential sugar, cinnamon, and rose water are missing. The apple pie crust here is also strange, made with water, butter, and saffron heated together, with flour added and two egg whites. The crust is meant to be free standing, that is, a "coffin," but whether it was eaten or not is uncertain. There are other meat and poultry pies, fritters of various sorts, as well as a "short paest," which is almost certainly intended to be eaten. It is made simply with fine flour (as opposed to coarse needed in a free-standing pie), water, butter, and saffron, with two egg yolks. It also says "make it thynne and as tender as ye maye," a sure sign that it was supported in a dish and eaten.[15] Into the tarts go various kinds of fruit: gooseberries, medlars, damson, strawberries, flowers like borage or marigolds with egg yolks and curds, or even beans.

In *The Good Huswifes Handmaide* of 1588 there is a similar recipe for pastry crust based on egg yolk, flour, butter, and water boiled together. The directions specify, without giving precise measurements, not to use too many egg yolks, "for if you doe, it will make it drie and not pleasant in eating," nor too much butter, which will make it too short, and it will not raise. That is, it would not hold its form in a free-standing pie. This at least is evidence that pies could be both self-supported "coffins" and eaten.[16] The author also offers two other variations that appear to be completely unique. One crust uses butter and ale boiled with flour, eggs, sugar, saffron, and salt, the other almond milk, flour, oil, and saffron, which is suitable for Lent. Strangely, Lent was still observed in Protestant England, ostensibly to support the fishing industry and to keep beef abundant and its price down. At least that was the claim. In any case, this book offers many pie recipes, referred to as "baked meates," which include chickens, mutton, veal, or venison, often combined with fruits, spices, sugar, and butter. In this respect they are close relatives of those being made on the Continent. Some of these contain whole deer or wild fowl, though, so it seems these could not have been sliced as a pie. Instead, the contents were scooped out or sliced off, and some of the crust was placed beside the fillings as they were emptied. It is *The Good Huswifes Handmaide* that contains the recipe for oysters baked in a pie, "shels and all."[17]

There are dozens of pie and tart recipes included, but perhaps none as

intriguing as the "tart to provoke courage either in a man or woman." The
context of the courage is left ambiguous, but it is most likely sexual. The
tart is made with a quart of wine with two scraped burre roots (burdock,
Arctium lappa), two quinces, a potato, and an ounce of dates, all boiled
until tender and passed through a strainer. To this is added eight egg
yolks, brains from three or four male sparrows, rose water, sugar, cinna-

mon, ginger, cloves, mace, and sweet butter. It is cooked in a chafing dish
of coals between two platters—in other words an approximation of the
Italian *testa*. It is there boiled "till it be something big."[18] The directions
to boil suggest that there is no crust, but it qualifies as a tart because of
the shape, in the end something like a frittata.

The baking directions in Thomas Dawson's *Good Housewife's Jewel* go
somewhat further in technical development. There are still free-standing pies made of coarse rye flour, some with bones inside. The normal
procedure was to parboil the meat, let it dry, perhaps press it, and then
cook it in the pie. After baking, a sauce would be poured in the top and
it would be left to thicken. However, there are some recipes calling for
boning the contents—as with a turkey pie, though the bird is left whole
and trussed, pricked with cloves, or larded.[19] However, there are also
recipes made of a fine pastry with egg yolks and butter, as well as sugar,
if desired. Dawson also mentions that some people add beef or mutton
broth and cream as the "true seasoning," which may suggest a traditional
or preferred method. Even more exciting is a true puff pastry he calls a
butter paste. It is probably not the first recipe of this kind, but it shows
how the art of pastry making was developing. It is a standard dough made
from flour, eggs, cold butter, water or rose water, and spices. It is beaten
then rolled out into two or three sheets, which have butter placed on top.
The sheets are folded and rolled out again five or six times, which encases
the butter and causes the flaky dough to rise when it is baked.[20] With the
exception of the eggs, puff pastry is made exactly the same way today.

Interestingly, a similar though more complicated recipe for puff pastry
exists in Lancelot de Casteau a few years later, where it is called leafy
pastry of Spain. His is layered with melted pork fat and rolled. It bears
a striking resemblance to Scappi's flaky pastry recipe cited above. Some
of the language appears to be taken directly from Scappi.[21] Why Lancelot
associates it with Spain is unclear, though he may have pilfered it from
Granado—who took it from Scappi.

The development of pastry making in Spanish cookbooks follows
roughly the same course as in England. In fact, one of the most popular
types of pastry there is called an "empanada Inglesa" and was generally

made with meat off the bone, fish, or vegetables. A major difference in the pastry itself, although here too containing eggs and sugar, is the use of pork fat. *Pastelones,* for example in Maceras, contain cut-up lamb, chicken, pigeons, or rabbit, along with egg yolks, spices, and beef marrow (*cañas de vaca*), and are made with a flour and lard paste.[22] Elsewhere, in a truffle pie he calls for suet (*manteca de ganado*).[23] For the most part pies are made from butter, though. Maceras also offers empanadas made in the shape of a *barca,* or flat-bottomed ship—roughly equivalent to the English coffin—made to fit around a piece of meat like a beef loin or a bustard, a kind of waterfowl.[24] Both were meant to keep seven or eight days, and so were most likely served at room temperature. That such creations were meant to be decorative exhibition pieces for the chef is evident in remarks such as "make the pastry curiously, putting into the dough the design that the master likes."[25] Montiño has completely separate coverage for the arts of pastry making, biscuits, and conserves. The court of Spain in the seventeenth century was absolutely insane for little pies, fritters, and similar tidbits. Practically every ingredient he treats gets put into a pastry.

The French sources too show an obsession and apparent expertise in pastry making. Over the border in Liege, Lancelot has a *paste de bugnolle,* or fritter, that is a precise choux paste recipe, such as are used in profiteroles or cream puffs. It is made with a *chopine* of cream (a half pint)[26] and a bit of butter heated with flour in a pan, into which are broken four eggs. The mixture is stirred until combined, and four more eggs are added. Then, more melted unsalted butter is added and the dough cooked until it comes together. The dough can be squeezed from a syringe or cut into strips and fried in butter, or baked in the oven on parchment paper in little rounds.[27] In his section on *tourtes,* Lancelot explains another typical procedure in pastry making. The standard dough is made of fine flour, eggs, butter, and a little water. He then explains, "so the pastry will not be tough, beat the pastry for a quarter of an hour."[28] What this would do is thoroughly break down the glutens in the flour, leaving a light and delicate crust. The fillings for these tarts, in this case *blancmange,* in others could be chopped veal, or chopped spinach and parmesan. These are thus pies in the modern sense of the word, which could be sliced and served in wedges.

The development of pastry crust reaches its fully modern form in seventeenth-century France. *Le patissier François* of 1653, attributed to La Varenne, was translated into English by one Monsieur Marnette.[29] It is the most comprehensive book on pastry written up to that time.

It contains the old inedible dough made with rye flour and hot water, made into a crust two or three inches thick and intended "to bee sent farre off," presumably to be eaten while traveling or as a gift, not just sent away.[30] The fillings for these are quite traditional: venison and game, and spices. The crust here is definitely merely a container, because he claims that if the contents are not completely eaten, the lid can be restored and it can be reheated later.[31]

There is also here the classic French pastry dough made with a " . . . peck of flour formed into a hill with a well (or 'fountain') in the middle, into which 2 lbs. of butter are added, 3 ounces of salt and $^1/_2$ pint of water."[32] This dough is floured, rolled out, and used exactly as pastry dough is today. Significantly, it contains no eggs or sugar. There is also an extraordinarily thin pastry dough made of sheets of flour and water dough layered with butter, folded over, and rolled over and over again to the thickness of a "shilling peece in silver," and laid in a pie plate.[33]

The author has some interesting comments about baking technology. He directs his comments at ordinary households as well as large professional kitchens, because he says that in homes, curious housewives have small ovens just for pies, probably set into the wall by the hearth. These are contrasted with portable ovens made of brass, into which presumably coals are heaped,[34] but most people use "covered tart pans, wherein they bake their delicate cakes, Tartes, and exquisite pyes."[35] These were, in effect, metal versions of the classical earthenware *testa*. Elsewhere, he elaborates that in baking tarts, it is best to use copper pans "trimed and glased within side" and buttered. These can be used in an oven or in hot cinders with a copper lid, onto which cinders or charcoal is heaped and placed in the corner of the fireplace.[36] A glazed copper pan does not seem to mean tinned on the inside, which is the usual procedure. It probably means enameled—which is essentially a silica glaze much like those used on pottery, but here lining the pan, as is done with Le Creuset pots on cast iron.

That French pastry making was departing from practices elsewhere in Europe can be gleaned from a few of the author's comments. The garnishing ingredients within pies were to a certain extent similar: cockscombs, sweetbreads, artichoke bottoms, and mushrooms, but this is what he says about musk—which was still fashionable elsewhere: "Some curious pallats do steep half a grain of Musk with a drop or two of Rose-water, and do pour it into the said pye in their filling of it up, but the sent of the Musk doth for the most part offend the Female sex, and some Males too: wherefore it is far better omitted; and deemed best not at all to put in any."[37] This is a good indication that aromas, which of course were originally intended to arouse both male and female, were now being gradually banished from elite cookery.

Pasta

It is hard to determine the extent to which sixteenth- and seventeenth-century elite diners enjoyed pasta. Naturally, the majority of recipes came from Italy or were borrowed from Italian cookbooks—usually Scappi. We do find pasta in medieval cookbooks. In fact, the earliest recipe for ravioli is, believe it or not, in an English cookery manuscript.[38] In the early seventeenth century, Lancelot du Casteau offers recipes for ravioli, or as he calls them, *raphioulles*.[39] There is no reason they should have been borrowed from an Italian source, except for the name and that they use "parmesin"—one with chopped veal, the other with spinach. In any case, pasta was most common in the Italian city-states, and it is fairly certain that it entered Europe via Italy.

As we know, the ancestors of pasta existed in classical times (*laganae, itria*), and some kind of pasta was certainly present in cultures of the Middle East. In Italy, pasta is first recorded in a Genoese document as early as 1279 that mentions macaroni—which was not yet tubular, but probably meant a kind of dumpling more like the modern gnocchi. This explains why they roll downhill so easily in Boccaccio's Land of Bengodi in *The Decameron*. In succeeding centuries there was extensive trade in dry pasta throughout the western Mediterranean. By the Renaissance, most of the forms we would recognize as pasta existed: vermicelli (long strips), pappardelle, lasagna, and stuffed pasta like ravioli and tortelli. There was not yet a generic term "pasta" (which merely means dough and could refer to pastries, pies, and so forth), but the word *macaroni* came closest to a catch-all phrase.

It is also clear that people throughout the peninsula had very different ideas of what the term macaroni meant. Macaroni in one text could be a long flat strip (as in *macaroni ala zenovese*), or a rolled string (as in *romaneschi*), or a hollow tube (as in *macaroni siciliani*), which was rolled on a long iron stiletto. All these forms are found in Martino in the fifteenth century. In other texts such as Messisbugo's, macaroni are made with flour, bread crumbs, eggs, and spices, and are really dumplings, more like modern gnocchi.[40] There are also variants of *maccheroni Napoletana* and *macheroni Romaneschi;* the former are long straight ribbons but are made of a mixture of fine flour (*fiore di farina*), egg, sugar, and fresh bread crumbs soaked in rose water, the latter made from a similar dough though rolled around a stick to become tubular. From the fifteenth to the sixteenth century at least, the terms and methods are not consistent at all. What this suggests is that though the generic term *macaroni* was recognized throughout Italy, it differed radically from place to place, and each variant was primarily identified with a specific city.

Judging from the numerous pasta-makers' guilds that sprung up in the sixteenth century, as well as the accumulating civic legislation about prices, locations of retail shops, and quality control, all this evidence suggests that pasta was a popular food by this time.[41] But we are still hard-pressed to construe it as a dish enjoyed frequently by elite diners, and revealingly harder-pressed to find recipes. Tomato sauce will not show up on pasta until the nineteenth century. In the sixteenth and seventeenth centuries it was usually cooked in broth or, during Lent, in water and sprinkled with sugar and cinnamon.

Importantly, pasta is rarely considered a dish in its own right in the early modern period. When formed into shapes, it is often merely a filler in soups or a garnish for other dishes. When in sheets, it is just a wrapping for fillings, an alternative way to form what would ordinarily be pies or pastries, that is, a variant of pastry dough. As Serventi and Sabban say in *Pasta*, "the dough had no culinary value of its own; it served only to protect the delicate stuffing," and "As for the dough it is absolutely superfluous except to contain the stuffing."[42] Sometimes the dough for ravioli is omitted entirely and it is served without a wrapping, or equally strange is that lasagna could be made with chicken skin instead of dough.

Of greater significance is the absence of a separate first course containing pasta. This was not the result of some intentional apastasy, but rather that starch in general appeared everywhere and anywhere in a meal. In cookbooks of the early modern period, pasta was never given a major role. It appears here and there—always in fresh form, so there was obviously no social stigma against eating pasta. But there may have been a stigma against eating dried pasta products. By the end of the sixteenth century, these were being produced on an industrial scale, even apparently using mechanical extruders. There is no doubt that physicians considered these dense (al dente) pasta products indigestible, along with all things made from unrisen dough—including crackers and *azima* (matzoh). This advice may have been internalized by elite diners, because when pasta does appear it is invariably the lightest, thinnest, and most tender handmade fresh pasta, and it is cooked until practically mush: half an hour or more in some cookbooks. It was clearly not the pasta itself that elite diners were interested in.

Then there is the paucity of recipes. The few pasta recipes featured in Scappi's monumental *Opera* of 1570 are a soup of tagliatelli, three recipes for soup using the three different kinds of macaroni (either ribbons, hollow tubes, or gnocchi), three tortellini recipes, and one for a ravioli without a casing.[43] Pasta also appears briefly in Book III in recipes for Lent, where it is not cooked with meat, and then it is mentioned in Book VI for convalescents, where the author suggests a few chopped meat or fish mixtures that can be used to stuff ravioli. In total, there are about ten or twelve recipes, in a book of 1,066, which means about 1 percent. Elite diners, in this case the papal court, were not terribly interested in pasta. It is certainly nothing like the staple it would become in later centuries. It may have been popular among other social classes, but the point here is that it was nothing like a food that could be considered quintessentially Italian.

Starches and Pasta

Scappi's contemporary Alessandro Petronio (who was also working in the Vatican as a physician; they may have known each other), in his *Del viver delli Romani et di conserver la sanità,* an encyclopedia on contemporary Roman food practices, does not mention pasta. At about this same time, the Florentine cookbook author Domenico Romoli, in his list of all possible dishes that can be served, singles out three maccheroni dishes for Lent—Florentina, Napoletana, and Romana—again suggesting the association for each variety is local and there is no form that is common everywhere.[44] Moreover, this is three recipes among 301 without meat. For meat days he lists capon covered in *anolini* or maccheroni, also pappardelle, either alla Romana or alla Fiorentina, and capon ravioli (what he calls vermicelli here is not pasta but syringed butter or ricotta).[45] These recipes are among 360, not including sauces, salads, and soups (though there are two ravioli soups and one with pasta vermicelli). In any case, the percentage of pasta recipes is roughly the same as Scappi's—about 1 percent.

By the seventeenth century, cookbooks and menu lists still offer no more than a scattered few pasta recipes. Only Giovan Battista Crisci's *Lucerna dei Corteggiani* mentions different types of pasta, but this was in Naples, where pasta seems to have gained wider acceptance than elsewhere. In mid-seventeenth-century Bologna, in Giovanni Francesco Vasselli's *L'Apicio,* the only dish that comes close to renowned Bolognese tortellini is here associated with Lombardy and is called *tortelli alla Lombarda.* The tortelli are stuffed with pounded pheasant, eggs, cheese, pepper, crushed mostaccioli, and covered with butter, cinnamon, and parmesan, and garnished with sugar.[46] But there is no lasagna, vermicelli, tagliatelli, macaroni, or any other form of pasta. Judging from contemporary banquet books that list long menus, pasta products were not something elite chefs were terribly interested in serving.

Of course in the ensuing centuries, pasta would grow more important, particularly among average eaters. When industrial production stepped up and extruded pasta became more prevalent throughout the peninsula, pasta did become more of a national dish, which it remains to this day. The evidence of cookbooks in the sixteenth and seventeenth centuries, however, suggest that it was not yet an object of reverence, certainly with nowhere near the status of pastries, or even bread.

CHAPTER 7

Wine and Alcohol

The first two centuries of printed culinary literature are surprisingly reticent on the topic of wine. The banquet organization guides always discuss the separate kitchen department and staff devoted to serving wine, and cookbooks often specify certain types of wine to be used in cooking. About the wine itself they offer few clues about taste and what was appreciated in a fine wine, apart from the preference for certain types such as Malvasia and occasional comments about the age or color of wine. Fortunately there is a fairly large body of literature devoted specifically to wine, much of it medical in nature, but nonetheless providing explicit details about drinking practices among the elite, which the writers considered ruinous to health. For example, physicians decried putting ice or snow in wine. Some insisted that it should be cut with water and only under certain circumstances drunk undiluted. Others elaborated complex criteria for judging the quality of wine and what types are best for what individuals, and where in a meal they should be consumed. In each case their criticisms detail what were common practices among elite diners but that have left no record in the culinary literature.

There are also a number of books about viticulture, the wine trade, and even satirical works about the pleasures of drinking, all of which provide certain kinds of information that can round out a decent picture of what the culture of wine consumption was like in the sixteenth and seventeenth centuries. It was in many ways diametrically opposed to the culture of wine that would emerge in modern times. Perhaps most important, if strange according to current tenets of wine appreciation, is that wine was often served adulterated. Drinkers preferred it sweet, even with sugar added to mimic more expensive heavier wines from hotter climes. They also had no qualms about adding spices, herbs, and other flavorings to wine. Moreover, the art of distillation had recently emerged from the alchemist's laboratory and had entered the confectioner's kitchen. Like many other medicinal substances, alcoholic distillates—cordials, aperitifs, juleps (all of which are direct ancestors of the liqueurs and mixers we still know today)—made an easy transition from pharmacy to banquet table. What were first offered as drugs, for a wide variety of ailments as well as for longevity, were increasingly taken under any pretext or solely for pleasure. Increasingly, these products began to supplant consumption of ordinary wine, especially at the end of the meal. Distillates and flavored wines would not have serious competition from other beverages until the introduction of coffee and tea, which filled a different culinary niche of daytime drinking, for the most part.

Naturally, alcohol abuse was one of the major concerns among critics of banqueting, along with eating too great a variety of foods in one sitting without any order or reason, a rebuke it is easy to understand, because there was continual quaffing and toasting throughout a meal. It was believed that wine in excess added too greatly to the internal vital heat of digestion, totally subverting it, much as throwing too much wood on a fire suffocates it. This then leads to a corrupt "concoction" in the stomachand the rising of cloudy vapors that then surround the brain, making one dizzy, incoherent, and eventually julepated. It was, in a sense, merely the mechanical force of fumes obfuscating the spirits coursing through the brain that caused drunkenness. Not only was this a concern among physicians, who offered their own preventive measures as well as remedies, but one can imagine that in a court fraught with political intrigues and rivalries that keeping up the pace without losing one's senses became a very real consideration. As with the food consumption in general, early modern diners had to choose among various rival claims: drinking for pleasure, for health, or in moderation for the sake of morality. The culinary writers will have the first word.

From a culinary point of view, wine and various close relatives were an indispensable ingredient in many recipes. Many sauces were based on wine—such as the *salsa reale,* which is made from sugar, vinegar, wine, and cinnamon.[1] Wine was also used to make biscuits, pastry, and gelatins, and finds its way into numerous stews and fricassees. White wine was a common ingredient in the sixteenth-century French cookbooks. Verjuice, made from unripe grapes, had since the Middle Ages been one of the most important condiments, as had *sapa*—grape must cooked down by one-third, and its close relative *rob vini* or *arropa* in Spanish, which is reduced wine. Vinegar too, of course, was central to the medieval kitchen but by the early modern period was increasingly supplanted with aromatic versions, particularly rose- or cinnamon-scented vinegar.

For drinking, however, even the most extensive texts say little about wine as a beverage. Scappi identifies a handful of wine types used in cooking, but not much more.[2] In general, his preference was for sweet, thick wines from southern Italy, Greece, or Crete. Malvasia, or what in English is called Malmsey, is the variety most often mentioned. It is usually a golden, thick but not turbid, and aromatic wine. Just as with the preference for perfumed foods, so too are light-colored and perfumed wines favored. Scappi mentions Moscatella made from Muscat grapes, another aromatic wine, but he also names lighter local varieties such as Romanesco and Trebbiano. A far more detailed source for understanding the variety of wines appreciated by the papal court in the sixteenth century is a letter written by Sante Lancerio about what could be found among Roman wine merchants.[3] The author was *bottigliere* for Pope Paul III, so he may have actually worked right beside Scappi and handed him the bottles that went into his sauces. Mentioned first, perhaps not coincidentally, are Malvagia from Crete, sweet and drier varieties, Moscatello from Ligura, and the lighter or, as he says, more subtle Trebbiano. Greco is another wine frequently encountered in the literature, the name of which actually comes from the grape variety, not from a Greek origin. Sante describes in detail several different types, and from his descriptions it is clear that what he valued most in wine is the clarity, golden hue, perfume, and that the wine not be excessively sweet—but probably quite so by modern standards—and that it not be too *fumoso*, which refers to strength and the ability to send fumes up to the brain, or cause inebriation.[4]

Wine and Alcohol

Sante mentions dozens of other types of wine, of great interest to economic historians and oenophiles. Sorting out the sources and names here would be superfluous, but it is important to note that the author makes specific claims about the organoleptic properties of each wine, its color, texture or turbidity, taste, and aroma. Clearly the court contained discerning drinkers. He usually notes whether the wine had any medicinal properties, if it might be phlegm reducing, oppilative (clog causing), or dangerous for people prone to certain humoral ailments. That is, for Sante, both gustatory and medicinal considerations played a role in his comments.

At about this same time, Giovanni Battista Scarlino came out with his own vernacular poem in terza rima about the diversity and quality of wines that could be bought in Rome.[5] He insists that he personally investigated all the wines that arrived by boat at Ripa on the Tiber. He posits that despite popular taste, Greco is not the best wine that can be bought, but rather Malvagia, which comforts the brain, chest, and heart.[6] Moscatello is also superb, Chiarello is good in all seasons, and Guarnaccia is fine if not too sweet—and Scarlino even wishes the Pope would pass a decree to commandeer the entire supply. These are all the same wines preferred by Scappi, incidentally. Scarlino sees nothing wrong with eating melons and pears with wine in summer, and concurs with other noble customs:

> vi avviso anchor che non facciate errore
> che Novembre per tutto Febraro
> s'usa vin grandi, e di dolci sapore

> be advised then not to make error
> from November through all February
> to use strong wines, and of sweet flavor[7]

Scarlino also approves of the fad for flavored wine and gives a recipe for hippocras—of which "every glass is worth a florin." It is made of two pitchers of magnaguerra wine, eighteen ounces of white sugar, one ounce of canella, four drams of grains of paradise, and three scruples of ginger, all left to soak for twenty-four hours.[8] To get a sense of these proportions, compared to the medieval versions, according to apothecary's weights there are eight drams in an ounce, which also equals twenty-four scruples. That means one-half ounce of grains of paradise and one-eighth ounce of ginger. The overwhelming flavor in this version is sweetness rather than spice.

At the same time and place that Sante was writing about wine, Scarlino buying it, and Scappi using it in the kitchen, a physician to Paul III wrote his own Latin treatise on the various types of wine, *De diversorum vini generum*. This was one Jacob Praefectus of Noto in Sicily. It is written as dialogue between three learned friends who describe a banquet. Their list of foods is entirely in line with what would have been served at the papal court, and consists primarily of "pheasants, heath cock, capons, guinea fowl, peacocks, geese, ducks, pigeons as well as tiny birds like thrushes and fig peckers," not to mention boar and roast suckling pig, artfully carved and served out.[9] The tables are also laden with cloths, golden cups, and ewers brimming with wine. There are pastries and songs to Bacchus as they drink some sparkling falernum.[10]

Somehow the physician among them slips away, but is brought back to offer a discourse on the qualities of wine. Apart from the usual medical warning about inebriation and the innumerable diseases it can cause, a conversation that one might think would put off the revelers at this stage, he warns against drinking chilled wine, how being drunk weakens the power to procreate,[11] and how all the odd things added to wine—such as sandalwood, rose, amber, lignum aloes, and musk—increase the likelihood of getting a bad headache.[12] These were all common courtly practices at the time. He also addresses the question of whether it makes sense to eat peaches and other fruits at the end of a meal with wine.[13] Like most physicians, he resolutely rejects the practice, contending the peaches corrupt, and the wine prematurely forces the fruit into the veins before being properly processed. Obviously courtiers paid little attention to these warnings. Banquets almost always include fruit and wine as a last or second to last course, to refresh the palate. It is nonetheless a fascinating example of how the concerns of health and gastronomy could directly clash.

Interestingly, it is usually physicians rather than cooks and culinary writers who expound on the topic of wine in the greatest detail. One particular controversy taking place in Verona in the 1530s is revealing in this regard. The argument was over the "temperature" of wine, which refers to the humoral effect it has on the body, rather than actual tactile heat or cold.[14] The details of the controversy, and whether wine is primarily a food or a medicine, are not directly relevant to cuisine, but in deciding whether wine heats or cools the body, moistens or dries, the physicians devised fairly sophisticated criteria for appraisal. Giovanni Battista Confalonieri, who initiated the controversy, insisted that it is not only the grape variety but the location and soil properties that affect the flavor of wine. Hence from the same grape can be made acrid or bitter wine, insipid or watery, or sweet and smooth.[15] Even the water quality can give wine the flavor of alumina, sulphur, salt, asphalt, and so forth.[16] Equally, some incite sleep, some are arousing, some loosen the digestive tract, others make it firm. Some cause headaches, others help relieve them. All these qualities depend on the particular variety, growing conditions, and wine-making skills of the vintner.

Confalonieri's combatant, Antonio Fumanelli, goes further in describing the various properties of wine and whether it is hot and moist and nourishing, or hot and dry and medicinal. In the course of his rather long-winded disquisition, he also inadvertently describes various courtly drinking practices. For example, he claims that one ought to drink between one and three times. It is not entirely clear if he means glasses or draughts, but the custom was to bring a full cup to anyone who requested it and then remove it. Four drinks he finds excessive, and if *meraca,* or undiluted wine, is brought first—as was the custom at banquets—successive drinks should contain more water as the meal progresses.[17] His insistence suggests that few people followed this advice.

The famous physician Girolamo Fracastoro was brought in to settle the dispute, and interestingly decided that wine is always, whether as food or medicine, a heating and drying substance.[18] It was clearly his own medical experience that informed his pronouncement and his understanding that wine dehydrates the body. It was these kinds of questions, and abandoning the opinions of the ancient authorities, that brought wine writers closer to a precise understanding of wine, as well as a critical vocabulary for discussing it. But once again, it was physicians rather than food writers who expounded on the topic.

This is also the case in the massive *De vini natura* of Gulielmo Grataroli. Although a good part of the work is a moralistic diatribe against drunkenness, in describing what kinds of wine are good for people of various constitutions he offers a good picture of the range of wines available at the time. Melancholics need sweet and aromatic wines, while bilious and sanguine people—the hot constitutions—need lighter white wines cut with water. Phlegmatics need old wine, though he believes that after seven years wine is really only good for medicine, not for nourishment.[19] Again, whether diners actually heeded this advice is impossible to say, but clearly the variety of options available in a banquet would have appealed to those concerned about health. Just as they could choose from a variety of foods in every course to suit their particular complexion, so too could they choose darker or lighter, heavier or thinner wines accordingly. Grataroli also distinguishes wine according to age, location, and whether it has been racked or separated from the lees. It is preferable if it has been, but actually will not last as long.[20] At this point wine was still kept in wooden casks; the wine bottle appeared only at the end of the early modern period, so presumably special care had to be taken to prevent it from spoiling. This is probably why seven years was considered the oldest wine drinkable with a meal. He also distinguishes between various generic categories of wine: *vinum ruffum* (a light red claret) is the best and generates the best blood, *subruffum* (a darker red) is crasser but still quite nourishing, while *nigrum,* or very dark wine, is too difficult to digest and is best left for young laborers.[21] *Citrinum* is a "subtle" wine—probably meaning dry and high in alcohol, and is the hottest of white wines. *Palmeum* is clear and aromatic and good for all ages and complexions, and seems to describe precisely those wines most esteemed on elite tables. Elsewhere he attests to the popular practice of drinking chilled wine in summer, made by suspending a vessel into an ice bucket with *nitre* (sodium nitrate), which lowers the ice water below the freezing point.[22]

Remarkably, Grataroli also offers advice about tasting wine and the importance of not eating bitter or too salty foods, which will affect the taste buds and one's ability to judge. In fact, eating very little before-hand is preferable, and never salty cheese or nuts or foods flavored with nutmeg or cloves, which will promote indoucement, that is, make any wine taste sweeter.[23] This advice was intended to detect fraud and spoiled wine, but it points to the fact, corroborated by the banquet management literature, that wine was commonly taken with cheese, nuts, and olives at the end of a meal.

Grataroli also goes into great detail about wine making, judging ripeness of grapes, how long to let wine sit in the skins, and so forth. In this section he also describes how to make various flavored wines, which regularly appear at the end of banquets.[24] Not only can sugar be added too, but citron, cloves, myrtle, or cypress leaves. Any number of herbs like southernwood, asparagus flowers, or fenugreek can be suspended in a linen bag in a cask of wine, as can spikenard, licorice, or ginger. Peach leaves or coriander remove bad odors, and if desired, one can even make wine with the aroma of goat. Germans purportedly like this, and it is made with goats' horns. Clary sage or horminum, another kind of salvia, give wine a musky odor. May wine, flavored with woodruff, is one of the few surviving descendants of this once common practice. Grataroli also offers recipes to make wine last longer, by adding almonds, raisins, gypsum, olive pits, or shells. Pine resin or myrrh also work.[25] One can also add any of the now rare medieval spices: zedoary, long pepper, grains of paradise, galangal, mastic, or camphor. The majority of these were primarily used in medicines or quasi-medicinal wine concoctions, the descendants of hippocras—the spiced medieval favorite.[26] A flap of salted pork skin tied over the bung hole, we are told, prevents corruption. Without lingering on the dozens of strange recipes he offers for improving defects in wine, it is important to note that there was no hesitation whatsoever to adulterate wine with a perverse array of ingredients. To turn wine to a lovely vermilion color one can use carrots, which were incidentally red rather than orange.[27] A Vernaccia or greenish wine can be made deep red with ivy charcoal and oak galls.

Most important of all, though, in cooking and in wine, was the infusion

of aromatics. Orris root, spikenard, and artemisia all lend their own se-
ductive scents. In compounds, wine becomes even deeper and more mys-
terious: one recipe for a claret includes ginger, galangal, nutmeg, mace,
cloves, pepper, cinnamon, spikenard, citrus peel, and honey.[28] There is
even a description of instant wine meant for sailors, made from must and
wine cooked down and dried in the sun and ground into powder.[29] Yet

despite his enthusiasm and recipes, Grataroli insists that such concoctions are intended to be medicinal but in his day are used to excess and
abused for pleasure—particularly the distilled drinks such as "nectar,"
which is served at sumptuous weddings and regal banquets. The scores
of sweetened and spiced drinks clearly ruin the taste buds and health of
the indulgent,[30] and diners are only induced to "inexplicable gluttony"
by the lascivious vessels and obscene goblets studded with jewels, which
one commonly finds on nobles' tables.[31] No doubt he had something in
mind like the mannerist cups with recumbent nudes perched on the rim,
which flirt precariously with the lips when drinking. Incidentally—and
this explains his attitude—Grataroli was a staunch Protestant, chased
into exile from Italy by the Inquisition and residing in Basel.

A fuller explanation of the distilled aromatic drinks so beloved by European courtiers can be found in the work of another Swiss writer, a contemporary of Grataroli, none other than Conrad Gesner, famed zoologist
and botanist. Why he chose to publish his work under the pseudonym
Euonymus Philiatrus is not clear, but the work was included in his *Opera
Omnia* nonetheless. Its short title, *De remediis secretis,* does not immediately reveal that the book is about medicinal distilled wine preparations.
Nonetheless, it was remarkably popular and was translated from Latin
into several European languages.

There were several printed books on distillation that predate this one.
Hieronymus Brunschwig's *Liber de arte distillandi,* appearing at the end
of the fifteenth century, was enormously popular and was followed by
several others. But this one seems to record more faithfully the kinds of
cordials that so appealed to elite palates by the mid sixteenth century.
Ostensibly, the book was intended to teach physicians how to concen-
trate the virtues of wine into a super-charged health drink. Aqua vitae,
the water of life, had been produced in the Middle Ages, but by the early
modern period it began to be more widely consumed, both as a medicine
and for pleasure. The rationale for medicinal use was that if wine was
nourishing and increases the vital heat and radical moisture, then the
super-rarefied form of wine should do so quicker and more conveniently

because it requires no digestion in the body. It is in a sense pre-refined. This was precisely why medieval alchemists such as Arnald of Villanova promoted it in pro-longevity regimens. If wine generates blood and has medicinal properties, why not take it in concentrated essential form?

Gesner's introductory discussion of the mechanics of distillation is both comical and revealing of contemporary mental constructs. In physiological terms, a distillation is what occurs when a volatile spirit excited by heat suddenly contacts a cool surface and liquefies. Spirits (a super-refined form of nutrition) flow around and nourish the brain. When the brain is accidentally chilled, as in a "cold" distemperature, those spirits are distilled and return to liquid form, usually dripping from the nose in what was called a rheum, or flux. In describing the distillation of wine (an analogue of blood), Gesner explains that it too is rarefied through heat, and the essential vapors rise up. They are then cooled in what he calls the "head" (*capitellus*) and flow through the "nose" (*nasum*) of the alembic into another vessel. Alcohol is produced from wine through the same mechanism as a runny nose.[32]

Of greater importance, Gesner explains that the qualities of a distillate are not necessarily the same as the original liquid. Absinthe distilled becomes sweet, while mint and basil have a bad odor when distilled. That is, only certain volatile elements are removed in the distillation process.[33] But in all cases, whatever is removed becomes more intense and powerful qualitatively. From wine, only the hot and volatile elements are removed, and this is why alcohol (or *aqua ardens*) is always without question extremely hot and dry.

Therefore, pure alcohol is ideal for all cold infirmities, particularly of the brain and eyes. Like wine it nourishes the blood, purges obstructions, counteracts poison, and chases sadness—and is thus ideal for melancholics and maniacs.[34] It also increases the substance of reproduction (*potentiam ad coitum auget*) and makes women more fecund. Women were thought to have their own form of sperm, an abundance of which causes fertility. In a nutshell, distilled alcohol had the power to make relatively weak wine obsolete as a medicine.

Interestingly, Gesner made a distinction between alcohol distilled from pure wine and that made from lees (which we would call grappa), which he considered the worst. He also recognized that grappa was increasingly becoming a regular part of people's diet, rather than a medicine. He says "aqua ardens or aqua vita which is extracted from wine, among us from the lees, is sold by the vulgar so much that some almost make a meal of it."[35] This provides some evidence that alcohol was becoming increasingly popular and was not unaffordable, again giving it greater power to displace wine as the ideal self-prescribed medicine.

That alcohol could make this transition from medicine to recreational drink is not surprising. Gesner himself concedes that these new drinks have their appeal. Regarding gin he says, "juniper berries infused in wine [and distilled] make it the best and most suave aromatic liquor."[36] But this is not as useful as the quintessence itself, from which all elements have been removed, leaving behind only the pure incorruptible spirit. This is accomplished through successive distillation in a hermetic vessel, and presumably what Gesner was able to achieve was something clear, pure, and of very high alcohol content.[37] If wine prolongs life, then the incorruptible quintessence of wine is the elixir of life itself.

Naturally, Gesner cannot go so far as to claim we can prolong life beyond the time appointed to us by God—this would give alcohol the power of conferring immortality, something only possible through salvation, but this is the next-best thing.[38] He even speculates on, and regrets the difficulty of, distilling human blood as a medicine. Procuring sufficient quantity for viable production seems to have been something "prohibited by religion,"[39] but he does seem to have experimented a bit with quintessence of blood.

Far more marketable were the many spiced aromatic compounds, the ancestors of most modern vermouths, cordials, and flavored sweetened liquors. Gesner and many other authors offered hundreds of recipes. The importance of these is that around the sixteenth century and over the course of time, these drinks supplanted wine as a medicine, making the entire debate over wine's medicinal virtues obsolete. The argument for including wine in an ordinary diet, and particularly its power to nourish the body, also lost its appeal for physicians as humoral physiology was gradually and only impartially replaced with chemical and mechanical theories in the late seventeenth century. After this, wine logically could only be taken for pleasure, and this in a sense freed people from the burden of having to defend their consumption patterns as therapeutic. Of course, drinking for one's health continued for several centuries more, but the rationale that it is nourishing became more difficult to support. With even the most rudimentary forms of chemical analysis, it became apparent that wine is very different from blood. It also became increasingly obvious that wine is not terribly nourishing, and just as conceptually it became increasingly difficult to imagine blood converting into wine in what was once considered the miracle of the Eucharist, so too did it seem increasingly implausible that wine could be converted to blood in the body. The controversy over wine's role in health did not disappear, though the terms of the debate changed. There were new arguments to support moderate consumption, just as there were prudish physicians railing against alcohol abuse.

To return to Gesner and his cocktails, despite his claims of their medicinal virtues, it is clear that people drank them for pleasure, and that the final course of a banquet would have been incomplete without them.

Most of the ingredients are soaked in wine and then distilled, and they range from absinthe (the direct ancestor of the drink that entranced nine-teenth-century painters and poets),[40] cherries (an early form of kirschwasser), strawberries or peaches, to walnuts (still made at home in Italy, where it is known as *nocciola*), and roses (known today as *rosolio*).[41] He also uses lavender or dandelions. Now, to be sure, Gesner's aims were purely medicinal, despite the appeal of these beverages. He also distills drinks from frog sperm, cow manure, human excrement, and blood.[42] Nevertheless, the floral- and fruit-flavored cordials were bound to catch on as recreational drinks. Ironically, we have even forgotten that the word cordial originally meant a heart medicine, and aperitif something intended to open up clogs in the body's passages, not the start of a meal.

On a purely culinary note, Gesner also suggests that because alcohol acts as a powerful preservative (of the human body), one can also store fish and meat in it to prevent corruption.[43] There are also a wealth of recipes for cosmetics, essential oils, and hair dyes, but the most interesting are the super-complex spiced drinks. Once again we encounter nectar made with the full range of spices, but he adds that "if you wish to make this for a prince or the very rich, add to the above mentioned, the best aloe wood and leaves, of each a half ounce, a half dram of musk, and in place of honey use sugar most finely pounded in a mortar and then dissolved in wine." Furthermore this can be fortified with aqua vitae.[44] These comments suggest precisely the way that European taste would evolve over the following century, with expensive aromatics taking precedence over the standard spices, sugar replacing honey, and the recreational use of alcohol at first among the rich.

No discussion of wine in the sixteenth century could omit Andrea Bacci's *De naturali vinorum historia,* the largest, most comprehensive book on wine written at the time. The book's real value is his final section on Italian wines, delineating dozens of locales and wine-making styles. He is often criticized for borrowing extensively from the wine book of Etienne and for not knowing much about French wines. This reputation is unfair, for though he does borrow much information, and his knowledge of the medicinal uses of wine is wholly derivative, and he indulges in extremely long discourses about wine drinking among the ancients, his book is nonetheless a treasure trove of information about sixteenth-century drinking and even eating customs. For example, he tells us that to give astringency and to act as a preservative, winemakers added hops to wine (just as they did to beer for the first time in this era).[45] He also distinguishes between three different kinds of reduced must used in cooking: *passum* is merely reduced in the sun, *defrutum* is cooked down by half—offering a slightly caramelized or cooked flavor—while *sapa* is a dark, thick syrup cooked down to a third or even fourth of its original volume. All these are different from *vin cotto,* which was most frequently used in Italy in his day, but was almost unknown by the ancients.[46]

Bacci also discusses a kind of wine byproduct sometimes called *secundaria* or *Lora,* and in some places *Aquatis* or *raspatum*. In other texts it is called *aquarello*. It is basically the pressed-out grapes skins and pits collected after fermentation, to which is added water for a second light fermentation, and then re-pressed. Most wine authors deride this inferior wine as something suitable only for rustics, and much too cold and watery for delicate constitutions. Bacci, on the other hand, approves of it, saying it has a delectable taste and asperity, perfect for the summer. It is also used throughout Italy, he claims.[47]

Regarding the consumption of pure alcohol, he attests to the increasing and widespread practice. "Aquavit is used throughout the entire city today, nor do I find it praiseworthy to slug down a half ounce or even an ounce, as the vulgar do, on an empty stomach."[48] Clearly, what had started as a noble recreation had by the end of the century extended to nearly all levels of society. Bacci himself is amazed at how little writers say about this common abuse among the old (supposedly taken as a longevity drug) but even among youths and small boys.

The subsequent sections in Bacci discuss the properties of wine, and he religiously follows the ancient authority Galen in this regard, generally ignoring the fruitful dialogues of the mid century. But he does recount in great detail the various factors that enter into appraising wine: the age, color, taste, consistency, odor, and strength. The popularity of his work would at least keep these criteria in the minds of readers, both for reasons of health and pure sensory pleasure. For both cases it is once again sweet wines that take precedence. The sweet and unctuous are not only the most nourishing but pleasant in his mind. Anything with acrid, pontic, pungent, or astringent overtones is best taken as medicine.[49]

Perhaps the most interesting comments in Bacci's book relevant to the topic of fine dining are when he compares the raucous ancient convivia of ancient times to those of Rome in the late sixteenth century. Most authors contrast the frugal Romans of republican times with the drunken banquets of their own era. In counterpoint, Bacci claims that meals among the papal court are positively frugal. "In our times we have mediocrity and honesty in princely meals, especially in the Roman Curia we see frugality and moderate laudable splendor."[50] This would appear to support evidence that the popes had begun to eat much less lavishly following the reign of Pius V and particularly in the wake of the Council of Trent. The culinary literature of the same era, particularly the carving manual of Vincenzo Cervio and the management guides of Cesare Evitascandalo, the former written before and the latter published only a decade after Bacci in Rome, does not appear to suggest any toning down of splendor in the Vatican. In fact, building projects and commissions would suggest precisely the opposite, but this may have been the result of a renewed energy in the baroque era. From Bacci's vantage point, and he had apparently been in Rome since 1552, the late sixteenth century was admirably sober.

Wine and Alcohol

CHAPTER 8

Nations

The firm association of specific recipes, ingredients, and ways of dining with particular nations is an indication not only that some European states were beginning to forge distinct identities in the early modern
period but that they were also codifying what might be called national cuisines. Both natives and foreigners began to have a clear idea, for example,
that *olla podrida* was a Spanish dish, game pie was English, and omelet was
French. Like defining a national poetry, architecture, music, or language,
food can be an invaluable tool for fostering allegiance to the nation-state.
The ordinary experience of eating is invested with symbolic meaning that
induces subjects to identify with the state and feel that they belong to a
greater whole. In the context of formal state functions, eating a national
dish signifies solidarity with one's countrymen, and sends a formidable
message of identity to foreigners. Equally, serving a dish associated with
the nation of an honored guest can be a gesture of friendship, while it reaf-
firms the difference of the stranger. Cookbook authors, in labeling recipes
by nation of origin, provide evidence that states were indeed beginning to
form distinct culinary identities.

Eating a national dish, especially during official celebrations, is also an
act of patriotism, and the incorporation of such special food in a sense
situates one's nationality. Consider how effective the Thanksgiving turkey
is in the United States as a tool of assimilation. A national cuisine is an
artificial entity, and can be overtly propagandistic. It is also designed to
efface regional, minority, or aberrant foodways. Other times it is merely
the projection of a cookbook author who happens to be caught up in

the process of forming a national identity, though often official patronage provides the incentive. Whatever the impetus, the formation of the nation-state and the codification of a national cuisine usually progress in tandem.

If this is the case, then those nations that attempted to centralize and rationalize their governments in the early modern period should also have expressed some conception of a national cuisine. France, Spain, and England, just as they developed a xenophobic sense of all the strange things other nations ate, should also have tried to define their own cuisines. Conversely, those places that failed to unify, such as Italy, would not have developed a standard repertoire of recipes and foods that could be considered quintessentially Italian, but rather would have maintained regional or civic associations for specific foods. That is, recipes would have been considered Florentine, Roman, or Lombard rather than Italian, because there was no Italy per se.

What exactly constitutes a national cuisine and why does it emerge in the sixteenth and seventeenth centuries? It has long been commonplace to assert that medieval cuisine was essentially international, much like the Gothic arts. There were regional variations, and of course ingredients differed from place to place as did certain preferences, but it is still hard to argue against the idea that the same basic flavor combinations and recipes circulated throughout Europe prior to the early modern period. Rulers were first and foremost interested in eating the same dishes that other rulers ate, and thus manuscript cookbooks across Europe aspired to re-create the international favorites. *Blancmange,* cameline sauce, *bruets,* and *mirraust* appeared everywhere. Similar spices were used; almond milk or sweet-and-sour dishes were served at all European courts.[1]

Most important, medieval cookbooks rarely labeled recipes by nation of origin, although there are some exceptions. Compilers either understood that a basic repertoire of procedures and flavors were common to all of them, and ignored what were certainly regional differences among the food habits of ordinary people, or they truly had little idea of what would constitute a typically French or Spanish dish. Stereotypes, of course, existed, but no clear conception of national cuisines. Even when an author did differentiate between varieties of a particular recipe, for example the English broth, German broth, or Hungarian broth in the *Vivendier,*[2] it is nearly impossible to understand why the recipes are given such names. The German version is any kind of broth with almond milk and spices, the English contains chestnuts and liver, and the Hungarian blood. These appear to be merely exotic names attached to the recipes, when in fact they are fairly typical of ingredients and flavorings found in any European court.

Because authority in the Middle Ages was for the most part decentralized, there was little official incentive by means of patronage to define what the foods of an entire nation might be. The nobility were not yet inextricably drawn into the royal court, where they followed the king's taste, but rather presided over their own small courts that competed with and imitated each other. National rivalries had not yet sought to draw firm territorial and cultural lines that accentuate differences along the margins rather than similarities. For instance, people on the border of France and Spain had much more in common with each other than they would have had with either of their respective capitals. But when Paris and Madrid sought to govern and effectively tax and perhaps mobilize these people in war, it became important to stress national allegiance, national language and culture, and indeed national foodways. These attempts at unification were not always successful, and arguably it was not until after the age of revolutions, in the modern era, that nationalism played a decisive role in shaping culture. But the effort of defining national recipes did begin in the early modern period and is related to the development of the centralized nation-state and the royal court.

One could easily argue that cooking in the sixteenth and seventeenth centuries was still to a great extent international. Perhaps cosmopolitan would be a better term because recipes were presented as foreign and characteristic of particular nations, rather than popular among many countries. To be more precise, medieval cookbooks mostly presented multinational recipes that were common across Europe, as well as in the Middle East. Early modern cookbooks increasingly presented native dishes, along with older favorites, and recipes associated with foreign nations.

A question that must also be seriously explored is whether these associations truly reflected national recipes or were merely extended attempts to offer interesting foreign dishes by adding a few strange ingredients. In other words, when an author claims that a particular dish is French, was this an actual distinctive recipe found in French sources, or merely something made up by the author and given a fancy name? Does the proliferation of recipes associated with far-off places merely reflect these authors' desire to offer more strange and exotic fare, but little that is authentic? Of course modern chefs are not immune to this practice either, but today we can recognize clear and real differences between cooking among European nations. Was this also the case in the sixteenth and seventeenth centuries? For example, were the handful of odd, sweet, egg- and milk-based soups Messisbugo identified as Hungarian really from Hungary or were they labeled "Ongaresca" merely to sound exotic?[3] Did cookbook authors think they were relating authentic foreign dishes, even though they willfully or otherwise substituted ingredients, adapted methods, and changed recipes to suit their own tastes? Authenticity itself is difficult to define, but certainly when a recipe is taken directly from a foreign cookbook the author's intention to present a genuine foreign dish can be trusted.

Ironically, recipes were usually "borrowed" without attribution. Thus we find Scappi's Roman recipes translated into Spanish in Granado, borrowed in Dutch cookbooks,[4] and adapted into French by Lancelot de Casteau or into German by Rumpolt. All this is evidence that in most European courts, chefs were happy to present foreign recipes with no attribution or association whatsoever. They obviously borrowed from each other willingly. But at the same time, authors increasingly labeled recipes by nation of origin, and the more strongly the state demanded national allegiance, usually in moments of crisis, the more urgent the need to define culture and food in terms of nation.

To further define what constitutes a national cuisine, it should be stressed that it is imposed from above for political reasons, rather than a spontaneous grass-roots accumulation of traditional practices. The term must, therefore, be disassociated from any notion of folk culture. In the late nineteenth century, folk culture and peasant cooking was appropriated as representative of national character. If a recipe (or music or craft) was indigenous and had grass-roots origins, it qualified to be considered national, even though these were almost always regional or local in origin. This was obviously done to claim an authentic (and ethnic) pedigree for cultural products as distinct from arts conforming to aesthetic values originating in professional, academic, or foreign circles. Of course in the process of claiming folk culture as national, these forms of culture did become academic or professional—think of *Grimm's Fairy Tales,* vernacular country churches, or the music of Bartok or Sibelius. Folk culture as a concept, however, will seriously confuse any discussion of early modern Europe because peasant foodways were rarely if ever adopted by people higher up the social ladder. If anything, it was elite habits that slowly trickled down.

Another term, *popular culture,* is useful today when one is speaking of a national cuisine. It identifies those practices, ingredients, and recipes that transcend regional peculiarities and can be recognized as typical by both natives and foreigners. Wurst and sauerkraut for Germans, paella for Spaniards, and fish and chips for the English are all iconic popular foods of these particular nations. A food can, however, become truly popular throughout a country though not be representative of a nation or constitute a national dish—Indian food in England or Chinese food in the United States. Equally, a food stereotype may be exaggerated by outsiders but never be universally popular. The French eating frogs is an example of this. The term *popular cuisine* for the early modern period is also misleading specifically because there is no way to discern what most people cooked. We can extrapolate information from culinary litera-ture, especially negative comments about what peasants ate, and there are records relating to agriculture and trade, but there is no way to be sure what would constitute a popular cuisine. Cookbooks reveal almost exclusively elite cuisine.

A national cuisine, then, is something indigenous, recognized through-out a nation and by outsiders as typical and as expressive of that nation's culture. It can originate in any social class, though is usually the cuisine of the court, and most important it is something fabricated. That is not to say that there is something false or deceptive about it, but people have to be informed that it is national. Rarely are national cuisines invented from scratch without regard to historical precedents, though. There are always native ingredients, cooking methods, and finished recipes that compete as candidates for being characteristic expressions of a particular people. But this process also always involves defining what is atypical of the national character, what is imported, foreign, and other. That is to say, the process of codifying a national cuisine always involves excision of everything that refuses to follow the national model, whether the product of native soil or not. Extraneous practices must be artificially assimilated or banished.

Like a national cuisine, the nation-state is itself an artificial construc-tion imposed on heterogeneous peoples for the purpose of controlling, taxing, and using them for reasons of state. Ethnic minorities must be assimilated or marginalized, local dialects must be subsumed, indepen-dent sources of authority must be surrendered to the centralized state. As part of this process, foreign dishes and aberrant foodways must be identified as such and in extreme cases shunned or outlawed. This is precisely what happened in Spain, following the expulsion, to recipes associated with Jews. The more desperate the effort to create a national identity, the more rigid the definition of the national cuisine will be.

This is especially the case when the state is threatened from outside, and equally when it is newly unified or has recently gained independence. Germany in the late nineteenth century is a perfect example, as are all the eastern European democracies formed in the wake of World War I from Finland straight down to the Balkans. The same is probably true for the former Soviet republics today, all struggling to define their own culture after decades of assimilation.

In the sixteenth century it was war, colonial and mercantile rivalry, and most of all an attempt to draw the geographical, cultural, and political periphery into the center that urged states to define their national cuisines. For France it began with territorial and administrative expansion; with Spain it was joining disparate kingdoms into one Catholic monarchy; for England, too, it was a matter of religion and centralization. That distinctive national cookbooks appeared at the same time is no coincidence.

Italy

Without such pressures, it is also apparent that a national cuisine would never develop. The negative example of Italy will be a good place to begin. That is, in a place that resisted unification, retained its local autonomies, and resolutely refused to become a nation, such questions of national character remained muddled and inchoate. In Italy in the early modern period, regional identification or primary allegiance to the city rather than a larger state remained much stronger than any sense of nation, or of Italy as anything other than a geographical appendage hanging below Europe. Here it was more proper to speak of Venetian cuisine, Tuscan cuisine, Roman, Lombard, because this was the level of political organization.

That Italy failed to unify in the early modern period mostly owed to forces entirely out of her control. It was the invading armies of those states that had already unified and centralized (France and Spain and later Austria) that prevented it. Perhaps Italy would have become a nation-state on its own and would have created a distinct national cuisine. In fact such a thing is difficult to recognize, and there does seem to be some connection between political disunity and culinary heterogeneity. That is, a series of ingredients, cooking procedures, and recipes that could be considered familiar throughout the peninsula and identified as typically Italian by outsiders is surprisingly hard to define for the early modern period.

Italian food authors frequently identified recipes by nation. "This is a French dish, Spanish dish, Turkish," and so forth. These authors' and their patrons' willingness to try foreign dishes and identify them as such without appropriating them is itself revealing. Just as xenophobia in dietary literature goes hand in hand with the formation of the nation-state,[5] this may be why Italians never really become xenophobic in terms of food. Not only are Italian authors not afraid of foreign and exotic recipes, but they also seem to have little sense of what is uniquely their own cuisine as different from other nations. Cookbook authors rarely, if ever, mention that a recipe is Italian. Messisbugo offers two lone examples; the first is a *potaccio alla Italiana,* which is meat cut up, browned in fat, and simmered in broth with chestnuts, spices, and apples.[6] There is also what he calls a *fracasea Italiana,* although it does not seem to be a fricassee at all, that is roasted veal's kidney pounded with egg yolks and spread on toast.[7] Neither of these recipes was recognized as Italian in any other cookbook native or foreign.

Of course, why would we expect authors to label dishes Italian if writing for an Italian audience? The point is, they were not writing for an Italian audience, but rather for Venetian, Lombard, Tuscan, and Roman audiences. This is why they consistently labeled recipes with these names, or sometimes even with specific cities. Scappi's *Opera* sometimes reads like a compendium of regional cuisines, and he often needs to explain what an ingredient would be called in another dialect, again pointing to the fact that there was not yet a national cuisine. Romoli's lists of all possible dishes label them either by country or by Italian region, not as Italian.[8]

Food writers did recognize certain unique Italian ingredients. These would have existed however the cuisine developed. Authors everywhere associate Italy with artichokes, and note that Italians use olive oil or lard rather than butter, wine instead of beer. Across Europe there were many foods frequently associated with Italy, or at least with the Mediterranean—olives, anchovies, lemons. Each of these unique ingredients was the result of climate and topography and agriculture; none was a deliberate culinary choice. You might even say that certain cheeses, especially parmigiano or equally popular ones from Piacenza, Lodi, or all these sometimes just associated with Milan, were universally recognized as originating in northern Italy. These of course would become elements of a national cuisine as it later developed. But cooking techniques, flavor combinations, recipes, and uses of ingredients that one could immediately identify with the nation appear to be absent. Pizza Margherita is probably the best example of an Italian national dish today. Created to honor Queen Margherita of Savoy, according to the legend, this red, white, and green dish, like the new flag, was subsequently adopted as quintessentially Italian. In 1889 Italy was still a relatively young nation. Whether the story is true or not, pizza did become an iconic national food, even though it originated in Naples.

Given its reputation today, pasta might be the dish we would most expect to be considered quintessentially Italian, but in fact, pasta dishes varied wildly across the peninsula. Macaroni could refer to gnocchi made with bread crumbs, flat sheets, or hollow tubes, and most important, these were always associated with specific cities, not Italy as a whole. Outside Italy, cookbooks take scarcely any notice of pasta at all. It would not become a national dish until produced on an industrial scale and in dried form, after which it could be exported in much greater quantities.[9]

In the sixteenth and seventeenth centuries, despite the fact that Italian recipes do have an impact on European cooking, primarily through publication or adaptation of Martino via Platina and borrowing from Scappi, there is little indication that outsiders recognize any recipes or techniques as uniquely Italian. Within the peninsula and through Europe, associations are with particular regions. Nowhere was a complete conception of recipes or dishes that are specifically associated with Italy alone and as a whole.

For example, in the greatest of Spanish cookbooks in the baroque era, Francisco Martinez Montiño's *Arte de cocina* of 1611, we find many national dishes: *cordero a la Francesa,*[10] *capon a la Tudesca*, and *ave a la Portugesa,* as well as a Portuguese rice dish, a spinach dish, and a few others. There is an *empanada Inglesa,* but not a single recipe labeled Italian. Only one recipe, *ciruelas de Genova,* (sugar plums)[11] comes close, but that is an association with the city. In Italian cookbooks these are also labeled as Genoese.

English sources offer a little more. Robert May's *The Accomplisht Cook* reveals the author's very catholic, continental tastes. He includes six recipes he identifies as "in the Italian fashion." They might not be what we would consider particularly Italian, but similar recipes can be found in contemporary Italian cookbooks. May's are a boiled bullocks cheek garnished with flowers and served with mustard.[12] It is unclear if this is a real *mostarda di frutta,* or English mustard. There are fritters made of cheese that can be made of Holland cheese or "parmisan grated."[13] There is an Italian pudding that turns out to be a bread pudding, and suet with dried fruits, eggs, and cream, which really seems like an English dish italicized, as do many of his recipes.[14] There are minced pies in the Italian fashion (minced veal, suet, salt, gooseberries, verjuice, currants, sugar, and saffron). This could have been taken from an Italian cookbook, except for the gooseberries. There is also a "Dish in the Italian fashion"[15] that is a simple pear tart, and then finally Italian chips, a paste of flowers and gum arabic rolled in sheets stacked and cut to look like marble.[16]

In France, the sixteenth-century cookbooks mention Castilian, German, and English dishes but no Italian ones. A century later, La Varenne offers a handful of foreign recipes: English, Portuguese, and a few Spanish, but nothing on Italy. His one pasta recipe, a pottage of fideles, is presented as French. It is found in Provence. Nor can one find many traces of Italian cooking in other French cookbooks of the era, and none in LSR. The only major French cookbook that records what were considered Italian recipes is Pierre De Lune's *Le Cuisinier* of 1656. Many dishes are labeled by nation—mostly English, Spanish, Swiss, or German—but there are a few Italian ones. *Potage de levraut à l'italienne* is a quartered young hare fried then simmered in broth with dried fruits, cinnamon, white wine, and served with citron slices and pomegranate seeds.[17] That comes as close to early modern Italian cookery as can be found. There is a similar fricassee recipe in Scappi, and it seems that spices and dried fruit were the signature flavors associated with Italy.

De Lune also has *Pigeonneaux à l'italienne*,[18] a *Paté de godiveau à l'italienne*[19] (a pastry of veal with dried fruits, spices, pistachios, and sugar), also very typical of the period, and *feves à l'italiene*.[20] But just as often there are dishes identified with cities: *Oeufs à la Milanese*,[21] *Crepes à la Florentine*, *Bonnets au fromage de Milan*, *Potage de fidellis de Gênes* (Genoa).[22] This may not be of any great significance, but it does mean the author had as many associations with Italian cities as with Italy as a whole, whereas any other foreign provenance he mentions is always by nation. It suggests that Italian cities have as much cultural capital as Italy as a whole.

In the end, it appears that culinary associations within Italy were primarily with city and region, just as peoples' personal allegiances would have been. With a few exceptions, foreign cookbook authors also have a hard time conceiving of a distinct cuisine for Italy. As we know, such a thing certainly did develop, particularly in the nineteenth century. By the time Pellegrino Artusi was writing his *Science in the Kitchen and the Art of Eating Well*,[23] an Italian cuisine was in place, even though based on regional recipes, which seems to support the contention that national cuisines develop along with nation-states themselves.

France

The evidence for the development of a national cuisine from a positive angle can be found in cookbooks written in the various nation-states. Ironically, France was the last to publish cookbooks of a national character, but after La Varenne's *Cuisinier Francois* and the *Patissier Francois,* they never ceased, from the mid seventeenth century to the present. The titles themselves reflect a desire to inform outsiders as well as natives about typically French cooking. That Louis XIV consciously promoted French culture, arts, and language is a well-known fact. The codification of a national cuisine was part of this whole process, and in many ways, especially toward the later seventeenth and early eighteenth centuries, it was significantly different from the cooking styles covered in this book, and uniquely French. Accounting for the previous century is more difficult.

Apart from the numerous editions of the medieval *Viandier de Taillevent,* attributed to Guilaume Tirel though actually containing much older and newer material, there was a spate of cookbooks in the sixteenth century with different titles.[24] Each is essentially a reprinting of an earlier version, sometimes adding new recipes, but also often adding older medieval ones. This attests to a demand in France for cookbooks, and in many respects the new recipes do represent a departure from medieval cuisine in essentially French patterns. The increasing use of butter, wine, herbs, and aromatics, one could argue, presages later developments in French cuisine.

The question is, however, was there a French cuisine recognized as such by cookbook writers elsewhere?

Were outsiders beginning to have a clear conception of truly French dishes? Messisbugo has many French recipes, which is not surprising considering that Ferrara had a French duchess, Renée of France, and sheltered many French Protestant exiles. What is remarkable is the number of dishes labeled French that can be found in contemporary French cookbooks such as the *Livre fort excellent.* One is tempted to wonder if Messisbugo saw a copy of the book or was informed of its contents by a visiting French courtier. For example, his recipe for *uova alla Francese* consists of ten eggs or merely egg yolks cooked in a half pound of butter in a silver platter placed on hot coals. It is almost exactly the same as the French recipe for *Doeufz poches au beurre.*[25] Messisbugo's *Fracasea Francese,* a fricassee — which denotes chicken or another meat cooked then cut up and sautéed in butter or fat (which Messisbugo preferred) — has its counterpart in the banquet menus of the *Livre fort.* A recipe for *Fracasea in altro modo* is essentially the same as the French fricassee recipe and consists of liver and onions fried and then braised in a sauce. Related fricassees are even found in Willich's *Ars Magirica* and in the *Proper Newe Booke of Cokerye* with the corrupted name *Frasye,* which is made of chicken giblets, heads, and feet. All these cookbooks are roughly contemporaneous.[26]

Messisbugo identifies another recipe as French, a *pastello batutto alla francese di carne di vitello, o castrone,* which is a pasty of parboiled veal leg chopped fine with kidney fat, seasoned with ginger, pepper, nutmeg, and saffron plus whole cloves, encased in a crust with a bit of prosciutto and onion that can be added as well. With the exception of the last two ingredients, the same recipe can be found in the *Livre fort.*[27] Whether Messisbugo saw this book and adapted it to local tastes is perhaps less important than his clear recognition that there are distinctively French dishes, many of which foreshadow developments normally associated with the following century.

For example, Messisbugo offers a recipe for little French tarts made with milk. The dough is nearly the classic *pâte brisée* one can find in the *French Pastry Chef* in the next century,[28] except that this contains egg yolks (which would make the dough tender, more like a *pâte sucré*) but is nonetheless a true French butter-based pastry filled with an egg custard.[29] A similar recipe is also labeled as French, which contains cheese and the wild fruit azaroles,[30] Liver fritters laced with sugar and raisins are perhaps harder to recognize as French from our vantage point, as is a soup called *capirotta francese,* which is pheasant or capon or even veal roasted, finely chopped, and served on toast with broth poured over.[31] A similar French *minestra* is made of herbs and is served on toast with fried slices of meat.[32] There are many similar potages in the first pages of La Varenne. Obviously Messisbugo could not have found them there, but there does seem to be something truly French about these recipes, and the titles are not just added for exotic effect. This is an indication that France was beginning to forge a national culinary identity recognizable to outsiders.

For some inexplicable reason, there are no French recipes in Scappi. Romoli has only one French recipe: a French beef pie, or rather *pasticcio,* that employs an extremely sophisticated technique. The loin of beef is parboiled with a piece of lard or prosciutto. A pie casing is formed and is baked blind filled with flour, which is then emptied. The beef is placed inside with the lard, broth, pepper, and spices, covered, and finished in the oven.[33] There are many other French recipes in Romoli's list of all possible dishes that can be served, including shrimp in a French sauce, French moray eel soup, tench soup, sparrow soup, the belly of tuna in pastry, and other pastries made with ombrina (a kind of fish, croaker), plus another of cream. He also lists as French dishes suitable for meat days sweetbreads, the *fracassea alla Francese,* presumably the same as that mentioned previously, as well as the *capirotta*—both of which he may have learned about from reading Messisbugo—a dish of brains, stuffed kid's pluck (*coratelle*), kid and pork with lemon, French fritters, and various pastries made from goat, kid, brains, poultry, and several others, including an herb tart.

The recipes most frequently associated with France are pastries, hardy soups, or fricassees. This is true not only of Italian sources but throughout Europe. In English sources of the mid sixteenth century we find recipes similar to those considered French in Italy. *A Proper Newe Booke of Cokerye* offers an egg tart as "After the Frenche Fashyan,"[34] which is similar to Messisbugo's. *The Good Huswifes Handmaide for the Kitchin* of 1588 has chickens boiled in the French fashion, as well as French tripe and French calves' feet. A French pottage consists of chopped mutton ribs, boiled with carrots and onions.[35] There is little indication in these recipes why they were considered French, though. Thomas Dawson gives a bizarre technique that is similar to recipes cited by later authors as French. In this case he uses pigeons half roasted on a spit, then coated in a pudding batter of herbs, egg yolks, bread, and spices. These are then wrapped in parboiled cabbage leaves, bound tight, and boiled in beef broth. Cabbages also go in the pot. They are served in a dish with broth poured on top and garnished with fruit.[36] Similar recipes appear through the next century, though not made with pudding batter.

In the next century there was more consistency among authors about what constitutes French cuisine. Perhaps the most interesting source is John Murrell's *A New Booke of Cookerie* of 1615, which contains a good proportion of recipes labeled French. If these do reflect what he claims to have observed as a "Traveller," the book constitutes one of the most important sources for French cooking in the period preceding La Varenne. His claim of authenticity is not easily substantiated, but there are decent clues that it does reflect actual practice as part of a national cuisine. The book opens with a number of new French dishes, including a capon boiled and larded with preserved lemons, served in mutton broth with candied fruit. Three recipes for leg of mutton claim a French provenance: boiled, hashed, and roasted.[37] The one procedure that seems to link many of these recipes, though, is what the author calls "to boyle" but is in fact a kind of stew. Most of the main ingredients are also stuffed. For example, pigeon are stuffed with herbs and put into a pipkin, a small earthenware vessel with legs, placed over coals. They are then stewed in mutton broth, seasoned with spices, and thickened with rice.[38] Likewise, rabbit is stewed in mutton broth and green vegetables and thickened with bread and butter. Chicken receives a treatment with the same basic structure with mutton broth, and Murrell even suggests that you can use water if you prefer, but mutton broth is preferable, and "the French men follow the other way and it is the better." This then appears to be a standard and truly French type of preparation, instantly recognizable both to the author and his readers as something new and foreign. A chine of mutton or veal (the backbone where the ribs are attached) is prepared in the same French fashion as well, boiled with lettuce, spinach, and herbs and thickened with bread and hard-boiled egg yolk.

Robert May, though his recipes are far more complicated and elaborate, repeated many of the same "French" recipes mentioned in Italian sources. His Capons in Pottage in the French Fashion[39] is clearly a descendant of the same dish Messisbugo had in mind, though garnished with marrow, sweetbreads, and lemon. Another Pottage in the French Fashion[40] is also a cousin of Messisbugo's French herb *minestra* containing meat, plus oatmeal, and a variety of herbs such as spinach, lettuce, endive, and cauliflower, served over bread "sippets." In all, May has fifteen recipes labeled French, and among them various pies, though there is no obvious reason why some are identified as French. One pie is merely minced meat, pine nuts, and grapes or gooseberries, the other a sort of modified *blancmange* tart of pounded almonds, cold turkey, butter, lemons, and sugar with a handful of garnitures.[41]

Another indication of what the English thought of French food can be gleaned from a small contemporary anonymous cookbook called *The Compleat Cook,* which appeared in 1658. It advertises itself as an international cookbook of Italian, Spanish, and French dishes. In fact, the recipes are mostly English, but there is a pig dressed in the French manner that is warmed over a fire, skinned, cut, and stewed in white wine, broth, onions, and butter, and served on slices of bread with the liquid poured around—merely a variation of the pottages mentioned above.[42] So too is the odd way of preparing a rump of beef, which is parboiled, slashed, and seasoned, then braised in red wine with onions, capers, and lettuce and also served in a bowl on buttered toast.[43] Ducks are given the same treatment: partial roasting then simmering in wine with chestnuts, oysters, and onions, or lacking these with artichoke bottoms, turnips, cauliflower, bacon, or sweetbreads. Again, it is served in a bowl on toast.[44] Clearly this presentation was firmly associated with France. The author also records practically the exact same French minced veal pie that appears in other cookbooks.[45] It is made with dried fruit, spices, sugar, and verjuice, and clearly was identified with France through much of Europe.

In William Rabisha we are also given recipes for boiled fowl, which in this case are not roasted first but are stewed in wine and broth with standard garnishes of the era, including artichokes, cockscombs, spices, barberries, and pistachios. The whole is served with marrow bones and asparagus, once again on toast.[46] It is essentially the same recipe that had been circulating since the sixteenth century as French, here gussied up in the English baroque fashion.

The anonymous *Archimagirus Anglo-Gallicus,* which advertises both English and French contents, has a leg of mutton that is boned and stuffed with a mixture of egg yolks, marrow, bread, and cream and studded with dates, raisins, and herbs. The whole is sewed up and stewed in broth.[47] Revealingly, this is almost the same recipe offered by the Spanish cookbook author Montiño for *Una pierna de carnero á la Francesa,* and like all the recipes mentioned above, it is served on toast with the broth on top.[48] Clearly, both north and south, this was a recognizably French dish, with numerous variations on the basic technique. Back to the *Archimagirus,* the book was printed from a manuscript belonging to Theodore Mayerne, who was physician to Charles I, so presumably the recipes date to the 1630s or so. The exact same recipe found in *The Compleat Cook* for ducks also appears here, but it is not entirely certain whether this work was the source, because they were both printed in 1658.[49]

Not only do cookbooks in many languages refer to French dishes, but by the seventeenth century there is consistency among these sources about what constitutes typically French cuisine. Although a repertoire of French cuisine replete with carefully defined procedures, sauces, and named dishes would not be developed until the latter seventeenth and early eighteenth centuries, it is clear that the efforts of French chefs were well on the way toward defining the national cuisine, as is evidenced by the fact that outsiders could recognize it. That this happens precisely at the time France develops as a powerful nation-state, with wars of religion in the past, does not appear to be coincidence.

Spain and Portugal

The case of Spain is somewhat different. Interestingly, Italian authors of the sixteenth century do not often associate recipes with Spain, but rather with Catalonia. Messisbugo records a variation on *sfogliatini,* which are little folded sweet pastries, the Catalan version of which is colored green with parsley or beet leaves and filled with raisins.[50] He also mentioned a kind of Catalan cheese recipe. Romoli also has only a Catalan dish that is made of little chickens roasted then cut up and stewed with lemon slices.[51] The only recipe Scappi associates with Spain per se is the *olla podrida*—or what he calls *oglia potrida*. It appears in most sixteenth- and seventeenth-century cookbooks, varying in form and ingredients, but always recognized as Spanish.

Evidence that this dish was not only popular but widely recognized as Spanish can be found in an unlikely source: Andrea Bacci's enormous Latin treatise on wine. Tucked within a chapter on ancient convivia is an account of a meal served by his patron Ascanio Colonna to Philip of Nassau, who arrived in Rome as a delegate from Philip of Spain in November 1595. Clearly the dish was meant to honor the Spanish, and Bacci even provides a recipe. With precise measurements it is worth repeating, because it is the prototype of a recipe that would survive throughout Europe for centuries. His *olla* contains ten pounds of beef and the same of mutton, three pounds of cured pork belly, six pigeons, ten quails, one pound of truffles, six thrushes, one capon, six pounds of turnips, six fennel bulbs, two pounds of lucanica sausages, one pound of red chickpeas, six onions, and when in season twelve little birds such as larks, figpeckers, or attagena (heathcocks), four cardoons, two cabbages, salt and aromatics, and some sugar.[52]

To return to Scappi, apart from his *olla* recipe, he only mentions Spain once again, calling for Spanish honey in a recipe. Had these cookbooks been published in the years when Spain was an active aggressor, we might not be surprised to find few Spanish recipes. But there were many associated with Germany, and of course the Empire and Spain were both linked, and soldiers from both places arrived on Italian soil. The majority of these cookbooks were published after those conflicts, anyway. More likely is that Italians had cultural links with the eastern coast of Iberia, and shared many culinary traditions. Catalan cooking was something they were familiar with to some extent. Rupert of Nola's Catalan cookbook was written in the court of Naples, and even Martino had Catalan recipes in the fifteenth century; many borrowed from Rupert word for word or in scaled-down versions. Thus despite the union of Castile and Aragon, Italians seem to have had stronger associations with the separate older kingdoms, though they only mention Catalonia.

The culinary associations with the nation of Spain did eventually emerge, though. The *olla podrida* continued to appear, as did a type of sponge cake called *pane di Spagna* that became practically universal as a garnish in baroque cooking. In general it is in the seventeenth century that recipes are labeled Spanish. In 1596 Englishman Thomas Dawson offered a Spanish way to make candied dried peaches, which is surprising given that the two countries were still at war.[53] Later English cookbooks offer more. Robert May describes how to make Spanish meatballs made from leg of mutton and suet, stewed in broth.[54] There is also a recipe for eggs in Spanish fashion scrambled with sherry, sugar, and orange juice that he calls *wivos me quidos*, which appears to be his quirky spelling for the Spanish phrase *huevos mejidos*, which means mixed or scrambled eggs, and is still made with sugar and milk and taken to cure colds. A similar *frittata alla Spagnuola*, or more properly a tortilla made with onions, was served by Vasselli in mid-seventeenth-century Bologna.[55]

Vasselli also provides a recipe for *capirotata*, or *zuppe Spagnuole*, which, though it does not yet resemble the dish that is now known by that name—which is a sweet bread pudding, is associated correctly with Spain. Here it is veal cooked on a spit and shredded and served with biscuits soaked in Muscat wine, cheese, egg yolks, cream, crushed mostaccioli, quince paste, squash, and plums in syrup.[56]

The Compleat Cook includes a Spanish cream, which is really just an odd way to make cream rise from fresh milk,[57] as well as a pap and an olio,[58] regarding which the author has some very particular preferences. It is made from bacon, beef, ears, trotters, and pigeons, as well as peas and chestnuts. Everything is flavored with leeks, garlic, pepper, and cloves, and perhaps most important, saffron soaked in broth. He insists on using an earthenware pot as well, and that oil should never be added, nor herbs, and that the broth should be drunk from a porringer rather than a spoon, and the only sauce for the meats should be sugar mixed with mustard. Whether the author is relating what he knows to be the authentic recipe or merely his own taste preference is unclear, but he certainly believed that most people ruin the dish by throwing in incongruous ingredients.

Elsewhere, in Liege, Lancelot de Casteau labels a puff pastry recipe as Spanish.[59] It is made from a standard dough with eggs, which is rolled out and brushed with pork fat to keep the layers separate, rolled up again, chilled, and then cut to form little pasties, which are filled with a spiced mutton and suet mixture and baked. In seventeenth-century Mantua, Stefani has a Spanish *bianco mangiare* that differs little from any other recipe except that it is made with regular milk rather than almond milk.[60] He also has a *latte alla Spagnuola*, which is milk cooked gently with eggs, sugar, and musk, all of which is browned on top with a hot shovel, like a flan.[61] Without lingering on such details, by the seventeenth century, authors do label recipes as Spanish, but there does not seem to be great consensus among them about what dishes are quintessentially Spanish. No one seems to have known about dishes that later became firmly associated with Spain—paella, gazpacho, *cocido,* and so forth, but then these sorts of recipes cannot be found in Spanish cookbooks yet, either. Not that cookbooks necessarily reflect the full range of dishes eaten. What can be said is that though Spain did produce several cookbooks, many features of which would eventually come to be associated with the nation, cookbook authors outside Spain did not have an extensive idea of what the cuisine was like, apart from a handful of scattered recipes. It was, nonetheless, a beginning.

The same is true of Portugal. Romoli lists three recipes in succession as Portuguese: a suckling pig on a spit, as well as lamprey roasted on a spit, and sturgeon fried in butter and served in a sauce of fried onions, herbs and spices, and wine, colored with saffron.[62] Lancelot records a Portuguese chopped veal pie with eggs and chopped fruits in syrup.[63] In England *The Good Huswifes Handmaide for the Kitchin* of 1588 includes a Portuguese dish called *fystes,* which are balls of suet, egg yolk, bread crumbs, currants, and spices boiled in sherry, as well as Spanish *balles* and *balles* of Italy, the former of mutton and the latter of veal.

La Varenne has a Portuguese egg dish that is made of egg yolks and sugar syrup cooked together and placed in a cone of paper, cooled, turned over on a plate, and garnished with sugar, candied lemon peel, and flowers.[64] Robert May has a similar dish, though served without the conical flourish,[65] as well as some marzipan tarts.[66] A "Portugall Dish" in the mind of *The Compleat Cook* is the guts, livers, and gizzards of capons soaked in wine and roasted on a skewer, and basted at the end with mutton gravy, orange juice, and saffron.[67] Again, though there were not a handful of recipes everyone recognized as Portuguese, the effort to label certain dishes as such was widespread.

Germany

The case of Germany, as a geographical and linguistic entity rather than a political one, generally supports the idea that political unity and national cuisines progress together. There would not be a nation Germany until 1870, yet some recipes were identified as German long before then. German chefs were even singled out as particularly proficient.

Many came to cook in Italy; Matthia Geigher is a prime example. This perhaps explains why it is usually Italian chefs who recognize German dishes. The *Livre fort excellent* does have two German dishes, though: a *chapon au brouet dalemaigne* and *lymatz dalemaigne*.[68] The former is a spiced almond and red wine broth with roasted capon that looks suspiciously medieval. The latter is sage-flavored water, flour, and eggs made into a dough that is fried in butter. Why these are considered German is not clear. But this recipe is similar to one recorded by Messisbugo about the same time.

Messisbugo often uses what he calls a *pasta tedesca* for pastry recipes. It is a dough made of three pounds white flour, three pounds milk, one pound butter, three ounces rose water, one pound sugar, a pinch of saffron, twenty egg yolks, and ten whites. The dough is then cut into various shapes and pan fried in butter. (The recipe converted and reduced to one-fourth roughly equals two cups flour, 1.5 cups milk, one stick of butter, one-half cup sugar, five yolks, two or three whites, saffron, and a dash of rose water. It is similar to an American biscuit dough rather than a pastry crust.)[69] Messisbugo also includes a classic apple pie and considers it German.[70] There is also a typical medieval preparation of small birds or some other meat cooked in sweet wine, pepper, raisins, toasts and vinegar, and sugar and spices.[71] A beef loin marinated for five or six hours in wine and vinegar, coriander, fennel, and salt and later roasted on a spit is perhaps somewhat closer to German cuisine as it would develop in the following centuries.[72]

In Romoli, an ombrina or similar fish *alla Tedesca* is cut up, washed in wine, salted, left for an hour, then the salt is rubbed off and the fish poached in wine and water, after which butter and spices are added. It is served with mustard, as Italians do it, or with a walnut sauce.[73] A comparable dish is made of brains and marrow.[74] In his lists of recipes there are a few more about which we can only guess — a *pasta Tedesca* filled with marzipan, boiled pike with flowers, German oysters, as well as the apple pie and beef loin, presumably like those from Messisbugo. But there is nowhere near the number of recipes in his list associated with France.

Rossetti's *Scalco* book lists dozens of dishes considered German. Unfortunately, the author provides only a list, no recipes, so it is rarely clear why he considers them German, although there are some clues. Beef loin in soup is labeled as German.[75] So too is stuffed beef loin in a pot,[76] as well as other recipes for beef with cabbage or onions bearing an undeniable resemblance to pot roasts of later German cuisine. Variations of these appear down the list using veal, mutton, or pork, so presumably, in the author's mind, they were procedures firmly associated with Germany, ones that could be adapted using a variety of ingredients. A number of birds such as crane, goose,[77] and various other wildfowl are stuffed *all'Alemana,* so this too must have been a familiar treatment. For the several fish dishes labeled German, there is not a hint what they might be. The German *suppa* he lists appears to be either almond milk or milk-based.[78]

Elsewhere in Europe, chefs are almost completely silent on the topic of German cuisine. Even Lancelot, right near the border, offers only a *lard d'Almagne,* which is essentially white and red almond paste layered together and sliced to look like bacon.[79] The lack of references may be taken as an indication that there was not yet a codified cuisine recognizable to outsiders, or at least it did not interest them, and it was not yet promoted as something typically German.

England

The final example will offer more evidence that the further the progress of nation-building, and the greater the recognition of a state as culturally unified, the more likely recipes were to be identified with the nation. England was first and foremost, and in practically all cookbooks, associated with pies. In Spain, Maceras offers five varieties of the *empanada Inglesa.* One is made with the head of an unspecified animal, probably sheep, which the previous recipes called for. Others are made with tongue, *turmas de tierra,* (truffles), gourd (most likely a European variety rather than squash, here called calabaça), and another with fish.[80] The association with England is somewhat surprising because the author was not a courtly chef, but rather a college mess hall cook. Nor is it likely that truffles or gourds would have been a common ingredient in England, so the association is a little perplexing, though the pasty itself is not. The author may merely be thinking that the pasty is English, and here are some interesting fillings that work in Spain. Montiño also mentions *empanadas Inglesas,* the form of which, we might assume, was recognizable in Spain.[81] Lancelot calls a similar dish *pastez d'Angleterre.* It differs in being made of lamb or goat meat.[82] La Varenne's version uses hare,[83] as does De Lune's.[84] Lancelloti was also serving *pasticii all inglese* to his Roman patrons in the seventeenth century.[85] By this time, however, it had taken on baroque form, filled with pounded veal, boneless pigeons, figpecker's breasts, Lucca sausages, cardoons, truffles, pine nuts, and other obviously un-English perversities. Although the fillings could change erratically, obviously the pasty is one example of a dish that remained common in England after four hundred years.

Apart from the pasty, in Italy the associations with England were rather more disparate. Messisbugo has a lean soup made from parsley roots,[86] though in England they might have been made from parsnip. His English fricassee is also perplexing. It is made of sturgeon boiled, cut up, and fried in butter and then mixed with orange juice, verjuice, vinegar, and spices. The dish can also be made with beef, veal, or shrimp.[87] Why there is an association with England remains a mystery, though, especially as the fricassee is usually considered French in origin. Romoli, even though he has dishes labeled Fleming, Slavonian, Polish, and Turkish, has nothing English; nor does Scappi. Similarly, in Rossetti's *Scalco* book there are dozens of dishes listed as French or German, even Polish and Bohemian, but none English.[88] Presumably the author knew about certain foreign techniques and had concrete associations with various countries, but none with England. Interestingly, he never labels dishes as Spanish either.

The *Livre fort excellent* labels two recipes as English: one *Taillis dangleterre,* which is multicolored gelatins,[89] and the other pike in an English sauce that is poached either in red wine or in beer and rosemary. A strikingly similar recipe for pike or other freshwater fish is found in the *Proper Newe Book,* though rather than beer, it is cooked in water and yeast. The French author came fairly close to capturing an actual English recipe.[90]

There remains the possibility that although the English did have a clear sense of their national culinary heritage, and practically everywhere they were already associated with roast beef, cookbook authors outside England were either largely ignorant of English cooking due to lack of immediate contact, or they were actively disdainful of a cooking they believed unworthy of their patrons. In either case, the dearth of references suggests that nations' culinary knowledge of each other was still necessarily limited. In the sixteenth century it is nascent, and in the seventeenth century more recognizable, despite authors' desire to show off their knowledge of foreign cuisines.

In the end it must be said that truly national cuisines, with fully developed and easily recognized stereotypes, only emerge after or at the end of the early modern period, at least in culinary literature. Then it is clear that food had become a tool of state and an instrument of both exclusion and national pride. Not surprisingly, just as the state in reality inched toward its modern form slowly and with fits and stops, so too did national cuisines. Some recipes are clear ancestors of modern ones, others were medieval remnants, and others disappeared entirely. The same is naturally true of political forms, art forms, and every other aspect of culture. Evolution rarely progresses in a straight line, but it should be clear in any case that while western Europeans were groping toward the development of the modern nation-state, they were simultaneously beginning to recognize national cooking styles.

CHAPTER 9

Staff and Carving

Apart from describing model menus and recording recipes, one of the major concerns of the culinary literature of these centuries was to describe the smooth functioning of the kitchen, pantry, and household in every stage of food acquisition, preparation, and presentation. Judging from the large number of books published on the topic, there was clearly a great demand for such information, particularly among fledgling courts where rulers felt the need to follow the latest fashions and throw banquets without any hitches. Equally important, this literature is specifically addressed to the potential *scalco* himself, usually one of good birth, if not noble, who must find patronage among these courts and in a sense sell himself and his skills. Though the *scalco* literature on the one hand serves as propaganda for the greatest courts, it also teaches the hopeful *scalchi* elsewhere how to run an efficient staff.

What is also evident in the literature is a growing bureaucratization of the staff, efficient accounting methods, and standardization of regulations by which the staff is expected to abide. In a sense, the business of banquet throwing is streamlined into a tight administrative machine, organized much like the modern state itself. The banquet staff, like political administration, is thus transformed from a miscellaneous collection of noble friends and relatives into an efficient and, most important, professionalized corps. One might say the same process occurs in the military, as the motley feudal army is transformed into a uniformed, salaried, professional and standing army. The kitchen undergoes much the same transformation.

Although it remained preferable to hire a *scalco* of noble blood—and some did actually attain knighthood for their service—it seems clear that in the course of the sixteenth and seventeenth centuries, an increasing proportion came from relatively humble backgrounds and were hired on the basis of merit rather than birth. One can easily understand how in the atmosphere of fierce competitive entertaining, achieving the most dazzling and perfectly executed banquet became more important than having someone with a noble ancestry. Nonetheless, there were specific qualities that were to be looked for in a *scalco*.

First, it is absolutely crucial to understand that the *scalco* was not the chef, nor was his position comparable to the maître d' in restaurant culture of classical French cuisine, even though the French often referred to this position using the term. Nor was he merely a banquet manager, though this seems the closest translation, though his duties were far more pervasive and complex. The *scalco* was the head of a rigidly departmentalized bureaucracy comprising the cook, who oversees the kitchen; the *credenziero*, who is responsible for an entirely separate kitchen staff that prepares the cold dishes that normally come out first or between hot courses; an official buyer; and an official stock manager or dispenser of ingredients. There could be many more officials as well, as will be described below, but these were in a sense the important second-in-command lieutenants who answered directly to the *scalco,* or general. The *scalco* was actually responsible for every staff member, but there was still a strict chain of command, with the chef, buyer, and so forth each having his own men to supervise.

In some courts and as a rule in France and Spain, the *scalco* was also the master of the entire household, or majordomo—an official court position going all the way back to Carolingian times. In France the term *maître d'hotel* was used precisely in this sense, for someone who not only managed the banquets but the entire household budget, with responsibilities for food and all other household concerns. In these countries, therefore, it was typical to have a noble serve, whereas in Italy it would have been the *scalco* himself. Ferrara, however, proves an exception to this rule. Both Messisbugo and Rossetti later in the century were masters of the household. According to Rossetti, in Germanic and Slavic lands, however, there was a master cook with supervisory status.[1] In Italy the general pattern included a *scalco* in charge of everything related to food, while another superior *maestro di casa* governed all household concerns and maintained the budget.

The *scalco* also normally managed the serving staff, and in fact he would personally serve the master presiding over the banquet and his table. The serving staff, particularly in larger households, would often also include sub *scalchi* (*sottoscalchi*), that is, several men whose job it was to serve lesser tables, but who were answerable to the head *scalco,* as were all the pages, bottle boys, napkin bearers, and other household staff. It was, without doubt, the strict division of labor that allowed this operation to function smoothly, and this rationalization and subordination of the staff hierarchy is its greatest accomplishment.

As for the *scalco* himself, there are numerous required qualifications. Antonio Frugoli explains the importance of the position. Incidentally, the *scalco* authors borrowed freely from each other, perhaps even more so than cookbooks, so no statement should be considered original. In the *scalco*'s hands rests not only the health of the Lord but his honor among his peers. Sloppy service or poorly prepared food will ultimately tarnish the reputation of the master and reflect poorly upon his judgment in choosing an incompetent steward. The *scalco,* because of his tending to the body of the master as first responsibility, is also his confidant, and one of the closest members of his personal circle. Along with those who dress him, entertain him, and take care of his horses, an astute *scalco* is indispensable.[2]

Because the health of the master is in his hands, it is also the *scalco's* responsibility to know the master's complexion, that is, his body's inherent predisposition in terms of humoral balance, as well as any infirmities to which he may be subject. It is the *scalco*'s duty to see that dishes are served to the master suitable for his complexion, age, level of physical activity, and that will not aggravate any existing condition. In some cases, therefore, the master is served food different from other guests, or more typically from the variety of dishes prepared, the *scalco* will see to it that only those appropriate will be presented on the master's table. Therefore the *scalco* must have intimate knowledge of what goes on in the kitchen and exactly what ingredients have gone into each dish, to be sure. For example, if the master's choler is raging, he is not served too many spices, or if he is in a melancholy mood or has a weak digestion, he must be served whiter and lighter dishes or restorative soups specifically designed for convalescents. Giovanni Battista Crisci insists that "the scalco must be prudent in thought for the health of his master, like a physician, observing when to give him good foods according to season."[3]

That both *scalco* and chefs took this quite seriously is evident in that Scappi's cookbook contains a whole section on foods for the infirmed, though it is not always clear why he thought they were appropriate. Equally, half of Romoli's book is about the humoral qualities of foods, digestibility, and other medicinal properties. A good proportion of Evitascandalo's *scalco* book describes the humoral qualities of every single ingredient that might be encountered. For example, he will tell you a lamprey is a freshwater fish good from February through May; it is temperately hot and humid in the first degree and offers abundant nutrition and is delicate in taste. It is good for every age and complexion, but tough to digest and offends the gouty. This precedes his culinary advice and suggested methods of preparation. There is no indication that the former information has any bearing on the latter, though, and it seems to be merely culled from a dietary text. The same is true of the medical advice offered by Fusoritto da Narni at the end of the carving book by Cervio. Strangely, it is in verse presumably easier to remember, but most of the opinions run directly counter to the culinary material. That is, there are instructions on how to carve wild game but then later this verse:

> Fa superfluità, e assai humori
> La carne selvagina, è malenconica
> E dar solo si deve à Lavoratori

> With superfluities and abundant humors
> Wild meat causes melancholy
> And you ought to give it only to laborers[4]

Medical information would remain a common feature in the *scalco* literature. Vasselli in the mid seventeenth century added second-hand medical opinions into his descriptions of specific ingredients and preparations. Such information, in most culinary texts, is largely superficial and never approaches the detail and complexity found in the dietary literature. Still, a decent knowledge of this kind of information was expected of the *scalco,* and apparently the buyers of these books were not surprised to find such information contained therein. In some courts, however, there was a permanent physician on staff who would attend to such issues, but the *scalco* was still the mediator between the kitchen and the physician.

Evitascandalo gives us a precise description of the ideal *scalco.*[5] He is ideally of noble birth, or at least well born and courteous. Twenty-five to sixty is the ideal age, but he must also have experience, less likely in the young, but also be energetic, less likely among the elderly. Strangely, if he is serving at court and noble himself, he is entitled to wear a hat and carry a sword. If serving clerics, a long cloak is more appropriate. Romoli prefers his *scalco* dressed soberly, wearing a small cap, but not like certain buffoons he has seen festooned in bright garish colors.[6] Apparently the position had not been professionalized to such a degree that an easily recognized uniform was developed, and of course the *scalco* would have preferred to associate himself with the nobles at court rather than the hired help. Rossetti insists that height is also a major consideration; the *scalco* must be able to peruse the entire dining area and keep a lookout for orderly service. He must not be so tall as to be clumsy, though.[7] Rossetti also had a certain obsession with both the polite manners of the *scalco* as well as his impeccable personal cleanliness. The popular image of everyone high and low encrusted with a patina of filth is clearly belied by such comments.

Rossetti is also explicit that the greatest difficulty the *scalco* faced was not in serving guests but in managing his own staff, keeping them honestly occupied, and most important, preventing theft. In fact, his obsession with this topic, one that it incidentally paralleled in political administrations of the period, appears to be the impetus for a strict method of accounting maintained by the *scalco*. It is not surprising that Italians would be expert in accounting methods, but applying them to the kitchen and serving staff is definitely a development that supports this idea of increasing rationalization of the banqueting business. Rossetti demands of each of his major officers that they keep a "list" or register of exactly what comes into the larder or kitchen, and exactly what goes out. Messisbugo kept his account books this way.[8] It appears that this was a system of double-entry bookkeeping of the kind invented in Italy in the Renaissance and regularly used by businessmen. Rossetti also insists that the buyer must list the quantity or weight of every item purchased, and the stock keeper must record everything he receives and everything handed over to the cook and *credenziero*. Periodically, normally every month, the *scalco* will personally check the account books, keeping his own records that can ultimately be presented to the Lord. Perhaps most important, each official keeping his own records acts as a potential check on the other. If their records do not accord, it would be clear where a theft had occurred. In this way the system is self-regulating and foolproof. Interestingly, it was precisely these kinds of internal checks that sixteenth- and seventeenth-century rulers were instituting to curb corruption within their administrations. Like a ruler, the *scalco* cannot oversee every single iota of food on its journey from market to plate, but this bureaucratic record keeping does let him oversee exactly what is going where and when, and how much it all costs.

The other advantage of this system is that it helped the *scalco* forecast requirements well into the future—to be well provisioned in the case of unexpected guests, or in the event of a war campaign. Both the *scalco,* chef, and the rest of the staff were expected to accompany the master in military ventures and feed the court in motion, which explains the need for portable cooking implements. In Scappi there is an illustration of an entire cooking kit that could be loaded on horseback. Although there is no way to tell how common the practice was, Rossetti even has his officers keep two separate account books, one for ordinary expenditure, designed for use in predicting future outlay, and another for extraordinary—special celebrations, wars, and the like, which can of course be presented to the master separately so he can understand the vast expenditure.

The most important part of the *scalco*'s daily routine, however, is designing the menu for the day's meals. It is for this reason, no doubt, that most of the information in the *scalco* literature consists of menus— sometimes mere listings of food served on various occasions, other times explicit enough to provide a skeletal recipe. That is, the *scalco,* although he does not cook the food himself, must be both gourmand, food stylist, caterer, and dining room manager rolled into one. The style and content of the meal are entirely in his domain, and thus the evolution of cuisine in these centuries largely owes to the aesthetic choices of the *scalchi* rather than chefs, as in our own day. He also chose the serving vessels, and one gets a vivid impression from the literature that the *scalco* would be watching over every plate before it was presented, suggesting an extra garnish here or flourish there, perhaps tasting a sauce to see if it was properly seasoned. Frugoli has him correcting the seasoning himself.[9] He would also be busy making sure the table was properly set and napkins exquisitely folded. Actually, the art of napkin folding was invented in this period. Practically no detail escapes his attention, down to the provisioning of toothpicks.[10]

The *scalco* also chose the room where the banquet or dinner would take place. There was not yet a permanent single-purpose dining room, so that in summer months the tables could be set up outside in the garden or a loggia; in winter he would choose the warmest room and be sure to have enough wood for the fire. Timing the courses was also extremely important, and it appears that in some places the entire service would be swept away between courses, while elsewhere there was a continual replenishment of empty dishes, with new foods gradually appearing on the table within each course. Rossetti's preference was to never see empty plates on the table.[11]

The head cook was one of the *scalco*'s prime lieutenants. He in turn had his own staff of cooks to manage, often dividing their duties into separate working spaces, effectively dividing the labor into specialized units. This was often a matter of practicality, as the pasta makers needed large tables where flour could be spread about, and the dairy makers needed a cool place to whip cream and egg whites and make cheese. There was also a separate space for sauce and jelly making. The cook was subordinate both socially and in terms of kitchen hierarchy to the *scalco*—he did not even design the menu, but merely carried out the orders of his superior.

Scappi, who was himself a mere master cook, offers some explicit details directed toward his apprentice, one Giovanni, who will presumably take over eventually. The cook must, first of all, know intimately the quality and proper season for every ingredient entrusted to him. This can only be learned through long and direct experience. Romoli says much the same: "A cook must be like an old doctor, aged in the art."[12] But he should not be too old to carry out his job. He must also be sober, and it is interesting that this is one of the most consistent comments made throughout the culinary literature—that the cook must not be a drunkard. The stereotype may have had some basis in reality for authors to make note of it.[13] Cleanliness and polite manners are mentioned throughout as well.

To the cook is left the task of organizing and maintaining the kitchen space and utensils. Scappi gives some detailed advice about using space efficiently, where to locate knives, and how to store cauldrons and pots in the open space above the workers' heads, suspended by chains. Certain ingredients are also suspended, probably to prevent rats from eating them, but they are also locked, so one might assume that this was to prevent theft as well. Another major concern was having water supplied for both cooking and cleaning, and Scappi suggests two tanks of around sixteen thousand liters each.[14]

The sort of inherent mistrust as was seen in the *scalco* and his subordinates is also expected of the cook. He must watch over the kitchen, not allowing strangers in, or even household members.[15] The logic of this is not only that the errant courtier may stumble in for a late-night snack and eat something important for the banquet, but that poisoning may have been a real concern within these courts. Without access to the kitchen, the potential assassin would be thwarted, unless of course he was in collusion with the cook. This explains the need for absolute fidelity among the food staff.

Scappi also gives us intimate details of the cook's life and living arrangements. First, in large households there were often two cooks who switched off every other week. On occasions when the service of both was required, it is evident from Scappi's comments that rivalry and contention was the norm. He suggests that they should behave as brothers and share duties equally. Although he does not speak of salary, he does specify that a precise formal contract should be made with both the *scalco* and the master of the house, delineating responsibilities and even a food allowance. The *scalco* will normally be given three pounds of bread and six *fogliette* (flasks) of wine per day, plus two and a half pounds of veal or mutton, a capon, or whatever else is leftover from the credenza, and on meatless days, eight eggs, or during Lent, two and a half pounds of fish. Scappi's assumption is that the cook should be fed as well as the nobles themselves.[16] In the courts of pope, emperor, and king, however, everything is "free," which presumably means the chef could take whatever he wanted without limit. The question remains, though, what exactly could he do with such quantities of food? This is clearly enough for a large family, and we might suppose the food is intended to be taken home. But Scappi also mentions that the cook should be given a furnished room with candles, a broom, and firewood, which implies that he sleeps there. It is also clear that the kitchen staff sleep there and are clothed. They too are given extraordinary amounts of food—a pound and a half of meat—and just a little less wine and bread than the cook.

Perhaps the most fascinating of Scappi's comments come in a brief paragraph in which he discusses the cook's perks. To him it was customary to save the ashes. This was merely a practicality, because they were used to make lye, which was then used to clean all the kitchen laundry. He also keeps the hides and feathers, perhaps to sell to leatherworkers and haberdashers, at a personal profit. But he is also given feet, heads, and innards, even though many of these are called for in recipes, as well as the used grease and cured fat that had gone rancid. What exactly he would do with these is not specified, but they may have gone into soap with the lye, or were perhaps sold for some other industrial use.

The next commander in the kitchen retinue is the *credenziero,* a word for which there is no suitable translation. The name itself comes from the table or credenza on which the food he prepares is placed. Credenza, like credence, implies trust, and according to some dictionaries the etymology of the word stems from the practice of having a servant taste the food intended for the master to make sure it was not poisoned. It is difficult to tell exactly what authors' comments mean when they say, "make the credenza of foods for the mouth of your Lord."[17] Vincenzo Cervio, in his carving book, does state explicitly that they make the "credenza" of Princes for two principal reasons: one for ceremony and the other for suspicion of poison. In many courts, such as in Urbino, there is no real need to do this, and it is continued only for the sake of pomp.[18] In any case, someone ceremonially tastes the master's dishes, but it does not appear to be the *credenziero.* Normally it would have been the *scalco.* There was no official "taster" with no other job function—someone of lowly birth hired solely to test the master's food. This seems to be the invention of modern fiction writers.[19] This is not, however, in any way to deny that there may have been real concerns over poisoning in these courts, and the many antidote recipes that line the pages of medical texts clearly demonstrate that people were afraid of being poisoned. They did spend a lot of money on items such as the bezoar—a calcinated deposit from the stomach of a ruminant, or even New World llama, reputed to ward off poison.[20]

In some courts the job of tasting was left to the *coppiero,* or cup bearer. Rabasco specifies that he both mixes the wine and water and then "makes the credenza, or test of the drink, having a vase thus prepared and separate from others, which is served to the master . . . (to secure his life from poisons) and he makes the test of foods and drinks." Crisci also assigns this task to the cup bearer, and it may be that by the seventeenth century the *credenziero,* being preoccupied with his own prep work, was left behind the scenes while an official trusted courtier was given the task of tasting.[21]

Nowhere was tasting the *credenziero*'s prime duty. He presided over an entire secondary kitchen staff whose responsibility was to arrange cold food in courses that began the banquet, and punctuated it by alternating with all the hot courses. Although this is never specified, it seems as if the *credenziero* was given cold leftovers from the day or evening before, items such as a cold capon or fish, which logically would have been first made by the cook. The bulk of items he prepared, however, were bought cheeses, olives, preserved meats and fish, salads both cooked and raw—everything we would consider antipasti or appetizers today. It also contained pies and pastries, and again, these may have been composed of leftovers. Recipes for pies and such almost always specify using cooked and cold meat, chicken, fish, and never, it seems, raw fresh ingredients. The importance of this type of service was that it could wait around for the hot courses or entertainments to conclude, so that there was never a halt in service.

It is not entirely clear whose responsibility the final fruit course and confections would be. There are clearly some dishes included there for which the cook is responsible, and there are recipes for these in all cook-books. On the other hand, by the end of the meal, most of the foods presented are cold conserves, fruits, and nuts, and would certainly fall under the purview of the *credenziero*. Obviously each court had its own particular arrangements. The Este court in Ferrara in Rossetti's time, for example, did not seem to employ a *credenziero* at all, though they did have a proliferation of other officials. The majority of authors consider this position essential, though.

Perhaps the most important job of the *credenziero* was designing and executing the sugar sculptures that graced every important banquet. His training was therefore primarily as a pastry chef and artist, rather than a cook. The most elegant arrangements meant to dazzle the eye were his domain. According to Frugoli, all the equipment necessary for decorating the credenza was his responsibility: plates and various vessels, some in the shape of eagles, lions, and other animals.[22] He would be expected to have a supply of spices and gold for gilding food, as well as alembics for preparing cordials and distilled drinks, not to mention a wide array of molds for cold gelatin presentations. It was the *credenziero* who prepared the majority of subtleties that were the central attraction of the banquet, and his skills clearly demanded that he be a skilled professional with extensive training.

The next official, and normally considered the most important beneath the *scalco* himself, was the *spenditore,* or buyer. There might be several of these in large households, shopping at different markets or for different types of provisions, or for ordinary versus extraordinary expenditures. Of the average courtly household, of the type Frugoli managed in Rome or later in Spain, we get a vivid picture of one man leaving every morning with his wicker basket, specially divided to keep separate the fish and meats from other goods.[23] Like other officials, he must be able to read and write, for he must coordinate the orders given to him throughout the house, for stocking the larder and for buying fresh food. His account book must also be arranged in distinct columns for inspection by the *scalco* or master of the household.[24] He is also given a certain amount of discretion in shopping, not only in choosing the best available produce but in buying certain rare items that happened to be available but were not thought of by the *scalco*. Thus the buyer has a definitive influence in the final form of the banquet and is the mediator between the farmers, butchers, and other vendors and those who prepare these goods.

Finally, among the upper echelon of the banquet staff there is the *dis-*

pensiero, the man in charge of keeping all provisions under lock and key, in fact two keys. Even he was not to be trusted, and when the larder was locked up it took another official to bring his own key and presumably watch while food and utensils were delved out.[25] His pantry contained not only all the dry goods and preserves but candles, plates, cups, cutlery, wine, absolutely everything necessary for dining. He would even keep fodder for the horses.[26] Like the other officials, he must also keep a strict account book so that the *scalco* can keep track of inventory and order fresh supplies when necessary. More important, he is in charge of guarding some of the most expensive objects owned in the court. The gold and silver vessels, which of course could serve as money in times of emergency, were in his care. He might thus be considered part banker and part stock supervisor. Almost of equal value were the spices and medicines placed in his trust.[27] This individual certainly has a major influence on the shape of the banquet because he apportioned the ingredients that would be used, but in some arrangements his job might be performed by the *scalco* or other official. Evitascandalo, for example, when describing the "officials" directly under the *scalco,* lists only three, without any *dispensiero.*

There were in some households a handful of other officials as well, the *bottigliero,* or wine steward, being perhaps the most common. Of course there was little choice of wine for individual diners apart from the few options that would be presented in each course. Rather than maintain the wine cellar, his primary function was to serve the wine with his own staff of pages, whose job it was to fetch cooled wine from a bucket, perhaps even iced, present the cup to the diner upon request, and then remove it. Not only were bottles not normally kept on the table, but even the cups were removed and washed after each drink. The pages were also charged with carrying water and towels for the elaborate hand washing that took place often at the start of a meal and definitely after the meal but before the confections. Once again, cleanliness was a major concern, even after forks would keep the diners' hands from being completely soiled. The most important job of the *bottigliero,* however, was actually mixing the wine with water, though as has been mentioned, sometimes a cup bearer would do this for the master separately. Within the wine steward's purview, therefore, is one of the major concerns among food authors in this period: the exact proportion of water to wine.[28] Should the wine be diluted a little, or should water predominate? Should the drinks be increasingly diluted as the evening wears on? What if one diner requests undiluted wine? What if someone has clearly trespassed his or her limit? In a sense, this official also serves as the sober bartender, a particularly important job when important officials are present in state functions.

In some courts there was a *canovaro,* or proper wine steward or cellar master, distinct from the wine server. In Ferrara, he was in charge of the wine barrels, pouring out whatever would be needed for each meal, as well as keeping a strict inventory of his holdings. Interestingly, Rossetti forbids him from eating in the wine cellar with his friends or pouring out wine without explicit permission. Presumably, for Rossetti to make special note of it, this occurred all the time.[29]

The other lesser officials would include a *panatiero* to supply bread, absolutely essential at every meal. His job is to measure the weight, number, and quality of breads served at each meal. He is not, however, a baker, but that someone was employed as such is evident from the presence of an official keeper of the granary, someone to hand out and measure flour whenever needed—the *Ufficiale delle Farine.*[30] Why this individual would be considered a high officer while the baker himself is not mentioned is not entirely clear. In smaller households, naturally, bread could be easily bought. Lastly, there was also an official hired merely to provision wood for the fires. As an essential part of the kitchen, as of course in the whole house in the colder months, he ranked among the middle cadre of the kitchen hierarchy.

Beneath all these officers there was the serving staff, often young nobles themselves being raised and trained in the household of a relative. This was a sure way to cement future bonds and networks of patronage. Such noble children in the household were kept apart from the kitchen boys who served as apprentices either in the kitchen, washing dishes, cleaning, or other jobs. They were obviously at the bottom of the staff hierarchy but could expect to move up the ranks over time with good performance and experience. But there is also ample indication that pages could become a major nuisance. Apart from joking around, stealing, or lying[31] (these after all were spoiled noble children, not hirelings), just getting them to perform their functions efficiently was difficult. Even when they presented or removed plates without spills or mishap, their presence could be annoying. Rabasco offers a little rhyme:

> Da Quattro cose Dio mi guardi, da servitor, che si riguara, da putta che s'affarda, da carne salata senza mostarda, e da picciol desinar che troppo tarda.[32]

> God save me from four things: a server who stares, a whore that puts on airs, no mustard with salted meat, a tiny dinner and a late seat.

It seems that this may be why many pages were told to keep behind the scenes when not needed; a bored boy can become a mischievous one. Of course in paintings depicting banquets they are always shown as perfect angels.

The stream of *scalco* literature continued unabated through the late seventeenth century, where this study ends. Two works in particular—Liberati's *Il Perfectto Maestro di Casa* of 1668 and the *A perfect School of Instructions for Officers of the Mouth,* as the title was translated from French (original 1676) by Giles Rose—deserve some attention for the way in which they exemplify the increasing bureaucratization and professionalization of courtly food management.

According to Rose, the demand for gentlemen to understand the art of management, carving, and linen folding had not changed in the past century. "It doth often fall out, that a man is put to the blush for shame that he doth not understand [carving and folding] . . .; and besides if any one hath a mind to serve in a great mans family, in the quality of a Master of the Household, or Steward, and is not well instructed what his charge is, but is ignorant, and to seek what to do; why, this Book will soon give him light in his business, how he shall behave himself in it."[33] What this suggests is that the managers were often not drawn from the ranks of kitchen or household staff, but that they moved into such service as a form of patronage, and had to learn the trade by reading rather than through apprenticeship or experience. Nonetheless, that this was considered a proper profession is evident from Rose's comments. The "officers" are divided somewhat differently in France now—there being a master as well as a carver, butler, confectioner, cook, and pastry chef. The master or steward has also begun to adopt a uniform, or at least a symbol of his profession: "le Maistre Hostel takes a clean Napkin, folded at length, but narrow, and throws it over his shoulder, remembering that this is the ordinary Mark, and particular sign and demonstration of his office."[34] In other words, there is an object intended to differentiate him from guests—even though he is still often a noble entitled to bear a sword and wear a hat, which he periodically doffs ceremoniously. But he still carries a badge of his station.

As for further specialization, apart from the carver, about which see in following passages, there was also a sommelier royale or butler in France and among the English who adopted this practice. His job is to set the table according to rigorous rules: to the right of each plate was a knife with the edge toward the plate, spoons with the brim downward, forks laid in straight lines but never crossed, bread on the plate, and the napkin on top.[35] Clearly the proliferation of regulations for cooking and serving reflected the rationalization of other sectors of classical culture at the end of the century.

Rather than the credenza officer as in earlier Italian texts, there is now a proper master confectioner. Just as sweets were increasingly marginalized to the end of meals, so too was this profession, although here he is still in charge of salads.[36] Apart from the professional specialization, what is perhaps most startling is the change in taste. Spices appear practically nowhere in the recipes. In fact, in a section where he has clearly borrowed some old recipes, Rose has absolutely no idea what "white powder" might be, and even a master French chef could not inform him.[37] The recipes are in fact from the *Livre fort excellent* of 1542, which makes them nearly 150 years old if not older. The point is, the cuisine had changed so dramatically that a recipe perhaps a century old had become unintelligible.

Although elite Italian cuisine did not undergo a comparable transformation, the increasing size, complexity, and specialization of the court appears to be similar. Liberati's work is actually directed toward the master of the household, in his case, papal. It thus contains much information that is not culinary in nature, but the proliferation of officers and increasingly ceremonial nature of service as well as its professionalization are much the same as with the French officers of the mouth. There is a strict chain of command descending from the major-domo, whose underlings as in an army must obey his supreme command without any contradiction.[38] Beneath him are various courtly officers: master of the chamber, master of the horse, master of the house, and down the line to the *scalco*. He governs these strictly by means of his "prerogative." Liberati's text is absolutely suffused with terminology taken from absolutist political theory.[39] There is also a superintendent general, an auditor, and a whole slew of specialized functionaries. For wine alone there is a wine steward, a cellar master, and servers. Furthermore, there is a *cuoco segreto,* or private chef, in a separate kitchen who cooks only for the prince. Though this was Scappi's title at the end of his life, there was no indication that such a person would never cook for other courtiers.[40] The *scalco* here, as before, still has charge of ensuring the healthful quality of the food served to the prince in consideration of his complexion as well as his personal taste.[41] He must also ensure that the food passes through as few hands as possible and that no strangers or even stray members of the household be allowed in the kitchen near food intended for the mouth of the prince. In any case, the officers have clearly multiplied, as have the basic kitchen staff and servers, but there remains one vital functionary.

Carving

Somewhat separate from this hierarchy, but absolutely essential to the entire banquet experience, was the *trinciante,* or carver. There were usually several, one for each table of four, six, or up to eight guests. These were nobles whose sole duty was to impress their peers with their feats of dexterous knife work. There is an entirely separate literature devoted only to carving, and it is clear that such men were normally not members of the household staff but rather peers who considered it an honor and privilege to carve at the table of one of their superiors. There are many suggestions, however, that this position too transformed from a courtier who took on the job of carving to yet another officer of the mouth.

The art of carving was nothing new in the early modern period. There were carving guides written long before the sixteenth century. The Spanish *Arte cisoria,* written in 1423 (though not published until the eighteenth century), is one example, and the Italian physician Michele Savonarola also wrote a carving book *De modis incendi.*[42] Wynkyn de Worde's *The Boke of Kervynge* is another English example published right at the start of the early modern era. Judging by the latter, the art was not yet highly refined, though, as the author insists that no more than two fingers and a thumb should be used to hold the fish, meat, or fowl while carving. This is not to suggest it was not dainty, and there is considerable care taken to cut and present crustless bread trenchers without touching them after carving.[43] The author also warns not to touch venison with the hand when slicing it for service—but most items are indeed held, not steadied with a fork.[44]

On the Continent, however, the customs had begun to change by the early sixteenth century, most dramatically in the carving of food perched on a fork in midair. Polyonimus Syngraphaeus in his book *Schola Apiciana,* printed in Frankfurt in 1535, describes the latest fashion for carving with the meat lifted high, and how delicate slices are let fall onto a plate. This is done merely for pleasure rather than necessity. "And this practice is common among some gentlemen . . . among the Germans today however they plainly act to the contrary."[45]

The carving tradition is in no way the invention of the late-Renaissance court. But it is here and especially in Italy that the art achieved its most elaborate form, and here that the carving literature proliferated. The most compendious text is without doubt Vincenzo Cervio's *Il Trinciante* of 1581, which was expanded in 1593 by the cavalier Fusoritto de Narni. Not only is every imaginable food item now carved before service, but the tools of trade are explicitly described, another measure of professionalization. Michel Jeanneret has suggested that skilled precision with a blade both here and in fencing were merely two sides of the same activity.[46] Here the carver is also exalted as the most trusted servant in the noble household. Ideally he is a noble, but the possibility that someone merely from a good family could also get the job suggests that it could be considered as just that, a full-time and permanent occupation.[47] Cervio insists that he must also be wealthy enough to be well dressed—and clearly buys his own attire, has servants, and his own horses. Again, the ideal at this point is that the carver be a wealthy noble at court, but the position is still considered a "profession."[48]

The true carver—as opposed to the many mere butchers Cervio has seen in various courts and those who carve out of sight, which he considers shameful—must perform his feats of carving *in aria* so that the difficulty and conquest of it is plainly exhibited to all present. This goes for large roasts as well as the tiniest little birds, fruits, and even eggs. Elsewhere in Europe, apparently, they were not as dexterous as at the Roman court, where the long fork and knife were used, though Cervio also contends that different cutlery is appropriate for different foods, too.[49] His specific directions are astoundingly precise, and there are even illustrations of tools, including a bone saw and hollow awl-like device for removing marrow. The long-handled egg-holder is perhaps the most bizarre.

The specific directions Cervio gives for carving individual items are absurdly detailed, and it seems impossible that anyone could actually follow his directions—especially with knife in hand. The instructions for carving a peacock take up five full pages and rival even the most precise anatomical texts of the era. The carver must of course be intimately acquainted with animal anatomy, absolutely expert with a knife and fork, as well as physically strong. Although some large animals are partially cut up before lifting into the air, whole roasts, no less than eight pounds, and often probably considerably heavier, are held up on fork prongs while carving. This seems to be a real concern for Cervio. In his entry for leg of wild boar he expresses concern that a young animal will be easy to carve, but a mature one will probably be just about the limit that can be handled.[50]

The carver was not merely someone who carves, though. He was the direct intermediary between the food and the diner. He disassembles the grand presentations into smaller portions and performs the same function as a waiter in a restaurant with tableside service, attending to the needs of each individual, even though the *scalco* actually serves the food. Cervio will even have him remain tableside to attend to his master rather than disappear after carving. There is also a separate carver for each table, and Cervio prefers that each attend to no more than six guests. In the entry for carving peacock, the carver prepares six separate platters in succession, each containing a portion of the choicest parts—a few thin slices of breast meat, a wing portion, sliced thigh, and so forth.[51] He is also expected, after attending to the master first, to keep filling plates wherever there is a need, and it appears that the intention was to keep the entire table filled with dishes at all times. There were, of course, several different foods within each course, so each diner had a vast array to choose from. The carver also sees to seasoning each plate with a bit of salt balanced on the tip of his blade, and also makes sure sauce is evenly distributed from the larger platter to the individual plates. That is, not only roasts were carved up, but any large whole food, as it was considered unseemly for guests to labor at cutting anything. To be noble is to have someone cut for you.

The carver also works through every course, from the credenza straight through the final fruit course, getting a break only between settings when the tables are cleared. His constant presence, as well as performance, no doubt served as a form of personal advertisement to those nobles present who might be useful in obtaining favors or patronage. His courtesy toward guests also advertised the power and personnel of the host, because on demand the carver would also be expert with a sword. It is almost as if the threat could be construed as explicit—this man is now carving out a turkey's gizzard, but tomorrow it could be yours if you cross me.

The practical skills of the carver are extremely extensive, as it seems most food emerges from the kitchen whole and is carved in the dining space. This includes tiny birds as well as prosciutto, salami, and bologna sausages, which are one of the few items he concedes must be carved resting in a platter. He also portions out boiled meats and soups or pottages with large contents. Pies too arrive in the dining hall uncut, but he seems to have little interest in these, as there are no skills to show off. Just be sure to give the most attractive and best cooked parts to your master, Cervio advises.[52] The carver also dissects fish, shucks oysters, and cleans crabs,[53] but his comments on fruit are the most interesting. Melons are, according to Italians, and when in season, the best fruit to eat. To carve them you start with a small fork and knife. The melon is first peeled in midair. What comes to mind, so often depicted in still life paintings, are the elegant spirals of whole peel that have been arrested in the middle of the procedure. A few slices are removed, the seeds discarded, and then the remainder carved into thin wedges. There are other methods as well.[54] Other "fruits" are also carved: apples and pears, even artichokes.

The addition to the text by Fusoritto da Narni contains some banquet menus, more directions for carving, but also some practical hints for the novice carver. "Be sure not to scratch your head, nor your beard, nor pick your nose, ears nor similar things, because all are nauseating and it will greatly displease the Lord to see such things."[55] The necessity of such advice perhaps suggests that not all would-be carvers understood the finer points, or practically anything, about service. There are also directions concerning wiping the platters with a napkin, and covering unseemly food parts. These comments suggest that even if carvers did not yet understand such things, they were nonetheless expected by the nobility.

The demand for carving books was not apparently met by Cervio's treatise, because several more followed in the coming years. Cesare Evitascandalo's dialogue on the carver, though written much earlier, was published in 1609. It also offers detailed instructions in a format designed to replicate the kinds of conversation that might take place between the novice and seasoned carver. The author's comments to the reader also indicate that carving had become something over-affected and ridiculous. He insists that decorum and poise is required and absolutely rejects the nonsense performed by charlatans and buffoons with a knife. Clearly in some courts, carving became a source of entertainment. It is also made absolutely certain that carving is a serious and "honored profession" rather than a casual sideline.

His particular advice about the carver's qualifications is similar to Cervio's. He should be old enough to keep a whole turkey aloft without obvious strain and sweating, but not a gray beard either.[56] He should also be properly proportioned physically, with graceful legs, big but not a giant. He should be able to stand still without moving his head or shifting his weight back and forth, nor should he speak unless posed a question.[57] He should be dressed well, but preferably in black or another somber color, not in red or yellow like a buffoon.[58] He should also bathe in perfumed waters; even though effeminate, it is allowed for the carver. Presumably, strong odors were seen as enhancing the dining experience rather than detracting from it.

The dialogue touches on the finer points of equipment, the different sizes of knives and forks appropriate for various animals, and how to clean them and keep them sharp, revealing a trick used by soldiers. The blades are stored in powdered lime or bran to prevent them from becoming dull.[59] In Scappi's description of the ray, we also learn that its skin was used by sword makers and other artisans to keep blade edges razor sharp.[60] Evitascandalo also discusses the polite way to serve and the ceremonies to be observed, believing that the tasting (credenza) done by the *scalco* is probably more for ceremony and to observe ancient usage than for real fear of poisoning. That possibility is not entirely ruled out, though tasting is often done in the kitchen.[61] The speakers then rehearse the details of service, how it is impolite to toss the food, how the plates should be filled and presented and properly dusted with salt.

The bulk of Evitascandalo's book recounts the proper way to carve every sort of food down to the tiniest truffle, but it appears that such detailed verbal instructions were not clear enough for the reading public. Carving books that followed were often illustrated, showing numbered steps for each incision. They are designed specifically with the professional in mind. Mattia Giegher's *Tre Trattati* of 1639 is typical of the development of this genre, offering step-by-step illustrations of how to pleat napkins, how to arrange plates and service paraphernalia, and most important, visual steps for carving. There is less amusing banter for courtiers and more practical guidance. The shape of the book itself, a long rectangular manual that will not topple if stood upright, suggests that this would be used by a working carver for practice. Giegher himself, working for the college of Germans in Padua for more than thirty years, is a good example of increasing professionalization. The illustrations are in fact much easier to follow than those in earlier texts, showing the exact placement of the fork, and the precise order in which each slice should be executed. For example, carving a turkey shows twenty-one separate steps, beginning with the neck and wings, on to the thighs, and proceeding to the breast meat and other parts.[62] Fruits are also carved into spirals, zig-zagged sections, puzzle-like presentations, and even in the form of a bird.[63]

A similar, if less detailed, carving book appeared in France a few years later, Jacques Vonlett's *La vraye mettode de bien trencher tant à l'Italienne qu'à la main* ... (1647). The title shows that both the Italian and variant modes were becoming fashionable. There is not much text and the illustrations appear to be pirated, but it at least shows that there was a market for this literature in France, and that there were local carving traditions in place as well. The turkey, for example, he says can be carved on a plate rather than in the air, and rather than broad slices, he makes one large cut down the breast and then cuts it into long, squared strips.[64]

The genre achieved further diffusion in the officers of the mouth text that appeared in France and was then translated into English in the 1680s. Although much is no doubt borrowed from earlier texts, there are extremely interesting details here regarding the carver. With napkin on left shoulder, he uncovers the meat, offers a slice of bread, and begins with boiled meats, proceeding through ragouts, stews, and finally the baked game, fowl, fish, and pies. He must not forget to place salt on each plate, as well.[65] The practical difficulties of having a standing officer to carve are made apparent by his comments that at weddings where there are many tables, if no carver is present, a gentleman should offer to serve the ladies and then sit down again. He believes this is not so "handsome or decent," but it shows that this was an art all gentlemen should be called upon to perform if necessary. The various Italian, German, and other ways to carve are here too illustrated. The turkey can be carved in two fashions, "either upon your Fork held up, or else lying in the Dish, as 'tis easie seen by the figure."[66] Each plate is given a portion of each section, and the preferred breast meat divided as the carver thinks best.

The art of carving had been disseminated in print nearly everywhere by the end of the seventeenth century. It became a central part of the dining ceremony, and as such, professionals armed with their instructional manuals joined the ranks of courtly officers. It is a good example of how nobles gained access to patronage networks and earned gainful employ at a time when military service was itself transforming into a professional occupation. It is also interesting that table-side carving is one of the last and vanishing remnants of fine dining in expensive restaurants, being replaced by plated food that has been prearranged in the kitchen. Ironically, it is also one of the few ceremonial acts still performed by the male head of the household in celebrations like Thanksgiving, a rudiment of this once noble art.

CHAPTER 10

Condemnation

The Sinister Side of Riotous Luxury

Nearly as quickly as cookbooks and banquet manuals were published, various kinds of writing proliferated condemning the eating practices of elites. Although ostensibly targeted at courtiers and their excesses with the intention of reforming them, these works would most likely have appealed to the kinds of people who would not be offended by the comments. What ruler wants to hear that his lavish display of wealth and power will ultimately mean the loss of his soul, health, or royal coffers? Apart from the select abstemious or parsimonious among them, few elites would have been interested in the literature condemning banquets. These works were generally written by and intended for people who are just outside the halls of power, but have direct glimpses of it. That is, these were either social aspirants chiding the behaviors of those whose ranks they wished to infiltrate—and their writings do sometimes smack of envy—or they are professionals, criticizing the behavior from one or several different angles.

Such works can be easily classified into separate categories. There are the moralistic Christian diatribes with a venerable history, mostly written by churchmen or those interested in public morality. By the early modern period there had amassed a significant body of literature against gluttony and drunkenness. These, critics argued, were deadly sins, likely to earn the indulgent a place in hell, perhaps not among the vilest of sinners, but if the late-medieval paintings of gluttons' eternal punishment is any indication, not a situation to be savored. In most depictions, the damned become food themselves, torn apart and devoured for eternity by a host of fiendish and sometimes perfectly preposterous demons. Like the paintings, the moralistic tracts aimed primarily at frightening people into frugality. Presumably, the illiterate masses would have rarely had the opportunity to eat in any lavish way, with the exception of holy feasts and carnival. Thus this literature was probably directed toward those with some expendable income, the moderately well-off family that can afford to live a little high on the hog year-round. Significantly, and quite unlike the classical ethical literature that stressed moderation in all things, the Christian tradition promoted asceticism and rigorous denial of sustenance as among the highest goal the holy person can achieve. To deny the body food is to purify the spirit, and only total self-destruction could be considered sinful.

By the early modern period this kind of literature was still being published and new works still written, but the classical emphasis on restraint and moderation was beginning to make serious headway, especially with the growth of humanism. Like the cleric, the humanist was also interested in curbing gluttonous appetites, but found that scare tactics were either going unheeded or had become comical. They turned more readily to satire, exposing the fictional glutton to the censure of readers through ribaldry. This had the effect of forcing self-examination. Because many of these works were written or translated into the vernacular, we must suppose not only a literate audience but those with at least enough income to be able to gorge themselves frequently. Apart from the restrained courtier, the humanist satires would have appealed first to academic types, not necessarily those with power but frequently close to it. Many of these texts also pose as histories of eating practices in ancient times, but in their descriptions of classical excess become warnings for their own era, headed on the same path of ruin. One might even consider the publication of Apicius in this light. There is no indication that ancient Roman cookery had any influence on the early modern in any way whatsoever. But Apicius, whom they took to be an actual historical figure, was always upheld as the prime example of gustatory excess. His cookbook, replete with flamingo tongue recipes and the like, was derided, not imitated. If the casual similarity to current banquets struck the reader, then the moral lesson hit home. Like Apicius, all gluttons end in ruin, in this case financial and suicidal.

The learned humanistic tracts promoting sobriety and moderation range from these fairly straightforward criticisms to those that are much more difficult to interpret, primarily because though they appear to have moralistic goals, they lavish so much attention on the grotesque, which becomes entertaining in itself, that it ceases to function as satire. In other words, Rabelais's *Gargantua and Pantagruel* is so absurdly excessive that no one could ever consider it a statement of real human practices. These are not humans, after all, and no human could ever compare his or her own behavior to the prodigious gluttony of these giants drinking gallons of wine, munching on whole oxen, tripe, sausages, and so forth. Gluttony here becomes comical but no longer satirical. Of course, the work is still a satire of various other genres, the heroic and epic especially, but it never gets the reader to wonder if his own behavior is gluttonous. The same can be said of Teofilo Folengo's *Baldus,* not really critical of anything, it seems, but a vast epic brimming with noodles and culinary tropes, and written in a perverse language not coincidentally called macaronic. The kreogyric, meat-induced encomia and mock-heroic poems like *In Praise of Sausages* by writers like Firenzuola and Berni function the same way. Although learned and witty, they seem to have abandoned any moralistic intention entirely. If anything, they actually flout it, usually praising those foods considered unhealthy by physicians and clerics.

Lastly, there is the vast medical literature against eating without rule or reason, at all times of day, or combining mutually antagonistic ingredients in deranged jumbles that can only subvert the entire system. A feature of early modern dietary literature from roughly the early sixteenth century onward is a persistent attack of courtly dining habits. These works were not merely fulminating against excess, but against disregard for the correct balancing of one's constitution, disregard for factors such as age, sex, and season, and almost complete disdain for eating foods digestible by delicate aristocratic frames. They were definitely written by outsiders who both understood courtly dining and had a vested interest in bringing about its destruction. With very few exceptions medical writers considered human health and gastronomy to be irreconcilable enemies. Despite Platina's valiant effort to speak of pleasure and health in one book, the first printed cookbook does a poor job of reconciling these two camps. The recipes of Martino are not written with health in mind, and Platina often had to remind his readers how unhealthy the dishes actually are. Domenico Romoli devoted half of his book to health issues, but these are conspicuously separate and relay information of a very different nature from the culinary sections. In cookbooks with special sections for convalescents—even Scappi contains one—there is practically no way to identify why such recipes are included, apart from the fact that they were considered "lighter" and more digestible. There is no indication that Scappi was familiar with the dietary literature at all. In the end, every pastry recipe, every exotic new way to stimulate the appetite and entice eager diners to excess, physicians considered an affront to their knowledge and experience. By the early modern period, medicine and cuisine were antagonistic topics.

Rather than recount the many ways clergymen, academics, and physicians loathed aristocratic dining, this chapter will mine their comments for details that are absent from the culinary literature. In other words, physicians, for example, reveal far more details about customs they considered reprehensible than any cookbook would. It is also information of a very different nature. Rather than merely prescriptive—cook this or serve this in this fashion—it is descriptive: do not eat as these people do, thus getting us perhaps one step closer to actual practice. Keeping in mind that all authors tend to exaggerate acts they hope to eradicate, negative comments are still useful in reconstructing a picture of elite dining in these centuries.

In practice, the majority of authors employ an admixture of Christian and classical criticisms of banquets, as they also often make use of medical arguments. Particularly for those works that are solely about banquets, the authors were willing to use any ammunition at hand. Such are works like Rudolph Goclenius's *De luxu conviviali nostri seculi ganeae artificibus, origine, auctoribus et asseclis,* published in Marburg in 1607. The title deserves comment. It translates as *On Luxurious Banquets* (though the classical term *convivial* is evoked here) of our times, and the makers, origins, inventors, and fans of gourmet foods. The word *ganea* originally denoted a rowdy, low-class eatery, and in some classical authors was equated with tavern food or take-out. The connotation by the early modern period, though, is precisely the same as that conjured by the word *gourmet*— snobbery, expense, pretension. In other words, this book is all about the stuff one should not eat. Goclenius was both a medical doctor and an academic pundit of sorts, and like many of these works his does not fall neatly into any one genre. It is written as an oration, so the rhetorical style can overflow with thundering phrases such as monstrous gluttony (*monstrificas helluatione*) and insane drunkenness (*ebriatate insanientium*) that somehow sound more frightening in Latin. Like most, he begins with descriptions of pristine simplicity and how humans became inured to excess in "our own era," which extends from classical times to the present.

He also insists, however, that there are pockets throughout Europe where people retain many of their original eating customs. Some people are practically wild, especially in the north of Germany, and many among the English. As a sign of this, he notes that they still bake large animals in pies, such as sheep and oxen.[1] What this suggests is that despite the occasional appearance of such items in early modern cookbooks, they might easily be considered backward and outdated. They are, of course, vestiges of medieval cookery.

Similarly revealing of early modern taste, Goclenius explains that the ancient Romans consumed very little meat, and so it is today among Italians who eat mostly herbs and vegetables—both cooked and raw.[2] He notes that they always start a meal with salad, and in summer sometimes eat just that—perhaps only of melons with some bread. Obviously, from his German standpoint this was rather extraordinary, but it provides a glimpse at what were considered standard practices, and in many instances confirms what is found in the culinary literature. For example, Goclenius says that Italians favor veal above anything else, but they will hardly ever touch mutton.[3] The French place perfectly absurd ingredients among their delicacies, like snails, frogs, and turtles.[4] He also repeats the standard food marvels of the day—food prohibitions among Jews and Hindus, the *astomoi* who live on odors alone without any food, and, most strange of all, New World inhabitants who make bread from odd roots like yucca.[5]

It is when commenting on the ancients, though, specifically Apicius, that he describes banqueting practices in his own day in greatest detail. Goclenius specifically mentions the sugar confections that appear in banquets and everything that comes under the category of *bellaria,* which means pastries and sweets that are brought out "more to be pondered than eaten."[6] This might be taken to mean that they were not necessarily eaten, nor perhaps even edible. While gums that solidified these structures were safe, the paint used in sugar sculpture may have rendered them inedible. Because the banquet menus do not describe how or if such scenes could be divided or eaten, this text offers a suggestion that they were not. A physician in the Netherlands, Ludovicus Nonnius, says that even the famous peacocks served in their feathers, though they really only appear in solemn banquets, are there more to please the eye than satisfy the appetite.[7]

Despite this, nobles did in Goclenius's estimation get fed, all too well. Their banquets outdo even those of ancient rulers, many of whom led sober and frugal lives. In comparison, the moderns are addicted to luxury. Some bear turgid swollen bellies of such size that "for many years they are not able to think about their private parts."[8] Moreover, some drink so much that their bodies grow effeminate and soft. Even women drink nowadays, many disguising the smell of alcohol on their breaths by eating anise comfits or fennel and coriander to cunningly fool their husbands or paramours.[9] This adds a whole new meaning to the use of spices at the end of the meal. As for the strange distilled concoctions meant to extend life, which combine wine with gold, silver, or mercury, Goclenius knows full well the real damage they do to human health, causing tremors, ruptures of the viscera, and a horrible wasting away.[10]

Perhaps as a direct observer of prodigious banquets, or treating patients who suffered from them, Goclenius concludes that it is precisely the luxurious profusion, intemperate drinking, and delicacies dreamed up by inventive chefs that ruins Christians' health and wastes their fortunes.[11] Not only that, but stuffed and drunk, people somehow believe they can be witty or conduct serious philosophical conversations, when in fact they say and often do the most imprudent and obscene things.[12]

Satires

There are some forms of satire with clear moralistic messages that are actually about totally different topics but are couched in the language of food, and therefore indirectly reveal information about elite dining. Pierre Viret's *Satyres Chrestiennes de la Cuisine Papal* (1560) is one such diatribe, a rabid piece of Protestant propaganda that equates the Roman Catholic Church with an elite banquet; priests are the chefs pandering to diners with their subtly disguised and venomous cuisine. The most remarkable thing is that the work is in verse and is padded with both French and Latin notes explaining the references. Viret also knew a great deal about cooking, remarking that Apicius and Taillevent knew nothing about the topic, and though there may be an honest man among them, such as Platina, they never served his cooking in Rome.

> I'en scay un de mon cousinage,
> Bon garcon, nommé Platina,
> Mais quoy qui'il die, plat il n'a
> Des viands de Cour de Rome
>
> I know one much like me
> A good fellow named Platina
> But what he said, they never plated up
> Among the foods of the Roman court[13]

Ironically, Viret is mistaken about that; Scappi served many dishes that were much like Martino's, found in Platina's *De honesta voluptate* in the previous century. What he probably meant, though, is that the cuisine was never tempered by good medical advice. The satire also points to the fact that Catholic theology, in his opinion like cookery, is a jumble of incongruous elements, disguised as something healthful but actually highly toxic. Equally in both, there is no consideration of cost. In this cuisine nothing is valued unless it is mixed up in a tart with expensive ingredients—a well-aimed critique. Worst of all, this cooking style spread from Rome to France and all of Europe, an interesting indication that at least one author saw both theology and culinary style traveling in that direction.[14]

Condem-nation

The most interesting of these satires concerns the kitchen and serving staff. Every rank in the ecclesiastical hierarchy is equated with an officer of the mouth. Augustinians scour the fields for anything to fry, Jacobins gather onions, and every monastic order takes bribes of andouilles to flavor their bouillon. The most delicate meats are brought in by cardinals, while theologians of the Sorbonne carefully turn the roast so it will not burn. Inquisitors are the ultimate gourmands: "Les gran-gousiers Inquisiteurs/De la foy, sont conquisiteurs."[15] The word *foy* here makes these both conquerors of liver and faith, a marvelous double entendre. Like chefs, clerics are always seeking new inventions, new combinations of the finest ingredients, "inventors of new broths" to satisfy their gullets. In the end, naturally, it is the pope's insatiable hunger that figuratively and literally devours his flocks, and the art the pope employs to enthrall his minions, Viret calls *gastrology*.[16]

The fourth satire equates kitchen utensils and serving dishes with the liturgical paraphernalia of the church: bells become cauldrons, napkins become vestry cloths, and an infinity of roasting irons becomes other instruments of the mass. The irony is made only more poignant when one realizes that the mass, *mensa,* means meal.[17] In the description of a papal banquet that follows, there is candlelight, washing of hands, the ceremonious entry of the salt, followed by white bread, wine, and soups. Then the next part of the "service" includes salads, apricots, and plums. Then follow various dishes such as veal liver, chickens in green sauce, roasted morsels, delicate wildfowl, sausages of every kind, hashes and *saupiquets, civets, porrets,* and *hoschepets.* Only at the end follow the vegetables, gilded turnip soup, and cabbage in pepper sauce. Naturally, spices flavor the entire the meal. Toward the end there is a fruit course of melons, olives, and artichokes, and to finish, dessert of fruit conserves and confections.[18] Every dish is equated with some part of the liturgy, and regarding the culmination, eating the body of Christ, he says, "Que pour vostre dernier renfort/Vous manger dieu comme un refort." For your last provision, you eat god like a radish.[19]

It is obvious that Viret has seen both banquets and masses and understands the structure, progression, and intricate details of both. He has no trouble equating the two, both in their lavish display, waste, and ability to dazzle spectators with theatrics. When Viret was writing this, the Council of Trent was reconfirming the theatricality of the mass, the importance of music, brilliant sights, and heady aromas in an attempt to win back believers. Viret sometimes explains these connections in the notes. This points to the fact that, the satirical intent of this piece notwithstanding, the closest relative to elite banquets in both form and function was indeed the mass after the Catholic Reformation.

The dazzling nature of banquets is captured in another work critical of elite cookery. It is one of the densest, most obscurely Latinate texts imaginable, and appears to be modeled after the *Hypnerotomachia Poliphili* (which itself contains some interesting banquet scenes). This too is in the form of a dream and is entitled *Comus sive Phagesiposia cimmeria somnium*—meaning the dream of a banquet thrown by Comus, the quintessential glutton. The author, Eyricius Puteanus, was a professor at Louvain whose vernacular name was Nicholas Pelloquin.[20] Apart from typical denunciations against luxury, there emerge some fascinating details the author apparently found revolting—not only the gems and perfumes and potable gold that one finds in a banquet, but the preposterous picking of teeth with silver toothpicks and generally effeminate behavior.[21] But it is the synaesthetic nature of banquets that he seems to find most deranged. Food is prepared not only for taste but for the eyes, and "very little do we eat: as if the throat alone can not capture gluttony, but we eat even with the eyes, and in the eyes is the gullet."[22] This suggests not only that the spectacle of food was perhaps of even greater importance that its taste, but that much of it was not actually eaten. The volume of dishes alone would suggest this, but here we have confirmation, particularly with dishes like swans replaced in their feathers and posed with Leda, or brightly colored foods in which gold and silver have been extravagantly swathed.[23] With these it is the ravishment of the senses, the fuliginous perfumes, the mesmerizing sound of fountains. The banquet itself, like a dream, mesmerizes the participants into a kind of stupor.

Although the details are infuriatingly difficult, there does not appear to be a great deal that discusses cuisine specifically, but rather the overall effect and dangers of banqueting. Puteanus is thus fairly typical of the academic author outside the social circles who would normally frequent grand dinners, and represents a distinct ideological position when it comes to food. Whereas rulers and their servants understood the value of grandeur and spectacle as propaganda, the learned critic sees only fortunes and health squandered for a night's fleeting amusement.

Another earlier work of this ilk, actually mostly a collection of works about banquets and carving, was published in 1534 under the title *Schola Apiciana,* by an author with the equally Latinate name Polyonimus Syngrapheus. Although some of the works included are purely culinary, the general tone makes clear that the whole is gently critical of contemporary banquets, and contrasts them with more sober affairs among the ancients. The title, perhaps suggested by the publisher, was from the very start explained—this will not offer recipes of Apician *popinae* (restaurant fare) but instructions for conducting a proper convivium according to both moral and medicinal dictates. Apicius was nothing but a glutton, and should not be imitated today. Rather the ideal meal should be small and intimate, among friends who bear no animosity, display no pride or envy, and come to the table as equals.[24] Clearly this was meant to contrast directly with the hierarchical and competitive nature of most courtly banquets.

The selections included to support this position come from some of the most revered humanist authors of the preceding generation: Giovanni Pontano's *De conviventia,* a tract against overindulgence replete with frugal classical examples to compare with the present, and also Erasmus's *Convivatoris officiis,* on the duties of banquet-goers, a pleasant dialogue advising readers not to drink unless they are thirsty, not to eat beyond repletion. The importance of these, again, is that they pose a rival aesthetic infused with an approach to food revived from ancient times and embodied in the simple symposium. They at once criticize elite banquets while standing just outside the door, offering an alternative to the meal as power play.

Through the sixteenth and seventeenth centuries, as humanist scholarship matured and traversed broader subjects, there emerged a number of food histories that recounted meticulous details of dining among the ancients. Though not directly about the early modern period, the authors sometimes added remarks about the present. Even tacitly, the deranged stories of Heliogabalus, Lucullus, Apicius, and the entire troupe of ancient gourmands was meant to be a warning to modern diners. All these men, and ancient civilization itself, were ruined by lavish eating and drinking. From the tomes of Stuckius, Jules Cesar Boulenger, Pedro Chacon (Ciacconius), and again Puteanus, the scholar could find models of both classical moderation as well as grotesque abandon, similar in these authors' minds to the feasts preoccupying European courts in their own day.[25]

Janus Cornarius (Hagenbut), a medical humanist and translator from Zwickau, Germany, in his *De conviviorum* of 1548, was among the few to make explicit comparisons between ancient and modern eating habits. For example, he mentions that although hops were known by Pliny, the ancients did not use them to clarify beer, as is done in the region of Hamburg.[26] He also compares the various drinking customs of peoples ancient and modern, and even mentions German drinking games, music, and typical stories told.[27] Naturally, the humanist prefers the pristine ancient forms, but in any case shows that topics dealing with cuisine, feasting, and drinking are sometimes discussed in unexpected places and often provide a counterpoint to the purely culinary literature.

Medicine

Without doubt the most explicit condemnations of elite dining are found in medical literature, both dietary manuals and general works about the qualities of food. Not only do they routinely identify ingredients that were associated with nobility, and they are remarkably consistent about these throughout Europe during the sixteenth and seventeenth centuries, but they also criticized specific fashions they considered injurious to health. Medical authors were unanimous in deriding the apparent lack of any order in sumptuous feasts, combining meat and fish in the same course, dairy products and ingredients of such wildly contrasting qualities and textures that they must totally subvert the human body. The very length of the average banquet, the apparent disregard for proper meal times, and of course the sheer volume, all gave these writers ample fuel for their tirades. Without lingering on the medical logic of their disquisitions,[28] more relevant for this discussion are the practices they mention that are generally unexplained in the culinary literature. For example, though the banquet books might mention that ice should be on hand for the *bottigliere,* it is only in the controversies among medical authors that we find the practice of cooling wine with ice or snow explicitly described and usually condemned.

The physicians, particularly in the latter sixteenth and seventeenth centuries, vigorously associate certain ingredients with nobles. In general, their opinions confirm the preferences found in cookbooks, although in some cases they seem to be ignorant of the latest fashions. Sometimes their criticisms seem directed at medieval cuisine and their stereotypical image of it rather than the innovative recipes current at court. It may also be that eating habits among all nobles were not quite as novel as some of the cookbooks suggest. For example, the Englishman Thomas Cogan knows well the universal courtly popularity for wildfowl. Pheasants are "a meat for Princes and greate estates." Poor scholars, who make up his audience, enjoy it only when they can get it, presumably rarely. Along with partridges, the great toil expended to catch these with hawks is no marvel because "every morsel (is) worth golde." He even knows how such fowl should be prepared; woodcocks and pigeons are stuffed with grapes as "cunning cookes have devised."[29] He understands too the value of porpoise and sturgeon, which for rarity alone "they bee esteemed of great estates."[30] The latter would remain popular, and in London a "feast royall" typically ended with sturgeon. Cookbooks had for the most part abandoned porpoise, though. This may have been a simple matter of nearly complete disappearance in European waters, but Cogan's countryman Thomas Moffett does concur that porpoise is an unsavory meat, "yet many Ladies and Gentlemen love it exceedingly, bak't like venison."[31] This may serve as a caveat that cookbooks do not necessarily reflect common customs that may be far more traditional.

Cogan also has some bitter words to say about gluttonous customs among nobles of his day, especially when they "prolong the time in eating two or three hours, with talking and telling of tales, as our manner is here in England at great feasts."[32] He also condemns eating many different kinds of food in one sitting, which was a standard complaint among medical writers. His comments on wine are also revealing: for breakfast a draught of strong wine with toast dipped in is in the "manner of noble men."[33] Interestingly, many people think it "princelike" to drink a lot after a meal,[34] but Cogan insists, "in our time, for that ryotousenes, and pleasure are growen to the fill, and infinit number are troubled with the gowt, for some never exercise themselves, and drink strong wines next their heart, and use immoderate lust."[35] At the very least this reveals the darker consequences of luxurious living, but it also shows that nobles drank alcohol for supposedly medicinal purposes—the phrase "next their heart" means as a cordial. That he then gives recipes for aqua vitae and the like is a bit surprising, but this does confirm many of the fashions prescribed in the culinary literature.

Jean Bruyerin-Champier rails against the use of condiments invented by ingenious gluttons, calling all cuisine a kind of adultery, but he considers this art merely the "heaping together of flavors," which seems more characteristic of earlier cookery.[36] He traces the practice of bifurcuition—cooking meat in two separate media, in this case boiling meat first before roasting over coals—back to ancient times, and confirms that it is still done among Frenchmen to make "carbonarias." This too, by the evidence of cookbooks, was becoming outdated. Roasting ducks cut up rather than whole, which even courtiers do, he believes is less a matter of style than a practical solution to quickly feeding unexpected guests. They also can be mixed into composed dishes that way, and become tender more quickly.[37] This is a thought-provoking hypothesis, especially considering the time it takes to roast a whole duck. It may indeed explain the culinary fashion.

Early in the next century, Joseph Duchesne, physician to Henry IV and evidently quite familiar with courtly habits, nonetheless denounces them. Today, people eat "without rule and measure, meat after meat, and we try to only please our tongue and palate with delicacies (which we know are very expensive). Nor are we content to heap plate on plate, meat on meat, but it is also necessary to have many diverse salads, many diverse fruits both cooked and raw, as appetizers and desserts. So many strong flavors, such a diversity of fish, and different types of salted meats, unsalted, boiled, roasted, to which we can add infinite pastries and baked goods."[38] Like the moralists, he would prefer we lived as our ancient forebears on bread, milk, and honey, perhaps some herbs and fruits. We would live much longer and be happier if we did.

An Italian Protestant exiled in Switzerland, Gulielmo Grataroli, is of much the same sentiment. Many leisured people "addict themselves to voluptuosnes and bellychere, to wallow in their disordered and lascivious appetites, tendryng and cockeryng their wanton carkases . . . [like] a great many Princes and Potentates."[39] These comments are typical of the entire dietary genre, especially among Puritanically minded authors. They reveal not only the consequences of extravagant banquets but how they were perceived or interpreted by those lower down the social ladder. Thomas Moffett explains the strange effect of eating through the night: "it is day with them as it is night with us, so courtiers and Princes eat when others sleep: and again (perverting the order of nature, and setting as it were the Sun to school) sleep out the sweetest part of the day, where in others eat and work."[40]

Giorgius Pictorius's dialogues on maintaining health put common attitudes toward courtiers in a humorous light. One character named Poligolo starts ranting against courtiers' eating every imaginable food in abundance, mixing flesh and fish, and persisting despite their becoming sick. His interlocutor Teofrasto comments that he knows their customs so well, perhaps he has eaten with them, to which he replies: no, I just happened to be nearby in a tavern and noticed that they eat like pigs, others like dogs, lions, or asses. At the royal court there are a great multitude of drunks as well.[41] Being accused of partaking in such antics seems to have been a real concern, and Poligolo had to distance himself from courtly behaviors as an outside observer, which of course the majority of these physicians were.

Not all physicians were entirely critical of the court. Those perhaps too close to rulers and in their direct employment would have found it harder to be so. Giovanni Ludovico Bertaldi, working for the Duke of Savoy, is a good example. Bertaldi essentially stuck annotations of his own onto an older dietary work, but they are in effect separate works. He reveals many courtly customs of the time without really offering his opinion on them. For example, he mentions that at the table of his master, they eat peach pits like almonds.[42] The nobles also enjoy chestnuts cooked in a perforated pan over coals, and cook them into biscuits made with wine.[43] Princes especially like deer. They "eat the tender points of their horns, the ears, the extremities of the lips and nose, especially with onions, aromatic spices, and fat, with lemon juice, and this meal is very celebrated."[44]

The dietician's comments are also particularly interesting when considering how ordinary people emulated the behaviors of their superiors. Melchior Sebizius tells us that pastry bakers make an innumerable variety of confections both elegant and subtle, delectable not only in flavor but to the sight. He continues that "their work is imitated by housewives everywhere, especially in weddings and elegant banquets" to adorn the dessert course, ingeniously made from eggs, milk, and butter. He lists *globulos, placentas, liba, scriblitas, spiras.* What exactly these would correspond to in modern English is difficult to say because they are ancient words applied to early modern confections that were by then quite different. Judging from the shapes, they are probably fritters, cakes, biscuits, tarts, and spiral pastries. In any case, Sebizius naturally insists that all such "scitamenta seu ganeatae ciborum deliciae" ruin a person's health.[45] He does not, however, disapprove of all courtly tastes. "Veal's head is often served at princes' dinners boiled, most pleasing to the palate, especially those parts that are nearest the ears, laudably fat and tender."[46]

Although this brief recounting of the ways banqueting was criticized in early modern literature has only really scratched the surface, it does show that the topic was of great concern to many people beyond culinary authors. The fear, particularly among the moralists and physicians, was that the wanton habits of the elites would eventually trickle down to the masses, that someday they too would be imbibing cordials, feasting on pastries and sweets, and indulging in all manner of jumbled excess without regard to health or propriety. Of course, their predictions have largely come true, and although modern cuisine has evolved in ways they could never have imagined, our taste in many luxuries has its roots right here.

CHAPTER 11

Recipes

The following recipes have been translated directly from the primary sources without any adaptation for the modern kitchen. There is one recipe taken from each of the major sources used in this book. The intent is to provide examples of the various forms recipes might take in the culinary literature without tampering or substituting ingredients to suit modern tastes and technology. Recipes so adapted, of course, tell us nothing whatsoever about the past. The translations are not literal, but rather attempt to capture the directions as they were intended to be used in a real working kitchen. Thus the punctuation, or actually lack thereof, has been left intact. The recipes were chosen to illustrate various themes played out in this book, but they are also interesting in their own right, and would be perfectly suitable to prepare and serve today. In some cases, practical suggestions have been provided when a procedure would be difficult to follow. As a rule, though, modern equipment has not been substituted to save time or energy—a food processor cannot, for example, achieve the same results as a mortar and pestle. Some ingredients, perhaps only musk and amber, are nearly impossible to obtain today or are obscenely expensive. The vast majority can be found easily. Other ingredients cannot be sold legally—lungs and spleen, for example—so these have not been included. Only because it seems very unlikely that readers will want to cook a veal's head, guinea pig, and similar items, the following recipes are comparatively tame but are nonetheless representative of the tastes and textures preferred in the past.

1. Livre fort excellent (Paris, 1542, French)

This recipe is indicative of the increasing use of dairy in sauces and is rare in that it suggests flour as a thickener a full century before La Varenne. The white powder of ginger and sugar, as well as the sweetness and whiteness of the overall dish, is in keeping with sixteenth-century taste preferences throughout Europe. The directions for sugar candies mentioned in the recipe literally say "in the fashion of dragée," which is rather cryptic and may mean merely to coat the entire dish with sugar.

ABREMONT OF MILK

Take full fat milk, boil in a pot with fat bouillon, flour or bread crumb, white powder, and a little saffron. Sieve everything with your milk. And when it is boiled add in your eggs while stirring all the time, with enough salt and sugar, until thickened. Dress capons or chickens or serve in a plate garnished with sugar candies.[1]

2. Messisbugo (Ferrara, 1549, Italian)

Although the herbs may appear to be lost in the gargantuan proportions of this pie containing about three pounds of cheese and nearly two pounds of butter and milk, the eggs do allow it to set like a cheese quiche. The recipe can also be quartered easily to fit into a small pie plate, in which case use 1 fresh mozzarella, 1 cup of milk, 2 eggs, ¼ pound grated parmigiano cheese, and a stick of butter, plus a few slices of Tomino from Piedmont or a French Tomme de Savoie under the second layer.

FERRARESE HERB TART, OR ROMAGNOLA

Take a bunch of beet greens well washed and chopped very well, and place in a bowl with four fresh cheeses (povine) and four cups of milk, eight eggs, a pound of fat cheese, and a pound of fresh butter and a quarter of pounded pepper, and incorporate everything together well, and grease a pan with three ounces of fresh butter over which you place the first sheet of dough, and then over that the abovementioned composition which you spread over the sheet, having a pound and a half of fat tomino cheese in slices as thin as you can make them and spread them over the composition, and then lay on that the other sheet keeping the contents inside, then over that pour half a pound of melted butter, and place it to cook, and when it is almost done place over four ounces of sugar, then let it finish cooking.[2]

3. Romoli (Florence, 1560, Italian)

Macaroni was the generic name for any kind of pasta, and here they appear to be broad strips. The principal difference compared to modern fresh noodles is the use of milk, and obviously the seasoning with sugar and cinnamon—or canella. The combination actually works very well. Romoli normally used starches like this to garnish other dishes, but they could be served on their own as well, but not as a first course.

TO MAKE MACCHERONI ALLA ROMANA

If you wish to make a good plate of maccheroni, take two fogliete of goat or cow's milk, and having white flour, which you make into a dough with the milk, roll out thin leaves as when you want to make tagliolini, but a little larger. Place them to cook in a pot when the water boils, salted first. When they are cooked, place in a plate, having first grated hard rather than fresh provatura cheese, canella well pounded and sugar however much will seem convenient, everything incorporate together so that the maccheroni is covered in cheese, after which fill the plates.[3]

4. Willich (Zurich, 1563, Latin)

Willich's *Ars magirica* is one of the few books containing recipes written in Latin in the early modern period. Presumably this was not intended for working cooks but rather an academic audience. Nonetheless, it offers practical and detailed cooking procedures. For the little spears used to fasten the crab shells together, turkey lacing pins would work, hammered through the edges.

ON STUFFING CRABS

Cook these in water and remove the tough shells. However set aside the large shell separately which you replace. But little lion crabs with the neck, belly and shell removed, cut up finely, which you mix with fresh egg and season them with many aromatics and salt. You can even color it with saffron, and throw in chopped parsley leaves. But so that it coheres like gluten, some flour and raw egg will work, and thus you can judge when it's ready to stuff. Next you take the back shell, which you stuff. Not however so that it's overflowing, and close up with another back shell, so that the head can be seen on both sides, and they will join in no other way, this is not so much to be ornate, but is necessary. Next roast them fastened with three or four little spears and place on the grill over moderately lit coals. Or fry in a pan, with melted butter, however long it takes this same stuffing to be done, you fry. Serve them hot.[4]

5. Scappi (Rome, 1570, Italian)

The cut of meat Scappi calls for is the ribs of a castrato — that is, a neutered male sheep. Considering the age of animals available today, it is probably not very different from what is sold in this country as lamb. The directions in chapter 61 he refers to here suggest it be served with green sauce, which is based on parsley, spinach, sorrel, burnet, arugula, and mint, chopped together, with nuts if desired, and with sugar, salt, and a little vinegar. (VI, 197) The brisavoli he mentions separates the ribs, pounds the meaty part flat, and marinates them under weight with rose vinegar, pepper, cinnamon, salt, fennel pollen, or coriander before they are grilled. Fennel pollen is just that, the yellow powder shaken out of the fennel umbels, not the seed. The beauty of this recipe is that it presents various options for a single cut of meat, making the reader an active and creative participant in the cooking process rather than demanding strict procedures that must be followed to the letter, as in modern cookbooks.

TO COOK A RACK OF LAMB IN VARIOUS WAYS

Take a rack of lamb which has been tenderized for boiling; though for roasting, if the lamb is young, it is not necessary, it will be tender. If you want to boil it follow the directions given in chapter 61 for boiling water and salt, as has been noted. If you want to roast it, you need not blanch it, but place it raw on a spit stuck with cloves of garlic and rosemary leaves. But if it is lean you can blanch it in water and stick it with little bits of bacon. And wishing to grill it, first par-boil it, remove from the broth and let it cool, sprinkle with dry fennel pollen, crushed salt and bread grated and let it take on color on both sides on the grill. And serve it while hot with a sauce over it of rose vinegar, sugar and orange juice, and if you want to make brisavoli alla Venetiana rib by rib, follow the directions given for beef in chapter 7. The tenderloin beneath the kidney, even if small, can be prepared in all ways, as with the preparation of veal mentioned above.[5]

6. *Good Huswifes Handmaide (London, 1588, English)*

Turkeys were fairly new but immediately and enthusiastically adopted throughout Europe. This recipe employs a typical English procedure of splitting the turkey down the back; it is normally used with a chicken or spatchcock. The bruising of the bones is so that it can be laid flat while baking. Interestingly, this uses no spices for flavoring.

TO BAKE A TURKIE

Take and cleave your Turkies on the backe, and bruise all the bones: then season it with salt, and pepper grose beaten, and put into it a good store of butter: hee must have five houres baking.[6]

7. *Dawson (London, 1596, English)*

This recipe calls for dried white peas, which were the standard variety in medieval and early modern times before the green split pea displaced it. A liquid broth was often made from them as a substitute for meat broth in recipes for Lent. As a pottage, the peas should probably not be cooked to a smooth consistency. Obviously, sea mammals are not an option today, but chunks of swordfish or shark might give a vaguely comparable effect. The powder called for is merely a pounded spice mix including perhaps cinnamon, ginger, and sugar. This is, of course, the original "pease porridge hot."

FOR WHITE PEASE POTTAGE

Take a quart of white pease or more, and seethe them in fair water, close, until they do cast all their husks, the white cast away as long as any will come to the top. And when they be gone; then put into the pease two dishes of butter, and a little verjuice, with pepper and salt and a little fine powder of march. And so let it stand till you will occupy it, and then serve it upon sops. You may seeth the porpoise and seal in your pease, serving it forth two pieces in a dish.[7]

8. Lancelot (Liege, 1604, French)

The heuspot is a quintessential dish of the Low Countries and one that was enthusiastically adopted elsewhere. It is best made of cubes of veal slowly stewed. Later in the century the author of the Dutch *Verstandige Kock* identifies the variation with egg yolks as Spanish.[8]

HEUSPOT DE VEAU

Hotpot of veal being half cooked, marjoram and mint chopped together, nutmeg, a handful of Genoese capers, some butter, a bit of white wine or verjuice and butter, and let it stew well. If you wish to do it otherwise, take egg yolks and beat them with wine and verjuice, without putting in any herbs.[9]

9. Maceras (Salamanca, 1607, Spanish)

The prime ingredient in this recipe, if prepared before 1492, would have necessarily been an Old World gourd, probably in the lagenaria family. By 1607 it could very well have been a squash, as New World species were adopted very quickly in Spain, where they adopted the older term for gourd. The verjuice here (*agraz* in Spanish) should be any unripe or, if unavailable, tart grapes squeezed.

HOW TO COOK CALABASH

After cleaning the calabash, you put it to cook with salt, then leave it to drain in a colander, and take a bit of onion fried in suet or oil, and place the calabash to fry with the onions, and take pounded spices, and garlic, and deglaze everything with water, tossing it in a casserole with the calabash, and to that add four to six eggs depending on the calabash, some chopped herbs, sugar and verjuice, poaching the eggs with it. And when you serve it on the table, sprinkle on sugar and cinnamon for each. If you wish to fry them, make slices dusted with flour and crushed salt, and take the fat or hot oil, and fry them very well. Then after frying you can coat them again with eggs and a bit of flour beaten together, take the slices of calabash and dip in the batter, fry them, and being browned a lot, add honey, vinegar and spices and cook everything together, and add for each plate sugar, cinnamon, and garnish the plate well, for meat days and fish.[10]

10. Montiño (Madrid, 1611, Spanish)

The interest in this recipe for tasajos is not that this was a common food among European elites, but that it reflects a food useful for traveling and convenient in wild places and may provide a link to its popularity in the New World, though there made with beef, in the colonial era and later.

HOW TO HAVE VENISON JERKY

To salt a deer into jerky, after killing the animal, you then have to skin it, and cut it into small and large pieces that have few bones, or none, and strew on coarsely crushed salt, and hang them up in the air, and you need do nothing more. If you wish to have pieces of four pounds, place in salt three or four days, having purged the large bones.[11]

11. Murrell (London, 1615, English)

Although the combination of flavors here looks particularly perverse, the end result is merely a very savory kind of small meat loaf or if you will, the ancestor of the hamburger. Ground lamb or veal from the supermarket without the addition of suet works fine. Marigold petals from the garden can be used if not sprayed with chemicals, but can easily be left out. The currans are tiny raisins "of Corinth" available everywhere; the bread should be dry crumbs, and the sippets merely slices of toast. This is a good example of the kind of "subtlety" most households could afford to try as it contains no terribly expensive ingredients.

A FOND PUDDING

Take either Mutton, Veale, or Lambe, roast or raw, but raw is better. Mince it fine with Beef suet: take Spinage, Parsley, Marigold, Endiffe, a sprig of Time, and a sprig of Savory: chop them fine, and season with Nutmeg, Sugar, minst dates: take Currans and grated Bread, the yolkes of three or four new layed Eggs, a spoonful or two of Rosewater, as much verjuyce: work them up like Birds, Beasts, Fishes, Peares, or what you will. Fry them, or bake them, and serve them upon sippets, with verjuyce and White-wine, Butter, and Sugar: serve them either at dinner or Supper.[12]

12. La Varenne (Paris, 1651, French)

The potage is quite more than a soup. It is a thick broth with large chunks of meat or even whole animals, but all the ingredients are not slowly cooked together like a stew. Significantly the meat is not blanched or par-boiled as in many earlier recipes but is actually browned in the pan or over a fire which makes the final dish darker and more savory. Flouring the turnips would also add to the final thickness of the dish, though traditional soaked bread is also used. Importantly, this does not contain spices.

POTTAGE OF DUCKS WITH TURNIPS

After they are cleaned, lard them with bacon, then sauté them in a pan with fresh pork fat or melted lard, or even roast them on a spit three or four turns, then put them in a pot; next take your turnips, cut them as you like, blanch them, flour them and sauté in fresh pork fat or melted lard just until they are well browned, put them in with the ducks, and cook everything together, finally soak your bread so that it's thickened, if you have capers, add them in or a dash of vinegar, dress and garnish with turnips and serve.[13]

13. May (London, 1660, English)

Apart from the lingering fashion for spices here, the desire to keep the dish warm for service is interesting, as is the garnish of berries and toast (searced manchet).

OYSTERS IN STUFFADO

Parboil a pottle or three quarts of great Oysters, save the liquor and wash the oysters in warm water, then after steep them in white-wine, wine-vinegar, slic't nutmeg, large mace, whole pepper, salt and cloves; give them a warm on the fire, set them off and let them steep two or three hours; then take them out, wipe them dry, dip them in batter made of fine flour, yolks of eggs, some cream and salt, fry them, and being fryed keep them warm, then take some of the spices liquor, some of the oysters-liquor, and some butter, beat these things up thick with the slices of an orange or two, and two or three yolks of eggs; then dish the fryed oysters in a fine clean dish on a chafing-dish of coals, run the sauce over

them with the spices, slic't orange, and barberries, and garnish the dish
with searsed manchet.[14]

ᴄᴀ

14. Stefani (Mantua, 1662, Italian)

This is a sapor, a thick sauce served cold with meats. The closest available approximation of the Muscat variety would be a ripe and fragrant
Anjou or other golden pear.

SAUCE OF MUSCAT PEARS

Take four pounds of muscat pears not too mature, well cleaned and the
seeds removed, and that little bit of toughness that they have inside,
take one pound and a half of fine sugar, 9 ounces of rose water, six ounces
of white wine, and put everything to boil with the pears, being careful
that the fire be only coals. Wishing to make this sauce, use always a low
heat, when it is half cooked, and begins to get stringy, then begin to mix
it, without its being completely cooked. This sauce will last all winter,
when it is cooked well; pass it through a strainer and serve cold, sprinkled
with cinnamon.[15]

NOTES

Preface

1. See Flandrin and Montanari, *Food: A Culinary History* and Revel, *Culture and Cuisine* for an especially Francocentric view.
2. Rabasco, *Il convito,* 78.
3. Ibid., 79.
4. Ibid., 112–13.
5. Ibid., 107. There are also, as Rabasco points out, feasts held on saint's days and carnival, as well as other forms of popular ceremonial meals, but these are rarely discussed in the elite culinary literature.

Chapter 1: Setting the Stage—Setting the Table

1. della Casa, *Galateo,* 93.
2. Rabasco, *Il convito,* 217.
3. Colonna, *Hypnerotomachia Poliphili,* 106–9.
4. Evitascandalo, *Libro,* 6.
5. Rossetti, *Dello Scalco,* 180.
6. Ibid., 131.
7. Scappi, *Opera,* 106–7.
8. Lancelotti, *Lo Scalco Practico,* 23–29.
9. May, *Accomplisht Cook,* 137.

Chapter 2: An Introduction to Ingredients and Wild Food

1. Ambrosoli, *The Wild and the Sown.*
2. Montanari, *Culture of Food.*
3. Rossetti, *Dello Scalco,* 294.
4. Peterson, *Acquired Taste.*
5. The first original cookbook in sixteenth-century France, *Petite Traicté,* first appeared between 1536 and 1538 and contained 133 original recipes. It was reissued, this time with 217 more recipes, as *Le livre de cuisine* in 1540, and reissued again in 1542 and 1555 as *Livre fort excellent de cuisine.* This is the text used here. Subsequently, fifty more recipes were added, plus 177 from the medieval Menagier de Paris and sixteen potages from the French version of Platina, and published

as *La fleur de toute cuisine* in 1542 by Sargent and then in 1548 by Cretien. This text was then republished as *Le grand cuisinier* in 1543–44 by Pidoulx—the other text I have used, along with the later 1575 edition of the same. See *Livres en bouche* for the genealogy.

6. *Livre fort excellent,* 27.

7. Lehmann, "Late Medieval Menu," in *Food in History,* 1:1.

8. Scully, *Early French Recipes.*

9. Heiatt et al., *Pleyn Delit,* Recipe #85.

10. Martino, *Libro de arte coquinaria.* An English translation of this edition has been published by the University of California Press in 2005 but was unavailable to me while writing this book. Also see Redon et al., *The Medieval Kitchen,* 82.

11. Adamson, *Regional Cuisines of Medieval Europe.*

12. Gazius, *Corona florida medicinae,* fol. fiii.

13. Sebizius, *Alimentorum facultatibus,* 370–71.

14. Messisbugo, *Libro,* 4.

15. Sebizius, *Alimentorum facultatibus,* 699.

16. Ibid., 704.

17. Ibid., 712.

18. Ibid., 1044.

19. Sala, *De alimentis,* 58.

20. Castellanus, *Kreophagia,* 147.

21. Sebizius, *Alimentorum facultatibus,* 926.

22. Ibid., 933.

23. Cogan, *Haven of Health,* 87, and Scappi, *Opera,* I, 31, and 39.

24. Scappi, *Opera,* II, 217; V, 103, 222.

25. Massonio, *Archidipno,* 288–89.

26. Cogan, *Haven of Health,* 55.

27. Ibid., 68.

28. Cardano, "De usu ciborum," in *Opera Omnia,* 58.

29. Massonio, *Archidipno,* 390.

30. Cogan, *Haven of Health,* 146.

31. Romoli, *La singolare dottrina,* 166–82.

32. Scappi, *Opera,* II, 95.

33. Rossetti, *Dello Scalco,* 479.

34. Ibid., 470–71.

35. Ibid., 476.

36. Ibid., 484–88.

37. Evitascandalo, *Libro,* 36.

38. Ibid., 37–38.

39. Montiño, *Arte de Cocina,* 167–78.

40. Ibid., 179–81. See also chapter 11 on recipes.

41. Lancelot, *Overture,* 14.

42. Ibid., 71.

43. Ibid., fols. K2–K4.

44. Stefani, *L'Arte,* 33.

45. Ibid., 35.

46. Mattei, *Teatro Nobilissimo de Scalcheria*, 1–7.

47. La Varenne, *The French Cook*, boar: 69, 73, 100–101; deer 70, 84, 110.

48. de Lune, *Le Cuisinier*, 365.

49. Ibid., 244–46.

50. L. S. R., *L'art de bien traiter*, 112.

51. Ibid., 48.

52. Gazius, fol. eiiiv.

53. Castellanus, *Kreophagia*, 152–53.

54. Cogan, *Haven of Health*, 122.

55. Thomas, *Man and the Natural World*, 116, 275.

Chapter 3: Dairy

1. Pantaleon da Confienza, *Summa lacticiniorum*, 9.

2. Willich, *Ars Magirica*, 226.

3. Messisbugo, *Libro*, fol. 77v.

4. Ibid., fol. 112–112v.

5. Ibid., fol. 106v mispaginated, should be 114v.

6. Ibid., fol. 79v.

7. *Livre fort excellent*, fol. 57–57v.

8. Scappi, *Opera*, 4.

9. Siraisi, *The Clock and the Mirror*, 263, note 50.

10. Ahmed, ed., *Proper Newe Booke*, 49. References to this work are drawn from this edition, which contains a facsimile.

11. *Livre fort excellent*, fol. 47.

12. Nonnius, *Diaeteticon*, 212.

13. Scappi, *Opera*, 68v.

14. *Livre fort excellent*, fol. 26.

15. Scappi, *Opera*, I, 8.

16. Ibid., 327v.

17. Ibid., 361.

18. Ibid., 51.

19. *Proper Newe Booke*, 50.

20. Ibid., 47.

21. Spenser, *British Food*, 123.

22. Dawson, *Good Housewife's Jewel*, 89.

23. *Livre fort excellent*, fol. 34v.

24. Ibid., fol. 10.

25. Ibid., fol. 17.

26. Ibid., fol. 19–19v.

27. Ibid., fol. 51v.

28. Ibid., fol. 64.

29. It is also in Le Ménagier. Eileen Powers, editor, suggests that it was made with almonds, garlic, and eggs. The dish, or at least the name, still survives, and

is still based on waterfowl or capon, though otherwise it scarcely resembles these early versions. Le Ménagier de Paris, *The Goodman of Paris,* 151.

30. Rabisha, *The Whole Body,* 39. As I was writing this, Prospect Books published a facsimile edition. This note appears in that version on page 105.

31. Ibid., 42.

32. Maceras, *Arte de Cozina,* 127.

33. Montiño, *Arte de Cocina,* 154.

34. Ibid., 383, 348, 203.

35. Ibid., 387.

36. David, *Harvest of the Cold Months,* 58–63.

37. Lancelotti, *Lo Scalco Practico,* 195–97.

38. Ibid., 42.

39. Ibid., 32. Another version includes kid's eyes, ears, and sweetbreads with cream, 238.

40. Ibid., 221.

41. Crisci, *Lucerna de Corteggiani,* 63.

42. Vasselli, *L'Apicio,* 47.

43. Ibid., 21.

44. Stefani, *L'Arte,* 14.

45. Ibid., 15.

46. Ibid., 27.

47. Ibid., 29.

48. Ibid., 57.

49. Ibid., 26.

50. Ibid., 73–74.

51. La Varenne, *Cuisiner,* 105.

52. Ibid., 57.

53. Ibid., 85.

54. Ibid., 99.

55. Ibid., 100.

56. Ibid., 128.

57. Ibid., 179.

58. Ibid., 167.

59. Ibid., 200.

60. Ibid., 128.

Chapter 4: Spices and Garnishes

1. Messisbugo, *Libro,* 42.

2. Ibid., 98v.

3. Ibid., 91.

4. Ibid., 88v.

5. Ibid., 72v.

6. Scappi, *Opera,* 8.

7. Ibid., 56.

8. Ibid., 59–61.

9. Ibid., II:8; II:91.

10. Romoli, *La singolare dottrina*, 132–33.

11. *Livre fort excellent,* fol. 13.

12. Ibid., fol. 27v. The typesetter seems to have used a gothic long *s* instead of a *j* in some numbers, and his mistake was perpetuated all the way into the *Grand cuisinier* of 1575 (fol. 64v–65), which copied these into a roman typeface. This particular spice mix recipe was left out of that collection for some reason, but the following one is transcribed, at times using *j* for *1* and at other times using *s*, or both. If the original typesetter meant something else by the long *s*, it still does not affect the tenor of the discussion here.

13. Ibid., 28.

14. Ibid., 38.

15. Ibid., fol. 11v.

16. Ibid., fols. 1, 3, 7, 9.

17. *Proper Newe Booke,* 13.

18. *Good Huswifes Handmaide,* 13.

19. Lancelot, *Overture,* 17.

20. Ibid., 32–35.

21. Ibid., 24–25.

22. Ibid., 87.

23. Maceras, *Arte de Cozina,* 15.

24. Ibid., 20–21, 27 calls for the same spices in a lampreda sauce.

25. Montiño, *Arte de Cocina,* 23–24.

26. Ibid., 25.

27. Ibid., 74.

28. Ibid., 64.

29. Stefani, *L'Arte,* 55, 66.

30. Ibid., 65.

31. May, *Accomplisht Cook,* 380.

32. *Larousse Gastronomique,* 545.

33. Viandier, Prescott Translation Web site: *http://www. telusplanet. net/public/prescotj/data/viandier/viandier1. html,* 34.

34. Messisbugo, *Libro,* 43v, 66.

35. Ibid., 51v.

36. Ibid., 54.

37. Ibid., 108.

38. Romoli, *La singolare dottrina,* 128.

39. Ibid., 130.

40. Ibid., 133.

41. Ibid., 144v.

42. Ibid., 151v–152.

43. Scappi, *Opera,* 21, 22, 22v.

44. Ibid., 26.

45. Ibid., 429v–430.

46. Ibid., 433.

47. Ibid., 24.

48. Rossetti, *Dello Scalco,* 102.

49. Ibid., 439.

50. Antonio Frugoli, *Pratica,* 2, 5.

51. Ibid., 52.

52. Ibid., 56.

53. Vasselli, *L'Apicio,* 2.

54. Ibid., 79.

55. May, *Accomplisht Cook,* 73.

56. La Varenne, *Cuisinier,* 132.

57. Ibid., 60–61.

Chapter 5: Vegetables and Fruit

1. Grieco, "Social Politics," 131–49.

2. Vasselli, *L'Apicio,* 51.

3. Stefani, *L'Arte,* 80.

4. Rossetti, *Dello Scalco,* 205.

5. Giacomo Castelvetro, *Breve racconto.* See also *The Fruit, Herbs & Vegetables of Italy.*

6. Massonio, *Archidipno,* 82.

7. Ibid., 240.

8. Ibid., 365.

9. Ibid., 371.

10. Ibid., 397.

11. Ibid., 155.

12. Ibid., 160.

13. Ibid., 348.

14. Ibid., 338–39.

15. Evelyn, *Acetaria,* 16.

16. Ibid., 34.

17. Ibid., 53.

18. Scappi, *Opera,* 74v–75.

19. Ibid., 76v.

20. Ibid., 362v.

21. Ibid., 59v, 148.

22. Ibid., 151v. *Molignane* is his odd term for eggplant, along with *pomi sdegnosi.* They are usually called *melanzane* or *meli insani.*

23. Ibid., 152.

24. Maceras, *Arte de Cozina.* 75.

25. Montiño, *Arte de Cocina,* 251.

26. Ibid., 258–59.

27. *Livre fort excellent,* 68, 72.

28. Ibid., 29.

29. Ibid., 33.

30. Lancelot, *Overture*, 10.

31. Ibid., 36–39.

32. Ibid., 40–41.

33. Ibid., 79. One wonders if he found this ravioli recipe in an Italian source. It is not in Messisbugo or Scappi.

34. Ibid., 125.

35. Rumpolt, *Ein new Kochbuch*, fol. 157b–59b.

36. *Proper Newe Booke*, 11.

37. *Good Huswifes Handmaide*, 5.

38. Ibid., 58.

39. Ibid., 60.

40. Ibid., 111.

41. Murrell, *Two Books*, 38–41.

42. May, *Accomplisht Cook*, 427.

43. Ibid., 426.

44. Ibid., 158–65.

45. La Varenne, *Cuisinier*, 95.

46. Ibid., 101–2.

47. Vasselli, *L'Apicio*, 50.

48. Ibid., 78.

49. Stefani, *L'Arte*, 84.

50. Scappi, *Opera*, I, 22–25.

51. Ibid., 80v.

52. Ibid., 92.

53. Ibid., 94v.

54. Ibid., 192–94.

55. Ibid., 327–28.

56. Ibid., 418–19.

57. *Livre fort excellent*, fol. 37.

58. Ibid., fol. 3.

59. Ibid., fol. 58.

60. Ibid., fol. 64.

61. Ibid., fol. 60.

62. Maceras, *Arte de Cozina*, 1.

63. Ibid., 139–40.

64. Montiño, *Arte de Cocina*, 468–70.

65. Ibid., 126.

66. Ibid., 133.

67. *Proper Newe Booke*, 11.

68. Ibid., 12.

69. *Good Huswifes Handmaide*, 31.

70. Ibid., 33.

71. Dawson, *Good Housewife's Jewel*, 94–95.

72. Ibid., 102.

73. Markham, *The English Housewife,* 104–9.

74. Murrell, *Two Books,* 17.

75. Ibid., 29.

76. Vasselli, *L'Apicio,* 37.

77. Ibid., 25.

Chapter 6: Starches and Pasta

1. Messisbugo, *Libro,* 40.

2. Platina, *De honesta voluptate,* 363.

3. Scappi, *Opera,* 335. The illustrations in Scappi's book do not depict an earthenware *testa* or any other ceramic vessel, though they are mentioned throughout the text. Either the illustrations were prepared independently or a decision was made to include only metal vessels. All show metal rivets. There are several illustrations of a *conserva,* though, which appears to be a metal version of the *testa,* though the lids are not concave.

4. Nonnius, *Diaeteticon,* 28.

5. Scappi, *Opera,* 335–335v.

6. Ibid., 339.

7. Ibid., 346.

8. Ibid., 365.

9. Ibid., 367v.

10. Ibid., 368.

11. Ibid., 385.

12. Ibid., 391.

13. Rossetti, *Dello Scalco,* 167–68.

14. *Proper Newe Book,* 42.

15. Ibid., 60.

16. *Good Huswifes Handmaide,* 22.

17. Ibid., 32.

18. Ibid., 39.

19. Dawson, *Good Housewife's Jewel,* 61.

20. Ibid., 71.

21. Lancelot, *Overture,* 66–67.

22. Maceras, *Arte de Cozina,* 24.

23. Ibid., 81.

24. Ibid., 34–35.

25. Ibid., 43.

26. La Varenne, *Le patissier.* The translator defines the *chopine* here, 21.

27. Lancelot, *Overture,* 19–21.

28. Ibid., 34.

29. La Varenne, *Le patissier.*

30. Ibid., 1.

31. Ibid., 51.

32. Ibid., 2.

33. Ibid., 6.
34. Ibid., 66.
35. Ibid., 21.
36. Ibid., 112.
37. Ibid., 70.
38. Heiatt, in Adamson, *Regional Cuisines,* 25.
39. Lancelot, *Overture,* 78–79.
40. Messisbugo, *Libro,* 52.
41. Serventi and Sabban, *Pasta.*
42. Ibid., 238–39.
43. Scappi, *Opera,* II, 173–81.
44. Romoli, *La singolare dottrina,* 168.
45. Ibid., 179.
46. Vasselli, *L'Apicio,* 47.

Chapter 7: *Wine and Alcohol*

1. Scappi, *Opera,* II, 267.
2. Ibid., I, 28.
3. Sante Lancerio in Faccioli, ed., *Arte della cucina,* 316–41.
4. Ibid., 319.
5. Scarlino, *Nuovo trattato.*
6. Ibid., Bii.
7. Ibid., Biv verso.
8. Ibid., Ci verso.
9. Praefectus, *De Diversorum vini generum,* 10v.
10. Ibid., 11.
11. Ibid., 38. "Temulenti enim in re Venerea imbelles sunt, quorum geniture aquosa est, et non prolifica." Scarlino said exactly the opposite in verse: "e'l coito incita, senza cui van saria Venere, e Amore." Civ verso.
12. Ibid., 43.
13. Ibid., 49.
14. See Albala, "To Your Health."
15. Confalonieri, *De vini natura disputatio,* 5.
16. Ibid., 13.
17. Fumanelli, *Commentarium de vino,* 32v.
18. Fracastoro, *Opera Omnia,* 234v.
19. Grataroli, *De vini natura,* 12–15.
20. Ibid., 58.
21. Ibid., 63.
22. Ibid., 346.
23. Ibid., 216.
24. Ibid., 80–88.
25. Ibid., 97–98.
26. Ibid., 109.

27. Ibid., 191.

28. Ibid., 200.

29. Ibid., 219.

30. Ibid., 261–64.

31. Ibid., 266.

32. Euonymus, *De remediis secretis*, 18–20.

33. Ibid., 24.

34. Ibid., 129–31.

35. Ibid., 120–21. "Aqua ardens, seu aqua vitae, à vino extrahitur, apud nos ex faecib. tantùm an iis qui vulgò vendunt, et ex hoc uno ferè victum quaerû."

36. Ibid., 137.

37. Ibid., 145–50.

38. Ibid., 205.

39. Ibid., 169.

40. Ibid., 46.

41. Ibid., 60, 68.

42. Ibid., 87–89.

43. Ibid., 202.

44. Ibid., 458.

45. Bacci, *vinorum historia*, 17.

46. Ibid., 23–25.

47. Ibid., 30.

48. Ibid., 42.

49. Ibid., 65.

50. Ibid., 148.

Chapter 8: Nations

1. Adamson, *Regional Cuisines*. Though the aim of this volume is to show that regional variations did exist in medieval Europe, much of the evidence could be used to support the opposite conclusion. The differences often appear to be mostly the result of geography and ingredients.

2. *The Vivendier*, Terence Scully, tr., 50, 49, 54.

3. Messisbugo, *Libro*, 81–82.

4. Notaker, "Comments on the Interpretation of Plagiarism," 70: 58.

5. Albala, *Eating Right in the Renaissance*.

6. Messisbugo, *Libro*, 92.

7. Ibid., 99v.

8. Scappi, *Opera*, 166v–182v.

9. Sabban and Serventi, *A Tavola nel Rinascimento*.

10. Montiño, *Arte de Cocina*, 51.

11. Ibid., 483.

12. May, *Accomplisht Cook*, 128.

13. Ibid., 171.

14. Ibid., 186.

15. Ibid., 249.

16. Ibid., 273.

17. de Lune, *Le cuisinier,* 255.

18. Ibid., 264.

19. Ibid., 372.

20. Ibid., 278.

21. Ibid., 273.

22. Ibid., 350.

23. Artusi, *La scienza.* See also the recent translation *Science in the Kitchen.*

24. See note above, Ch. 2 n. 5, and *Livres en bouche,* 94.

25. Messisbugo, *Libro,* 109; *Livre fort excellent,* xxxix.

26. Messisbugo, 99v; *Livre fort excellent,* xxxii; Willich, 178; *Proper Newe Book,* 75.

27. Messisbugo, 54; *Livre fort excellent,* liii.

28. La Varenne, Marnette, tr. *Le patissier,* 2.

29. Messisbugo, *Libro,* 56.

30. Ibid., 60.

31. Ibid., 58v., 73.

32. Ibid., 60.

33. Romoli, *La singolare dottrina,* 142v.

34. *Proper Newe Book,* 13.

35. *Good Huswifes Handmaide,* 15.

36. Dawson, *Good Housewife's Jewel,* 24.

37. Murrell, *Two Books,* B1.

38. Ibid., B2.

39. May, *Accomplisht Cook,* 67.

40. Ibid., 94.

41. Ibid., 233, 248.

42. *Compleat Cook,* 5–6.

43. Ibid., 45.

44. Ibid., 69.

45. Ibid., 17.

46. Rabisha, *The Whole Body,* 77, or 143 Prospect ed.

47. *Archimagirus Anglo Gallicus,* 30.

48. Ibid., 51.

49. Ibid., 44.

50. Messisbugo, *Libro,* 50.

51. Ibid., 106v., Romoli, 147v.

52. Bacci, *vinorum historia,* 166–67.

53. Dawson, *Good Housewife's Jewel,* 106.

54. May, *Accomplisht Cook,* 32.

55. Vasselli, *L'Apicio,* 47.

56. Ibid., 7.

57. *Compleat Cook,* 30.

58. Ibid., 92.

59. Lancelot, *Overture,* 66.

60. Stefani, *L'Arte,* 72.

61. Ibid., 73.

62. Romoli, *La singolare dottrina,* 162–3v.

63. Lancelot, *Overture,* 35.

64. La Varenne, *Cuisinier,* 97.

65. May, *Accomplisht Cook,* 438.

66. Ibid., 271.

67. *Compleat Cook,* 56–57.

68. *Livre fort excellent,* 56–57.

69. Messisbugo, *Libro,* 42. Another method is mentioned on 58v.

70. Ibid., 61v.

71. Ibid., 93v.

72. Ibid., 100.

73. Romoli, *La singolare dottrina,* 165.

74. Ibid., 74.

75. Rossetti, *Dello Scalco,* 455.

76. Ibid., 456.

77. Ibid., 477.

78. Ibid., 524–25.

79. Lancelot, *Overture,* 57.

80. Maceras, *Arte de Cozina,* 61, 64, 80, 99, 100.

81. Montiño, *Arte de Cocina,* 15.

82. Lancelot, *Overture,* 71.

83. La Varenne, *Cuisinier,* 65 and 110, which is practically the same recipe repeated.

84. De Lune, *Cuisinier,* 371.

85. Lancelotti, *Lo Scalco Practico,* 9, 187 and elsewhere.

86. Messisbugo, *Libro,* 74.

87. Ibid., 99v.

88. Rossetti, *Dello Scalco,* 451–530.

89. *Livre fort excellent,* fol. 5.

90. Ibid., fol. 8, *Proper Newe Book,* 45.

Chapter 9: Staff and Carving

1. Rossetti, *Dello Scalco,* fol. B3v.

2. Frugoli, *Pratica,* 1–2.

3. Crisci, *Lucerna,* 59

4. Cervio, *Trinciante,* 116.

5. Evitascandalo, *Libro,* 3.

6. Romoli, *La singolare dottrina,* 3v.

7. Rossetti, *Dello Scalco,* 1.

8. Ibid., 7, 13. Chiappini, *La corte estense.*

9. Frugoli, *Pratica,* 9.

10. Rossetti, *Dello Scalco,* 10.

11. Ibid., 43.

12. Romoli, *La singolare dottrina,* 5.

13. Ibid., iv–2.

14. Scappi, Scully, tr. This is Scully's calculation of the capacity in his forthcoming translation of the *Opera.*

15. Evitascandalo, *Libro,* 4v.

16. Scappi, *Opera,* 14–15.

17. Evitascandalo, *Libro,* 5.

18. Cervio, *Trinciante,* 16.

19. Elbling, *The Food Taster.*

20. There is a wonderful story told by Ambrose Paré about the French king Charles IX trying to test the efficacy of the bezoar. By chance, one of the king's cooks had been caught stealing silver plates and was condemned to death. Upon Paré's suggestion, the culprit was given the choice of immediate execution or poison with the possibility of being saved by the bezoar, in which case he would be set free. The poison of course killed him. See Magner, *A History of Medicine,* 166–67.

21. Rabasco, *Il convito,* 226; Crisci, *Lucerna,* 36.

22. Frugoli, *Pratica,* 5.

23. Ibid., 6.

24. Rossetti, *Dello Scalco,* 13.

25. Ibid., 17.

26. Frugoli, *Pratica,* 7.

27. Rossetti, *Dello Scalco,* 16.

28. Ibid., 29.

29. Ibid., 21.

30. Ibid., 18–19.

31. Crisci, *Lucerna,* 50.

32. Rabasco, *Il convito,* 21.

33. Giles Rose, tr., *Officers,* fol. A3.

34. Ibid., 4.

35. Ibid., 91.

36. Ibid., 126, 143–44.

37. Ibid., 292.

38. Liberati, *Il perfetto maestro,* Book II, 10.

39. Ibid., II, 13.

40. Ibid., II, 87.

41. Ibid., II, 45.

42. Savonarola is reprinted in Polyonymus; see note 45 below.

43. de Worde, *Boke of Kervynge,* 40.

44. Ibid., 42.

45. Syngraphaeus, *Schola Apiciana,* 28v.

46. Cervio, *Trinciante,* 59–60.

47. Ibid., 3.

48. Ibid., 4. "Ogni gentilhuomo ò qual si voglia, che faccia professione, deve sforzarsi con ogni suo potere di farla con la maggiore riputatione."

49. Ibid., 8.

50. Ibid., 44.

51. Ibid., 18–23.

52. Ibid., 62.

53. Ibid., 72–73.

54. Ibid., 76.

55. Ibid., 113–14.

56. Evitascandalo, *Dialogo,* 4.

57. Ibid., 21.

58. Ibid., 6.

59. Ibid., 11.

60. Scappi, *Opera,* 121v.

61. Evitascandalo, *Dialogo,* 14.

62. Geigher, *Li tre Trattati,* illustration #6.

63. Ibid., illustration #21.

64. Vonlett, *Le vraye mettode,* 15.

65. Rose, *Officers,* 24.

66. Ibid., 46.

Chapter 10: Condemnation

1. Goclenius, *De luxu,* 19.

2. Ibid., 20.

3. Ibid., 22.

4. Ibid., 28–29.

5. Ibid., 41.

6. Ibid., 57.

7. Nonnius, *Diaeteticon,* 239.

8. Goclenius, *De luxu,* 74.

9. Ibid., 83.

10. Ibid., 96.

11. Ibid., 98–99.

12. Ibid., 116.

13. Viret, *Satyres Chrestienne,* 6. A forthcoming edition from Librarie Droz, ed. Charles-Antione Chamay, ascribes this work to Theodore Beza, the Protestant reformer.

14. Ibid., 13.

15. Ibid., 25, 30.

16. Ibid., 40–41.

17. Ibid., 51–54.

18. Ibid., 60–74.

19. Ibid., 71.

20. Puteanus, *Comus sive Phagesiposia.*

21. Ibid., 17.

22. Ibid., 66.

23. Ibid., 68, 70.

24. Syngrapheus, *Schola Apiciana,* 3v.

25. Jeanneret, *Feast of Words,* 70–82.

26. Cornarius, *De conviviorum.*

27. Ibid., 36–39.

28. See my *Eating Right in the Renaissance.*

29. Cogan, *Haven of Health,* 133–34.

30. Ibid., 146.

31. Ibid., 165.

32. Ibid., 156.

33. Ibid., 215. He apparently got this detail from Leonard Fuchs, who disapproved. The School of Salerno, for some reason, thought it a good idea.

34. Ibid., 203.

35. Ibid., 219.

36. Bruyerin-Champier, *De re cibaria,* 40.

37. Ibid., 68–69.

38. Duchesne, *Le pourtraict de santé,* 246.

39. Grataroli, *Health of Magistrates and Students,* B4v.

40. Moffett, *Health's Improvement,* 293.

41. Pictorius, *Dialoghi,* 41.

42. Benzi and Bertaldi, *Regola della sanita,* 108.

43. Ibid., 185.

44. Ibid., 285.

45. Sebizius, *alimentorum facultatibus,* 114.

46. Ibid., 586.

Chapter 11: Recipes

1. *Livre fort excellent,* fol. 19–19v.

2. Messisbugo, *Libro,* 61.

3. Romoli, *La Singolare dottrina,* 192v.

4. Willich, *Ars Magirica,* 187.

5. Scappi, *Opera,* 36–36v.

6. *Good Huswifes Handmaide,* 26.

7. Dawson, *Good Housewife's Jewel,* 33.

8. Rose, *The Sensible Cook,* 50.

9. Lancelot, *Overture,* 11.

10. Maceras, *Arte de Cozina,* 83–84.

11. Montiño, *Arte de Cocina,* 185.

12. Murrell, *Two Books,* 28.

13. La Varenne, *Le cuisinier,* 117.

14. May, *Accomplisht Cook,* 387.

15. Stefani, *L'Arte,* 64.

GLOSSARY

A number of terms used in this book have been consciously invented to describe particular culinary procedures or eating habits unique to the early modern period. The following list includes all those used in the text as well as others that may hopefully come into common parlance. Many of these terms can easily be applied to other cuisines as well. At the very least, this is an attempt to begin the development of a richer critical vocabulary for culinary historians in the hope that our language will resist glossification.

adipatry. The tradition of using animal fat as the primary cooking medium. From Latin *adeps, adipis*—fat, and *patria*—fatherland.

albondiguillescent. A preference for small dainty foods in meatball form. From Spanish for little meatballs.

allosipid. A dish composed of a main ingredient seasoned with flavorings that contrast distinctly with that ingredient and often with each other, as well. A vinegar-based sauce on meat would be one example, or a spicy sauce on a bland food. In medieval and early modern Europe, the intention of such contrasts may have been in part to balance the humoral makeup of the main ingredient. Hot and dry herbs or spices counteract the potentially harmful effects of cold and moist foods such as watery vegetables and fish. The antonym, and the logic whereby sauces are created in classical French cuisine, is *homeosipid.* Here the main ingredient is seasoned with flavors that complement, and are generally based on a reduction made from the main ingredient itself, as with a reduced meat-stock-based sauce on meat.

aquamanibulence. Careful attention to hand washing and drying, from the late Latin term for a decorative vessel used to pour water over diners' hands. By the Renaissance, the aquamanile was usually in the form of a classical ewer and basin. Earlier examples may have been in the form of a lion or animal.

aristobroma. Food of nobles. Adj. *aristobromatic.* From Greek *aristoi,* the best, or noble, and *broma,* food.

arosmatic. The tendency to season foods with rose water, both sweets and savory foods, meats, fowl, and fish.

asotic. Wastefully lavish. Directly from the Greek *asotos.*

aspergamensa. Things scattered around the table, either for decoration, as with flowers, utensils or small dishes bearing salt, or condiments. From Latin *aspergo,* to scatter, and *mensa,* table.

atriplexy. According to early modern nutritionists, eating cold and watery vegetables on a hot day can lead to a sudden shock to the head, akin to an apoplexy (stroke), or perhaps in fact not dissimilar to a brainfreeze when eating ice cream. From Latin *atriplex*—orache, a watery, leafy green vegetable commonly used in salads.

aulificate. To act or bear oneself in accordance with courtly manners and customs. A particular obsession among upwardly mobile persons hoping to gain patronage, hence the large numbers of how-to books on the subject. From Latin *aulicus,* courtly, and *faceo,* to make.

auriphage. Preference for golden-colored foods and drinks, or when available, actual gold or gilded foods. Extends also to the craze for *aurantia*—oranges, whose name derives from the color gold.

bellariferous. Describes vessels designed specifically for bearing desserts and often carried out ceremonially. From Latin *bellaria,* desserts.

bifurcuited. A food subjected to two different cooking methods. Typical of medieval cooking, as when a piece of meat would first be poached, then roasted, or half-roasted then sauteed. To be distinguished from biscuit, meaning twice cooked.

blitulate. To cause other foods to seem flavorless, as when something mild follows a rich or spicy dish. From Latin *blitum*—orache, or flavorless.

bradomagiric. A preference for slow-cooking methods using indirect and low heat, as with roasts turned slowly on a spit adjacent to a fire or cooked in a covered earthenware vessel, or long-simmered in a pot. From Greek *bradus,* slow, and *magirici,* cookery.

cenamorous. An intimate meal, often laden with aphrodisiacs, whose intention is to arouse feelings of passion. From Italian *cena,* supper.

chromorexia. Desire or hunger for colored foods. From Greek *chrom*—color, and *orexia,* hunger.

cibouyant. Large morsels of food such as dumplings or ravioli served in a broth or other liquid. From Latin *cibus,* food, and English *bouyant*—to float.

cinnamophilia. The typical use of cinnamon as a universal flavoring on both savory and sweet dishes. Often found in conjunction with zucarophilia.

circumordicate. To eat around the edges of a food, with fastidious attention. From Latin *mordax,* to bite.

collyrasect. To cut vermicelli and similar long noodle forms, often with a notched rolling pin designed solely for this purpose. From Greek *collyra,* which some scholars define as a noodle or thin strip of dough.

consanguilate. To thicken with blood. From Latin *sanguis,* blood.

crapuliferous. Drinks designed to quickly cause drunkenness. Its antonym is *crapulifuge,* a common preoccupation among Renaissance food writers, cabbage being most commonly recommended. From Latin *crapula,* for the state of gluttonous drunkenness, and *fero,* to bear or lead in.

deipnomania. Excessive attention to one's food and eating it publicly as an outward display of wealth and power. From the Greek title, the first history of food, the *Deipnosophistae,* written by Athenaeus in the second century A.D.

digitescant. To eat with one's fingers. From Latin *digit,* finger, and *esco,* to eat.

discrumbination. To remove the upper crust of a bread before slicing for trenchers on which food is placed.

dissordinate. In culinary parlance, when multiple courses follow no particular order. As in the Renaissance, when most courses would contain meats, fowl, fish, soups, sweets, and so forth.

edofication. To arrange food in ways that imitate architectural forms. From Latin *edo,* to eat, and assonant with *aedes,* a building or edifice.

endore. To cover with a golden surface with egg yolks or actual gold. An English word that has passed from current usage.

epulism. A food or dish that is specifically associated with sumptuous dining, such as sturgeon or veal's head. Often a grand presentation piece, requiring hours of preparation and decoration. From Latin *epulae,* banquets. In adjectival form the word is *epulaic.*

esuricette. Something that stimulates a lapsed appetite, apparently a common occurrence, according to nutritional writers in southern Europe. It is distinguished from the modern usage of appetizers, which merely mean hors d'oeuvres. The esuricette can be used at any point in a meal. From Latin *esurit,* to hunger, and *cedo,* bring me, in the plural. The passive verb is *to esuricede.*

exaspissate. To spew out contents or juice when punctured. From Vulgar Latin *pissiare* and Middle English *pissen,* to squirt or pee, and sounds like *exasperate,* to breathe out, or frustrate.

exociboid. The tendency to prefer rare and exotic foods and preparations from other countries. From *exo-,* foreign, and *cibus,* food.

expotition. Going out with the conscious aim of drinking along the route, essentially a pub crawl. From Latin *potus,* drink.

farciful. Taken from Latin *farce,* to stuff, refers to all variety of stuffed foods, a separate category of preparation in the Renaissance regardless of ingredients, and usually classified as such in cookbooks. Foods that readily lend themselves to this procedure can be said to have farcility.

fictilicious. Being allowed to lick the plates, having no social stigma against doing so. Derived from Latin *fictilis,* earthenware, and *licit,* being allowed.

fleaded. Wrapped in a caul, a fatty membrane surrounding the kidneys, and roasted or pan-fried. The intention is that the caul self-bastes and keeps little morsels of food or small birds moist. From the Old English word for caul—*flead*. This procedure is currently in fashion.

flummery. A dish composed of cream and a thickener, but used in a general sense for any concoction, a mishmash, balderdash.

foculent. Cookware and cooking methods designed specifically for a stove top rather than a hearth. From the Latin *focula,* a little stove.

foredilection. Picking on food before it is brought to the table.

frixophobic. The fear of frying. Characteristic of medical advice from the sixteenth century onward.

frustulent. Covered with bread crumbs or crumbs used as a thickener for a sauce. From Latin *frustulum,* crumbs.

goutesque. The mixing of jarring, discordant flavors in a single dish. From French *goûter,* to taste.

hipocrasy. To adulterate wine with extraneous flavorings, as with *hipocras,* a spiced wine sometimes served hot.

hypocendric. Foods baked underneath coals; tubers such as truffles and later potatoes were typically cooked this way. From Greek *under,* and *cendre,* in French, coals.

indoucement. When something tastes sweeter in juxtaposition with a bitter or tannic food.

julepated. Befuddled by thick after-dinner cordials and potions. From Arabic *juleb.*

kreogyric. A poem in praise of meat, as with Firenzuola's In lode di salsiccia. From Greek *kreo,* meat, and assonant with *panegyric,* which could very well mean in praise of bread.

lupescence. The act of wolfing down one's food greedily.

mandorlate. To flavor with almond milk, typical in early modern Europe for Lenten dishes.

mantequated. The use of butter in contexts that now seem out of date, as with floating butter on top of a rum toddy, or eating it at the end of a meal, as the Dutch did in the past. From Italian dialect of the sixteenth century and Spanish *manteca,* butter.

masticulate. To chew expressively with an open mouth, considered vulgar.

melascescent. The preference for sweet-and-sour flavors. Directly from Latin words for honey and vinegar.

merimbibe. To drink wine straight, uncut with water, as was the custom. From Latin *meraca,* straight wine.

migasculate. To remove the soft, fresh, interior crumb of a bread, often used as a thickener. From Spanish *migas*—crumb. Still used to thicken a gazpacho, which apart from the tomatoes is essentially a medieval soup. Pine nuts or almonds would have been the original base.

monollaic. A meal cooked entirely in one pot, as with a hodge-podge or classic Spanish olla podrida, which translates literally as rotten pot or potpourri.

nefferent. From French nef, ship—a ceremonial vessel for holding salt; activities relating to the presentation and passing of the salt cellar or similar smaller vessels.

oleaffluent. Dripping with olive oil.

omnipotient. Willingness to drink many different alcoholic beverages in one sitting or together without attention to how they complement the food.

periprandial. The entertainments, frivolities, and diversions that normally appear around or between courses in a Renaissance banquet. They include music, plays, and dancing performances and may involve fireworks or water displays. Prandium or dinner was the larger meal of the day, eaten in the late morning.

pertracted. Stretched out, as with dough. From Latin *tracta,* a kind of pulled lasagne noodle.

pestolent. A sauce or ingredient that is pounded, and the general preference for smooth foods that have been pounded in a mortar rather than ground, as with chicken in the classic blamange of the Middle Ages and Renaissance.

polyopsony. Derived from Greek *opson,* things eaten with bread or as a condiment with a main ingredient, and Latin *opsonia,* a broader term referring to banquet foods. Many cuisines, particularly of the Middle Ages and Renaissance, present a main ingredient with a variety of sauces and flavorings that each individual diner can add at will. Rather than a sauce chosen and presented by the chef and pre-plated, this affords the diner a creative role in the ultimate flavor and texture of the dish when eaten, and in fact many different condiments can be added, creating many different layers of flavor. The term can be applied to a Southeast Asian meal in which several standard condiments are typically presented, or even to a hamburger on which the diner has a choice of ketchup, mustard, relish, and so forth. The antonym would be *monopsony.*

poultritudinous. The quality or expression of beauty in fowl as arranged on a platter whole. Related to *pulcher,* beauty in Latin.

profrigate. Describing the huge cold buffet set out on a credenza before guests arrive, stacked with fruits, cheeses, olives, fish, and preserved meats. From Latin *frigor,* cold.

ruscious. Dainties served on toast points or crackers. From Portuguese *rosca*—ship's biscuit.

salumberous. Covered in salt, either for preservation or baking in a crust. From Latin *umbra,* shade.

sarmassmalacious. To tenderize flesh by kneading and massaging it. From Greek *sarx,* flesh; *massein,* to knead; and *malac,* soften.

sartagisault. To flip in a frying pan. From Latin *sartagine,* frying pan.

soperific. Soup or stew served on a bit of dry bread that soaks up the liquid—sops.

stamegnosis. Understanding of what and how to pass foods through a sieve. From Italian *stamegna,* a sieve.

stilettite. The shape of noodles that have been formed by rolling around a long iron pin or stiletto, as described by Scappi in his *Opera.* Today, in extruded form these would be called *bucatini,* or when cut up, *maccheroni.*

terrasophy. The systematic appreciation and understanding of the relationship between the soil, climate, and production methods and the effect these have on creating superior and unique food products. Related to the French term *terroir.*

testastorrous. Describing the habit of serving food nestled between two plates, one upside down on top of the food, and then stacking these plates, tying them with a ribbon, and carrying the resulting tower into the dining room for presentation. From Latin *testa,* earthenware, and *torre* in Italian, a tower.

trinciant. Pertaining to the court officer assigned the duty of ceremonially carving all manner of meat and fruit before diners. From the Italian name for the carving officer, usually noble, known as *Il Trinciante.*

ungulant. Something that coats the throat with fat. From Latin *ungo,* to grease, and *gula,* throat.

viceravore. The willful presentation of and preference for organ meats, including many no longer commonly eaten, such as spleen and lungs, as well as fish intestines and liver. Related to this is the delectation of recognizable body parts such as eyes, ears, and testicles. An aversion to such items developed only gradually in the modern era.

BIBLIOGRAPHY

Adamson, Melitta. *Regional Cuisines of Medieval Europe.* New York: Routledge, 2002.

Ahmed, Anne, ed. *A Proper Newe Booke of Cokerye.* Cambridge: Corpus Christi College, 2002.

Albala, Ken. *Eating Right in the Renaissance.* Berkeley: University of California Press, 2002.

———. "To Your Health." In *Alcohol: A Social and Cultural History,* edited by Mack Holt. Oxford: Berg, 2006.

Ambrosoli, Mauro. *The Wild and the Sown.* Cambridge: Cambridge University Press, 1997.

Archimagirus Anglo-Gallicus. London: G. Bedell and T. Collins, 1658.

Austin, Thomas, ed. *Two Fifteenth Century Cookbooks.* Early English Text Society. Rochester, N.Y.: Boydell and Brewer, 2000. Reprint.

Bacci, Andrea. *De naturali vinorum historia.* Rome: Nicholai Mutii, 1596.

Barnes, Donna R., and Peter Rose. *Matters of Taste: Food and Drink in Seventeenth Century Dutch Art and Life.* Syracuse, N.Y.: Syracuse University Press, 2002.

Bensoussan, Maurice. *Les Particules alimentaires: Naissance de la gastronomie au XVIe siècle.* Paris: Maisonneuve et Larose, 2002.

Benzi, Ugo, and Ludovico Bertaldi. *Regola della sanita et natura dei cibi.* Turin: Heirs of Gio. Domenico Tarino, 1618.

Black, Maggie. *The Medieval Cookbook.* New York: Thames and Hudson, 1992.

Bober, Phyllis Pray. *Art, Culture and Cuisine.* Chicago: University of Chicago Press, 1999.

Bruyerin-Champier, Jean. *De re cibaria.* Lyon: Sebast. Honoratum, 1560.

Cappatti, Montanari. *Italian Cuisine.* New York: Columbia University Press, 2003.

Cardano, Girolamo. "De usu ciborium." In *Opera Omnia.* Lyon: Huguetan and Ravaud, 1663.

Carlin, Martha, and Joel T. Rosenthal, eds. *Food and Eating in Medieval Europe.* London: The Hambledon Press, 1998.

Castellanus, Petrus. *Kreophagia.* Antwerp: Hieronymus Verdussius, 1626.

Castelvetro, Giacomo. *Breve racconto di tutte le radici, di tutte l'erbe e di tutti i frutti che crudi o cotti in Italia si mangiano.* Web site: http://www.liberliber.it/biblioteca/c/castelvetro/index.htm.

———. *The Fruit, Herbs and Vegetables of Italy.* Translated by Gillian Riley. London: Viking, 1989.

Caton, Mary Anne, ed. *Fooles and Fricasees: Food in Shakespeare's England.* Washington, D.C.: Folger Shakespeare Library, 1999.

Cervio, Vincenzo. *Il Trinciante.* Rome: ad istanza di Giulio Burchioni, nella stampa del Gabbia, 1593.

Chiappini, Luciano. *La Corte Estense alla metá del Cinquencento: I compendi di Cristoforo di Messisbugo.* Ferrara, Italy: Belriguardo, 1984.

Cogan, Thomas. *The Haven of Health.* London: Thomas Orwin, 1589.

Colonna, Francesco. *Hypnerotomachia Poliphili.* Translated by Joscelyn Godwin. London: Thames and Hudson, 1999.

Colorsi, Giacomo. *Brevita di scalcaria.* Rome: Angelo Bernabo, 1658.

Compleat Cook, The. London: E. B. for Nath. Brook, 1658.

Confalonieri, Giovani Battista. *De vini natura disputatio.* Venice, n.p., 1535.

Cooper, Joseph. *The Art of Cookery Refin'd and Augmented.* London: J. G. for R. Lowndes, 1654.

Cornarius, Janus. *De Conviviorum.* Basel: Joannes Oporinus, 1546.

Crisci, Giovanni Battista. *Lucerna de Corteggiani.* Naples: Io. Domenico Roncagliolo, 1634.

David, Elizabeth. *The Harvest of the Cold Months.* New York: Viking, 1994.

Davidson, Alan. *The Oxford Companion to Food.* Oxford: Oxford University Press, 1999.

Dawson, Thomas. *The Good Housewife's Jewel.* With an Introduction by Maggie Black: Lewes, East Sussex, England: Southover Press, 1996.

De Lune, Pierre. *Le cuisinier.* In *L'art de la cuisine française au XVIIe siècle.* Paris: Payot et Rivages, 1995.

Del Turco, Giovanni. *Epulario e segreti vari.* Bologna: Arnaldo Forni, 1992.

Della Casa, Giovanni. *Galateo.* Translated by Konrad Eiseenbichler and Kenneth R. Bartlett. Toronto: Center for Reformation and Renaissance Studies, 1994.

Digby, Kenelm. *The Closet of Sir Kenelm Digby Opened.* London: H. Brome, 1669. Reprint: Totnes, Devon, England: Prospect Books, 1997.

Duchesne, Joseph. *Le pourtraict de la santé.* Paris: Claude Morel, 1606.

Ecole Parfaite des officiers de bouche. 1676. See Rose, translator.

Euonymus Philiatrus (Conrad Gesner). *De remediis secretis.* Lyon: Antonium Vincentium, 1562.

Evelyn, John. *Acetaria.* Reprint: Totnes, Devon, England: Prospect Books, 1996. (1st ed. 1699).

Evitascandalo, Cesare. *Dialogo del Trinciante.* Rome: Carlo Vilietti, 1609.

———. *Libro dello Scalco.* Rome: Carlo Vulietti, 1609.

Faccioli, Emilio, ed. *Arte della cucina: Libri di ricette testi sopra lo scalco, il trinciante, e i vini.* Milan: Edizioni il Polifilo, 1966.

Fernández-Armesto, Felipe. *Food: A History.* Basingstoke and Oxford: Macmillan, 2001.

Fiorato, Adelin Charles, and Anna Fones Baratto. *La Table et ses dessous.* Paris: Presses de la Sorbonne Nouvelle, 1999.

Flandrin, Jean-Louis, and Carole Lambert. *Fêtes Gourmandes au Moyen Âge.* Paris: Imprimerie Nationale, 1998.

——. *L'Ordre de Mets.* Paris: Odile Jacob, 2002.

Flandrin, Jean-Louis, and Massimo Montanari. *Food: A Culinary History.* New York: Columbia University Press, 1999.

Folengo, Teofilo. *Baldus.* Emilio Faccioli, ed. Turin: Einaudi, 1989.

Fracastoro, Girolamo. *Opera Omnia.* Venice: Iuntas, 1555.

Frugoli, Antonio. *Pratica e Scalcaria.* Rome: Francesco Cavalli, 1638.

Fumanelli, Antonio. *Commentarium de vino, et facultatibus vini.* Venice: Ioannis Patavini & Venturini Rossinelli, 1536.

Garcia, L. Jacinto. *Carlos V a la mesa.* Ediciones Bremen, 2000.

Gazius, Antonius. *Corona Florida Medicinae.* Venice: Ioannes and Gregorius de Gregoriis, 1491.

Geigher, Mattia. *Li tre Trattati.* Padua: P. Frambotto, 1639. Reprint: Bologna, Arnaldo Forni, 1989.

Gillet, Philip. *Par Mets et par vins.* Paris: Payot, 1985.

Glanville, Phillipa, and Hilary Young, eds. *Elegant Eating.* London: V & A Publications, 2002.

Goclenius, Rudolph. *De luxu conviviali nostril seculi.* Marburg: Guolgangi Kezelii, 1607.

Good Huswifes Handmaide for the Kitchen, The. Bristol, England: Stuart Press, 1992.

Granado, Diego. *Libro del Arte de Cocina.* Madrid: Sociedad de Bibliófilos Españoles, 1971. (1st ed. 1599).

Grand cuisinier de toute cuisine. Paris: Jean Bonfons, 1543–4?

Grand cuisinier, tres-utile & profitable, Le. Paris: Nicholas Bonfons, 1576.

Grataroli, Guliermo. *A Direction for the Health of Magistrates and Students.* London: William Howe for Abraham Veale, 1574.

——. *De vini natura.* Strasbourg: Theodosius Ribelius, 1565.

Grewe, Rudolph, and Constance B. Heiatt, eds. *Libellus de arte coquinaria.* Tempe: Ariz. Center for Medieval and Renaissance Studies, 2001.

Grieco, Allen. "The Social Politics of Pre-Linnean Botanical Classification." In *I Tatti Studies in the Renaissance* 4 (1991): 131–49.

Hartley, Dorothy. *Food in England.* London: Little, Brown, 1999.

Heiatt, Constance, Brenda Hosington, and Sharon Butler. *Pleyn Delit.* Toronto: University of Toronto Press, 1996.

Henisch, Bridget Ann. *Fast and Feast.* State College: Pennsylvania State University Press, 1976.

Hobhouse, Henry. *Seeds of Change.* New York: Harper and Row, 1985.

Hollingsworth, Mary. *The Cardinal's Hat.* London: Profile Books, 2004.

Holt, Mack, ed. *Alcohol: A Social and Cultural History.* Oxford: Berg, 2005.

Hugget, Jane, ed. *A Proper Newe Booke of Cokerye.* Bristol, England: Stuart Press, 1995.

Jeanneret, Michel. *A Feast of Words*. Chicago: University of Chicago Press, 1991.

Katz, Solomon H., ed. *Encyclopedia of Food and Culture*. New York: Charles Scribner's Sons, 2003.

Kiple, Kenneth, ed. *The Cambridge World History of Food*. Cambridge: Cambridge University Press, 2000.

L. S. R. *L'art de bien traiter*. In *L'art de la cuisine française*. Paris: Payot and Rivages, 1995.

La Varenne. François Pierre. *Le Cuisinier François*. Paris: Montalba, 1983.

——. *The French Cook*. Lewes, East Sussex, England: Southover Press, 2001.

La Varenne, François Pierre. *Le patissier francois*. Translated by Mounsieur Marnettè as *The Perfect Cook*. London: Nath. Brooks, 1656.

Lancelot de Casteau. *Overture de Cuisine*. Anvers/Bruxelles, Belgium: De Schutter, 1983.

Lancelotti, Vittorio. *Lo Scalco Practico*. Rome: Francesco Corbelletti, 1627. Reprint: Bologna: Arnaldo Forni Editore, 2003.

Larousse Gastronomique. New York: Clarkson Potter, 2001.

L'Art de la cuisine française au XVIIe siècle. Paris: Payot et Rivages, 1995. (L.S.R., *L'art de bien traiter*, 1674, Pierre de Lune, *Le cuisinier*, 1656, Audiger, *La maison réglée*, 1692).

Laurioux, Bruno. *Manger au Moyen Age*. Paris: Hachette, 2002.

Le Ménagier de Paris. *The Goodman of Paris*. Translated by Eileen Power. London: The Folio Society, 1992.

Lehman, Gilly. "The Late Medieval Menu in England—A Reappraisal." In *Food in History* 1:1.

Liberati, Francesco. *Il perfetto maestro di Casa*. Rome: Bernabò, 1668. Reprint: Bologna: Arnaldo Forni, 1974.

Livre fort excellent de cuisine. Lyon: Olivier Arnoulet, 1555.

Livres en bouche: Cinq siècles d'art culinaire français. Paris: Bibliotèque national de France/Hermann, 2001.

Llopis, Manual Martínez. *Historia de la Gastronomia Española*. Madrid: Editora Nacional, 1981.

Maceras, Domingo Hernandes. *Libro del arte de Cozina*. Salamanca, Spain: Ediciones Universidad de Salamanca, 1999.

Magner, Lois N. *A History of Medicine*. New York: Marcel Dekker, 1992.

Markham, Gervase. *The English Housewife*. Edited by Michael R. Best. Montreal & Kingston: McGill-Queen's University Press, 1986.

Martin, Lynn. *Alcohol, Sex and Gender in Late Medieval and Early Modern Europe*. New York: Palgrave, 2001.

Martino, Maestro. *Libro de arte coquinaria*. Edited by Luigi Ballerini and Jeremy Parzen. Milan: Guido Tommasi, 2001. Translated by Jeremy Parzen as *The Art of Cooking*. Berkeley: University of California Press, 2005.

Mason, Laura. *Sugar-Plums and Sherbet*. Totnes, Devon, England: Prospect Books, 2004.

Massonio, Salvatore. *Archidipno overo dell'insalata*. Venice: Marc'antonio Brogiollo, 1627.

Mattei, Venantio. *Teatro Nobilissimo di Scalcheria.* Rome: Giacomo Dragondelli, 1669.

May, Robert. *The Accomplisht Cook.* London: Obadiah Blagrave, 1685. (1st ed. 1660). Reprint: Totnes, Devon, England: Prospect Books, 2000.

Meads, Chris. *Banquets Set Forth.* Manchester, England: Manchester University Press, 2001.

Mennell, Stephen. *All Manners of Food.* Oxford: Blackwell, 1985.

Messisbugo, Christoforo di. *Banchetti.* Ferrara: Giovanni de Buglhat and Antonio Hucher, 1549.

——. *Libro Novo.* Bologna: Arnaldo Forni, 2001.

Moffett, Thomas. *Healths Improvement.* London: Thomas Newcomb, 1655.

Montanari, Massimo. *Alimentazione e cultura nel Medioevo.* Rome: Laterza, 1992.

——. *The Culture of Food.* Oxford: Blackwell, 1994.

Montiño, Francisco Martínez. *Arte de Cocina.* Barcelona: Maria Angela Marti, 1763. Web site: http://www.bib.ub.es/grewe/showbook.pl?gw57 (1st ed. 1611).

Murrell, John. *Murrell's Two Books of Cookery and Carving.* Edited by Stuart Peachy. Bristol, England: Stuart Press, 1993.

Naso, Irma. *La cultura del Cibo.* Turin: Paravia, 1999.

Nonnius, Ludovicus. *Diaeteticon.* Antwerp: Petri Belleri, 1645.

Notaker, Henry. "Comments on the Interpretation of Plagiarism." In *Petits Propos Culinaries,* 70: 58.

Pantaleon da Confienza. *Summa lacticiniorum.* 2nd edition. Lyon: Antonium Blanchard, 1525.

Paston-Williams, Sara. *The Art of Dining.* London: The National Trust, 1993.

Pérez Samper, María de los Angeles. *La alimentación en la Espana del Siglo de Oro.* Huesca, Spain: La Val de Onsera, 1998.

Peterson, T. Sarah. *Acquired Taste.* Ithaca, N.Y.: Cornell University Press, 1994.

Pictorius, Giorgius. *Dialoghi.* Venice: Vincenzo Valgrisi, 1550.

Platina (Bartolomeo Sacchi). *On Right Pleasure and Good Health.* Edited by Mary Ella Milham. Tempe, Ariz.: Medieval and Renaissance Texts and Studies, 1998.

Pleij, Herman. *Dreaming of Cockaigne.* New York: Columbia University Press, 2001.

Plouvier, Liliane. *L'Europe a table.* Brussels: Editions Labor, 2003.

Praefectus, Jacob. *De Diversorum vini generum.* Venice: Jordani Ziletti, 1559.

Puteanus, Eyricius. *Comus sive Phagesiposia Cimmeria.* Louvain: Gerard Rivi, 1611.

Rabasco, Ottaviano. *Il convito overo discorsi di quelle materie che al convito s'appartengono.* Florence: Gio. Donato e Bernardino Guinti, & Co., 1615.

Rabisha, William. *The Whole Body of Cookery Dissected.* London: George Calvert, 1682. Reprint: Totnes, Devon, England: Prospect Books, 2003.

Redon, Odile, Françoise Sabban, and Silvano Serventi. *The Medieval Kitchen.* Chicago: University of Chicago Press, 1998.

Revel, Jean-François. *Culture and Cuisine.* New York: Da Capo Press, 1982.

Riley, Gillian. *Renaissance Recipes.* San Francisco: Pomegranate Artbooks, 1993.

Romoli, Domenico. *La singolare dottrina.* Venice: Gio. Battista Bonfadino, 1593. (1st ed. 1560).

Rose, Giles, transl. *A Perfect School of Instruction for Officers of the Mouth.* London: R. Bentley, 1682.

Rose, Peter, transl. *The Sensible Cook.* Syracuse, N.Y.: Syracuse University Press, 1989.

Rossetti, Giovanni Battista. *Dello Scalco.* Ferrara: Domenico Mammarello, 1584. Reprint: Bologna: Arnaldo Forni, 1991.

Sabban, Françoise, and Silvano Serventi. *A Tavola nel Rinascimento.* Rome: Laterza, 1996.

Sala, Giovanni Domenico. *De alimentis.* Padua: Io. Bapt. Martinum, 1628.

Sante, Lancerio. "Della Qualità dei Vini." In *Arte della Cucina,* edited by Emilio Faccioli. Milan: Il Polifilo, 1966.

Santich, Barbara. *The Original Mediterranean Cuisine.* Chicago: Chicago Review Press, 1995.

Scappi, Bartolomeo. *Opera.* Venice, 1570. Reprint: Bologna, Arnaldo Forni, 2002.

Scarlino, Giovani Battista. *Nuovo trattato della varietà, e qualità de vini, che vengono in Roma.* Rome: Valerio Dorico, 1554.

Schivelbusch, Wolfgang. *Tastes of Paradise.* New York: Pantheon Books, 1992.

Scully, Terence. *The Art of Cookery in the Middle Ages.* Woodbridge, Suffolk, England: Boydell Press, 1995.

——. *Early French Cookery.* Ann Arbor: Univerity of Michigan Press, 1995.

——, ed. *The Viandier of Taillevent.* Ottowa, Canada: University of Ottowa Press, 1988.

——, ed. *The Vivendier.* Totnes, Devon, England: Prospect Books, 1997.

Sebizius, Melchior. *De Alimentorum Facultatibus.* Strasbourg: Joannis Philippi Mülbii and Josiae Stedelii, 1650.

Segan, Francine. *Shakespeare's Kitchen.* New York: Random House, 2003.

Serradilla Muñoz, Jose V. *La mesa del emperador.* San Sebastian, Spain: R & B Ediciones, 1997.

Serventi, Silvano, and Françoise Sabban. *Pasta.* New York: Columbia University Press, 2002.

Sim, Alison. *Food and Feast in Tudor England.* New York: St. Martin's Press, 1997.

Siraisi, Nancy. *The Clock and the Mirror.* Princeton, N.J.: Princeton University Press, 1997.

Spencer, Colin. *British Food.* London: Grub Street, 2002.

Stefani, Bartolomeo. *L'Arte di Ben Cucinare.* Mantua: Osanna, 1662. Reprint: Bologna: Arnaldo Forni, 2000.

Strong, Roy. *Feast.* London: Jonathan Cape, 2002.

Symons, Michael. *A History of Cooks and Cooking.* Urbana: University of Illinois Press, 2000.

Syngrapheus, Polyonimus. *Schola Apiciana.* Frankfort: Christian Egenolffs, 1534.

Tannahill, Reay. *Food in History.* New York: Crown Publishers, 1998.

Taylor, John. *Taylor's Feast.* London: J. Okes, 1638.

Thomas, Keith. *Man and the Natural World.* Oxford: Oxford University Press, 1983.

Toussaint-Samat, Maguelonne. *History of Food.* Oxford: Basil Blackwell, 1992.

Vasselli, Gio. Francesco. *L'Apicio overo Il Maestro de' Conviti.* Bologna: HH del Dozza, 1647. Reprint: Bologna: Arnaldo Forni, 1998.

Viandier, tr. James Prescott. Web site: http://www.telusplanet.net/public/prescotj/data/viandier/viandier1.html.

Viret, Pierre. *Satyres Chrestiennes de la cuisine papale.* Conrad Badius, 1560. Reprint, Geneva: M. Gustave Revilliod for Jules-Guillaume Fick, 1857.

Visser, Margaret. *The Rituals of Dinner.* New York: Grove Weidenfeld, 1991.

Vonlett, Jacques. *La vraye mettode de bien trencher les viandes tant à l'Italienne qu' à la main.* Lyon: 1647. Reprint, Dijon, France: Aux Editions du Raisin, 1926.

Wheaton, Barbara Ketcham. *Savoring the Past.* New York: Touchstone, 1983.

Willich, Iodoco. *Ars magirica. Hoc est, coquinaria.* Zurich: Jacob Gesner, 1563.

Wilson, C. Anne. *Food and Drink in Britain.* Chicago: Academy Chicago Publishers, 1991.

Wright, Clifford. *A Mediterranean Feast.* New York: William Morrow, 1999.

Wynkyn de Worde. *The Boke of Kervyng.* Lewes, East Sussex, England: Southover Press, 2003.

Young, Carolin. *Apples of Gold in Settings of Silver.* New York: Simon and Schuster, 2002.

INDEX

Abremont: recipe, 174; sauce, 50
absinthe, 113, 115
accounting, 143–44
adobo, 65
agronomic literature, ancient, 29
alcohol. *See* distillation
alembic, 148
alexanders (*Smyrnium olustratum*), 81
alfalfa for fodder, 46
almond, 30; milk, 46, 56, 136;
    toasted, 69
aloes, 109, 115
ambergris, 25, 30, 54, 60, 67, 71, 109,
    173
anchovy, 11, 25, 30, 51, 69, 124
ancients (Greeks and Romans), xi,
    167–68, 170
anise, 30, 164
aphrodisiac, 4
Apicius, Marcus Gavius, 29, 160,
    163–64, 167
apple, 51, 87; and onion sauce recipe,
    84; pie, 135; puffs, 88; sauce, 87–88
apprentice, 145, 151
apricot, 85
aquarello. See Lora
aqua vitae, 112, 116
arbutus (strawberry tree), 38
Archimagirus Anglo-Gallicus, 131
Arnald of Villanova, 113
aromatics, 30, 60–61, 100
Arte cisoria, 153
artichoke, viii, 11, 25, 28, 51, 67, 74–75,
    80–81, 124, 131; bottoms, 26, 68,
    81, 100

artificiality, 16
Artusi, Pellegrino, 126
asceticism, 160
ash, 146
asparagus, viii, 11, 28, 55, 78; cooking
    time, 81; flowers in wine, 111; tips,
    68; wild, 37
avens, 37
azarole, 84, 86

Bacci, Andrea, 115–17, 132
bacon, 51, 71
Bacon, Francis, 32
Bacon, Roger, 57
badger, 36
bain marie, 48
banquet: meaning of word, vii; politi-
    cal nature, xii
barberry, 67, 131
barley, 51
baroque, viii, x, 21–26, 53, 133; gar-
    nishes, 72
basil, 113
bastard (wine) sauce, 24
bay leaf, 15, 37
bean, 11, 28, 31, 74
bear meat, 36
beaver tail, 36
béchamel, viii
beef, 10, 130, 135
beer, 137, 168
beet, 74; greens, 49; pickled, 77
Bembo, Pietro, 17
Bernini, Gianlorenzo, 22
Bertaldi, Giovanni Ludovico, 171

Ken Albala is a professor of history
at the University of the Pacific. He is the author
of *Eating Right in the Renaissance, Food in Early
Modern Europe,* and *Cooking in Europe,
1250-1650.*

THE FOOD SERIES

A History of Cooking
Michael Symons

Peanuts: The Illustrious History
of the Goober Pea
Andrew F. Smith

Marketing Nutrition:
Soy, Functional Foods, Biotechnology,
and Obesity
Brian Wansink

The Banquet: Dining in the Great Courts
of Late Renaissance Europe
Ken Albala

The Turkey: An American Story
Andrew F. Smith

The University of Illinois Press
is a founding member of the
Association of American University Presses.

Composed in 10/13 Hoefler Text
by Celia Shapland
for the University of Illinois Press
Designed by Copenhaver Cumpston
Manufactured by Thomson-Shore, Inc.

University of Illinois Press
1325 South Oak Street
Champaign, IL 61820-6903
www.press.uillinois.edu